REVIEWS OF UNITED KINGDOM

STATISTICAL SOURCES

Volume III

Housing in Great Britain

and

Housing in Northern Ireland

Reviews of United Kingdom Statistical Sources

Editor W. F. Maunder

REVIEWS OF UNITED KINGDOM STATISTICAL SOURCES

Edited by W. F. MAUNDER

Professor of Economic and Social Statistics
University of Exeter

VOLUME III

HOUSING IN GREAT BRITAIN

by

S. M. FARTHING

Lecturer in Town and Country Planning
Bristol Polytechnic

and

HOUSING IN NORTHERN IRELAND

by

M. C. FLEMING

Senior Lecturer in Economics,
Loughborough University of Technology

Published for
The Royal Statistical Society and
the Social Science Research Council
by

HEINEMANN EDUCATIONAL BOOKS

LONDON

Heinemann Educational Books Ltd.

LONDON   EDINBURGH   MELBOURNE   AUCKLAND   TORONTO
JOHANNESBURG   NAIROBI   IBADAN   LUSAKA
HONG KONG   SINGAPORE   KUALA LUMPUR   NEW DELHI

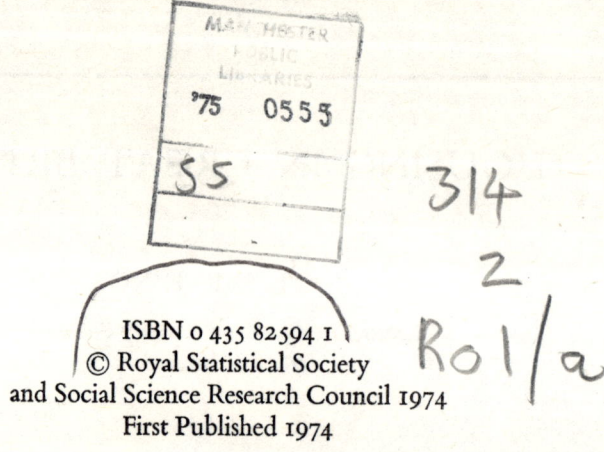
ISBN 0 435 82594 1
© Royal Statistical Society
and Social Science Research Council 1974
First Published 1974

For bibliographical purposes this volume should be cited as:
Farthing, S.M. and Fleming, M.C., *Housing in Great Britain and Housing in Northern Ireland*, Heinemann Educational Books on behalf of The Royal Statistical Society and the Social Science Research Council, 1974

Published by Heinemann Educational Books Ltd.
48 Charles Street, London W1X 8AH

Printed in Great Britain by
William Clowes and Sons Limited
London, Colchester and Beccles

FOREWORD

The Sources and Nature of the Statistics of the United Kingdom produced under the auspices of the Royal Statistical Society and edited by Maurice Kendall, filled a notable gap on the library shelves when it made its appearance in the early post-war years. Through a series of critical reviews by many of the foremost national experts, it constituted a valuable contemporary guide to statisticians working in many fields as well as a beachmark to which historians of the development of Statistics in this country are likely to return to again and again. The Social Science Research Council and the Society were both delighted when Professor Maunder came forward with the proposal that a revised version should be produced, indicating as well his willingness to take on the onerous task of editor. The two bodies were more than happy to act as co-sponsors of the project and to help in its planning through a joint steering committee. The result, we are confident, will be adjudged a worthy successor to the previous volumes by the very much larger 'statistics public' that has come into being in the intervening years.

Jeremy Mitchell

Secretary
Social Science Research Council

October 1973

P. G. Moore

Honorary Secretary
Royal Statistical Society

October 1973

MEMBERSHIP OF THE JOINT STEERING COMMITTEE

(February 1973)

Chairman: Professor Sir Roy Allen

Representing the Royal Statistical Society:

Dr W. R. Buckland

Miss S. V. Cunliffe

Dr S. Rosenbaum

Representing the Social Science Research Council:

Dr B. Benjamin

Mr E. Grebenik

Mr T. S. Pilling

Secretary: Mr D. E. Allen

Introduction

This volume forms the third in the new series which is the successor to the well-known *Sources and Nature of the Statistics of the United Kingdom*, edited by Professor M. G. Kendall and produced some two decades ago. During most of the planning period of the present project it was the intention to retain the original title, and the change was adopted, with some sentimental regret, to indicate something of the development in scope and approach which the new series is designed to incorporate. The two decades separating the projects have seen not only a vast growth in the data available but also a radical change in the attitude to their use; on almost any issue now at least the *desideratum* of factually based conclusions is broadly accepted. Recently the Younger *Committee on Privacy* has reported, and it is interesting to observe that one of their first steps was to commission a survey to discover what people actually think about their need for privacy; it is a fair bet that twenty years earlier the answer to the question would have been assumed in terms of fundamental principle.

The growth in data sources, of course, is not necessarily to be hailed with unmitigated glee. Obviously they are only genuinely 'available' if the person who needs the information knows where to find it, and probably there is a 'square' if not a 'cube' law between the difficulty of retrieval and the volume of material. Meeting this need is the basic purpose which the new series inherits from the old. Furthermore, a proliferation of data helps no one if they are unsuitable for his purpose. Considerations of this kind raise enormously difficult questions but the series aims to explore them as something more than an afterthought. There is no claim that authors produce all—or any of—the answers but it is hoped that they offer suggestions which will stimulate a needed debate and contribute to it.

The primary aim of this series is then to act as a work of reference to the sources of statistical material of all kinds, both official and unofficial, which fall under the fairly broad classification of 'economic and social'. The objectives under this heading are to enable the user to discover what data are available on the subject in which he is interested, from where they may be obtained, and what are the limitations to their use. Data are regarded as available not only if published in a normal printed format but also if they are likely to be released to a *bona fide* enquirer in any other form, such as duplicated documents or computer print-out. On the other hand, no reference is made to material which, even if it is known to exist, is not accessible to the general run of potential users. The distinction, of course, is not clear-cut, and mention of a source is not to be regarded as a guarantee that data will be released; in the twilight areas it may be very much a matter for negotiation. This applies with particular force to the question of obtaining computer print-outs of custom-specified tabulations. Where original records are held on magnetic tape it might appear that there should be no insuperable problem, apart from confidentiality, in obtaining any feasible analysis at a cost; in practice, it may well turn out that there are capacity restraints which override any simple cost calculation. Thus, what is requested might make demands on computer and programming resources to the extent that the routine work of the agency concerned would be intolerably affected.

The intention is that the sources for each topic should be surveyed in detail and the brief supplied to authors has called for comprehensive coverage at the level of 'national interest'. This term does not denote any necessary restriction to statistics collected on a national basis (still less, of course, to national aggregates) but that sources of a purely local character, without wider interest in either content or methodology, are excluded. Indeed, the mere task of identifying all material of this latter kind is an impossibility. The interpretation of the brief, of course, has involved discretion, and it is up to the users of these reviews to say what unreasonable gaps become apparent to them. They are cordially invited to do so.

The need for the treatment of sources, topic by topic in depth, is self-apparent; the reception given to the first series demonstrated how useful such a treatment can be. There is no dearth of admirable general guides but they leave the specialized enquirer (quite properly) without the guidance he is seeking. The *Fourth Report from the Estimates Committee* 1966–67 on Government Statistical Services made two recommendations, based on evidence in support of this view, which are worth quoting in full:

Recommendation (5):
There should be made available to the public a comprehensive guide to official and semi-official statistics which is revised periodically and which refers the user to explanatory matter and commentaries (paragraph 37).

Recommendation (7):
The CSO should ensure that the published series are regularly supplemented by comprehensive descriptions of the methods used in collecting primary data and in deriving secondary statistics.

It is known that work on implementing these proposals is in hand (see *Statistical News,* 14.15) but perforce has to take second place to the more fundamental commitments of the Government Statistical Service. However, even when completed it will be limited to public sector sources and not embrace all sources as is the intention of this series. Further, a personal view should contribute a more incisive critical evaluation than it is reasonable to expect from an official account. Consequently, for all these reasons there is unlikely to be any serious duplication between this series and the guides to be prepared by the CSO. In fact, as far as immediate policy is concerned, the early topics in this series have been selected to cover those areas where official documentation is weakest and to avoid those where it is strongest.

It is opportune to interpose at this point an acknowledgement of the heavy debt which the current project owes to official statisticians in a personal capacity and which, at least in an indirect sense, they see, no doubt, as a contribution in the spirit of the Estimates Committee's recommendations quoted above. Not only have some of them devoted a great deal of time both as members of the Steering Committee and as authors, but each topic almost invariably demands detailed consultation with Departmental officers. The extent of the help being received is indeed a very substantial part of the total effort but—let it be added hastily in order not to mar the co-operative and amicable relationship—there is no responsibility on the part of the Government Statistical Service for any errors which the editor may have allowed to pass undetected.

In the foregoing, mention has been made of the 'specialist enquirer' and it should be made clear that the typical user has not been envisaged as either a pure statistician or as an expert in the topic under review. Necessarily, in fact, he has been somewhat amorphous but the best working assumption seemed to be that he would possess some combination of statistical and subject matter interests. Among others, it is hoped that this would include staffs of economics and statistics divisions of large enterprises, civil servants and local government officials, politicians, market researchers, teachers, students and academic research workers.

To facilitate the use of the series as a work of reference certain features have been incorporated which are worth a word or two of explanation. First, the text of each review is designed, in so far as varying subject matter permits, to follow a standard form of arrangement so that users may expect a similar pattern to be followed throughout the series. The starting point is a brief summary of the activity concerned and its organisation, in order to give a clear background understanding to how data are collected, what is being measured, the stage at which measurements are made, what the reporting units are, the channels through which returns are routed and where they are processed. As a further part of this introductory material, there is a discussion of the specific problems of definition and measurement to which the topic gives rise. The core sections on available sources which follow are arranged at the author's discretion by production source, by subject subdivision, or by type of data; there is too much heterogeneity between topics to permit any imposition of complete uniformity on all authors. The final section is devoted to what has been mentioned already as a secondary aim of the series, namely a discussion of general short-comings and possibly desirable improvements. In case a contrary expectation should be aroused, it should be said that authors have not been asked to produce a comprehensive plan for the reform of statistical reporting in the whole of their field. However, a review of existing sources is a natural opportunity to make some suggestions for future policy on the collection and publication of statistics in the field concerned.

Secondly, detailed factual information about statistical series and other data are given in a Quick Reference List (QRL). The exact nature of the entries is best seen by glancing at the lists, and accordingly they are not described here. Again, the ordering is not prescribed except that entries are not classified by publication source since it is presumed that it is this which is unknown to the reader. In general, the routine type information which is shown in the QRL is not repeated verbally in the text; the former, however, serves as a search route to the latter in that a reference (by section number) is shown against a QRL entry when there is a related discussion in the text.

Third, a subject index to each review acts as a more or less conventional line of enquiry on textual references; however, it is a computerized system and, for an individual review, the only peculiarity which it introduces is the possibility of easily permuting entries. Thus an original entry in the index to the first review of Vol. I is:

Average expenditure handicapped persons services,

which is shown also as:

Expenditure handicapped persons services, average

as well as:

Handicapped persons services, average expenditure

The object at this level is merely to facilitate search by giving as many variants as possible. In addition, individual review subject indexes are merged into a cumulative index which is held on magnetic tape and may possibly be used to produce a printed version from time to time if that seems desirable. Computer print-outs of the cumulative index to date are available on application to me at the Department of Economics, University of Exeter. In addition, selective searches of this index may be made by the input of key-words; the result is a print-out of all entries in which the key-word appears in the initial position in the subject index of any review. Like the cumulative index itself, this is a facility which is not likely to be of considerable help until several volumes of reviews are in print.

Fourth, each review contains two listings of publications. The QRL Key gives full details of the publications shown as sources and text references to them are made in the form [QRL serial number]; this list is confined essentially to data publications. The other listing is a general bibliography of works discussing wider aspects; text references in this case are made in the form [B serial number].

Finally, an attempt is made to reproduce the more important returns or forms used in data collection, thus showing what tabulations it is possible to make as well as clarifying the basis of those actually available. Unfortunately there are severe practical limitations on the number of such forms that it is possible to append to a review, and authors perforce have to be highly selective.

If all or any of these features succeed in their intention of increasing the value of the series in its basic function as a work of reference it will be gratifying; the extent to which the purpose is achieved, however, will be difficult to assess without 'feedback' from the readership. Users, therefore, will be rendering an essential service if they will send me a note of specific instances where they have not found the help expected in consulting a review.

As editor, I must express my very grateful thanks to all the members of the Joint Steering Committee of the Royal Statistical Society and the Social Science Research Council. It would be unfair to saddle them with any responsibility for shortcomings in execution but they have directed the overall strategy with as admirable a mixture of guidance and forbearance as any editor of such a series could desire. Especial thanks are due to the Secretary of the Committee who is an unfailing source of help even when sorely pressed by the more urgent demands of his other offices. We are grateful to the Controller of Her Majesty's Stationery Office for granting us permission to reproduce Crown copyright material.

Stuart Farthing and Michael Fleming join me in thanking all those who gave up their time to attend the seminar held to discuss the first drafts of their reviews, which contributed materially to improving the final versions. We are most grateful to Paul Richardson of Heinemann Educational Books for all his help. The subject index entries for the first review in this volume were compiled by Mr David Oddy and for the second by Miss Barbara West, to both of whom we express our appreciation. Mrs Gill Skinner, of the Social Studies Data Processing Unit at the University of Exeter, has earned our sincere gratitude for writing the computer programs to produce the subject indexes.

University of Exeter   W. F. MAUNDER
November, 1973

5   Housing in Great Britain

by

S. M. FARTHING

Lecturer in Town & Country Planning
Bristol Polytechnic

Acknowledgements

Many people have given conscious and unconscious help and stimulus during the preparation of this review, and while making the usual disclaimers for responsibility I should like to acknowledge my debt to them.

Throughout the progress of the work I have received invaluable guidance and encouragement from Professor W. F. Maunder, the editor of the series.

In the University of Manchester thanks especially must go to Professor J. Parry Lewis for his guidance at crucial times in the preparation of early drafts and for contributing paragraphs and useful comments. I have also benefited on a number of occasions from discussions with Mr A. L. Traill

Without the help of various people in the Department of the Environment, this review would have been less complete. Mr A. Holmans was kind enough to read through and comment on an early draft and Mr W. Osborn clarified and commented on a number of doubtful points and made many constructive suggestions for improvement.

Finally I should like to acknowledge my debt to the Housing Research Foundation whose financial support of a similar project enabled me to carry out much of the initial research for this review.

Reference Date of Sources Reviewed

This review is believed to represent the position, broadly speaking, as it obtained at March 31st 1972. Later revisions have been inserted up to the proof-reading stage [May 31st, 1974] taking account, as far as possible, of any major changes in the situation.

Addendum

In addition to the continuing and inevitable process of change in procedures and in statistical reporting since March 1972, there have been two changes that have had a significant bearing on the situation as reported in this review. First, the Housing Finance Act 1972 has become law. In consequence, amongst other things, there have been substantial changes in the system of rents and subsidies for council housing. 'Fair rents' are to apply in both the local authority and private rented sectors with the exception of furnished lettings, and tenants in both sectors are eligible for rent rebates on the same basis.

The second major change has been brought about by the introduction of new procedures for identifying 'dwellings' in the 1971 Census. This is an important break with past practice and the new concept is explained in detail in Section VIII of the General Explanatory Notes to the 1971 Census. Since it was felt that the definition was simpler to apply, the gains in accuracy should outweigh any problems incurred in comparing the count of dwellings over time. However, because of errors in the application of the present and earlier definition, any precise estimate of the effect of definitional changes is, for the time being, extremely uncertain.

List of Abbreviations

DOE	Department of the Environment
FES	Family Expenditure Survey
GDP	Gross Domestic Product
GHS	General Household Survey
GLC	Greater London Council
GNP	Gross National Product
HMSO	Her Majesty's Stationery Office
HRA	Housing Revenue Accounts
IMTA	Institute of Municipal Treasurers and Accountants
MHLG	Ministry of Housing and Local Government
MPBW	Ministry of Public Building and Works
NBS	Nationwide Building Society
NHBRC	National House Builders Registration Council
PFU	Primary family units
PWLB	Public Works Loan Board
RES	Regular Expenditure Survey
RIBA	Royal Institute of British Architects
SDD	Scottish Development Department
WO	Welsh Office

Contents

Introduction

In recent years there has been an increasing emphasis on the need for quantitative information of all kinds by both Government Departments and by research workers and institutes. The field of housing has not been immune to this trend and the situation with regard to the collection of official statistics has improved considerably since R. Titmuss, referring to the period up to 1957, commented in the Foreword to [B 13] that 'The British people and their political parties, uninstructed in the basic facts and unaware of the extent of their ignorance, continued to grapple with their housing problems in the vocabulary of a class-conscious folklore inherited from the nineteenth century.'

An indication of the magnitude of the change in attitude can be gained by comparison of the wide range of statistics currently published with those mentioned in the paper by M. Bowley [B 2] which was published in 1952. Statistics collection is no longer seen solely or even mainly as a by-product of the administrative procedures of the housing section of the Department of the Environment (DOE) and there is a much wider appreciation of the need for statistics on all aspects of housing as a guide to government policy. Symbolic, perhaps, of this new spirit was the joint preparation in 1966 of Housing Statistics [QRL 26] by the Ministry of Housing and Local Government (MHLG), the Welsh Office (WO) and the Scottish Development Department (SDD) which represented an attempt to treat the field coherently. Mention, too, should be made of the paper by G. Penrice [B 14] in 1968 explaining the new directions, developments and objectives of statistics collection in the (then) MHLG.

The origins of central statistical collection, however, lie in the aftermath of the First World War when government involvement and intervention in housing led to local authorities being charged with the wholesale provision of housing accommodation. This led to returns for subsidy purposes from local authorities and similar returns from private enterprise who were also eligible for government subsidies at this time. Although the amount of information gathered today is much greater than half a century ago, local authorities in England and Wales are still required to make returns to the DOE (to the SDD for Scottish authorities) and because the government has much more direct regulation of their activities there is more information, for example, about new local authority housing than about private sector building. No government, however, can ignore developments in the private sector of the housing market and apart from information relayed in local authority returns steps have been taken to gather data for the assessment and forecast of trends. Of particular relevance has been the publication of statistics on the workings of the rent regulation machinery and the co-operation between the Building Societies Association and the DOE in the collection of statistics on mortgage advances.

One troublesome feature of the statistics on housing is that the house-building industry, whose activities cannot be ignored in any assessment of housing trends and prospects, was up to late 1970 more properly one of the responsibilities of a separate Ministry, the Ministry of Public Building and Works (MPBW) than of the former MHLG. In consequence it has in some cases been impossible to separate statistics relating to the house-building industry as such from those for the construction industry in general.* It is to be hoped, however,

---

* In this review of statistics interest in construction statistics will be largely restricted to those that can in fact be related to the house-building industry.

that the incorporation of both Ministries into the DOE and the expected appearance of a new publication, *Housing and Construction Statistics* [QRL 21] a combination of *Housing Statistics* [QRL 26] and the *Monthly Bulletin of Construction Statistics* [QRL 40] will go a long way towards improving this situation.

Not only has there been an extension of the coverage of statistics but there has also been an awareness of the needs of outside research interests. In many cases the Department is in the best position to take surveys and make estimations and calculations on particular aspects of housing and many of the results have been made available in the Supplementary Tables to [QRL 26], a development of considerable value to many workers in the field of housing. Nevertheless, there is always a tension between the statistical needs of government which tend to be geared to the specific policy of the period and the often more specialised needs of various research interests concerned with the 'housing situation'.

The production of statistics relating to housing, as in other fields in the social sciences, is thus confronted with the fundamental problem of quantifying and therefore measuring particular phenomena, a process which usually implies the formulation of an explicit definition. Definitions are however useful rather than true, and since interest in housing is so widespread any one definition will not necessarily meet the requirements for particular types of analysis. Take, for instance, the definition of the basic 'housing unit'. As we shall see later, for slum clearance purposes the unit adopted in the statistics is the 'house' but this may contain several structurally separate Census 'dwellings' (see Section 1.1). But the term 'dwelling' itself is not always suitable because it, too, can be restrictive when, for instance, the housing condition of households is being considered. Here some description of the actual accommodation occupied by households such as the 'household space' would probably be more useful (Section 2.2).

This is a problem that has to be faced squarely but cannot be entirely resolved. At least, if the definitions are explicit we know what the statistics show although it may not be what we should ideally like them to show, and, perhaps, too little effort is devoted to assessing conversion factors. The real problems are introduced when the definition is implicit and the measurement subjective as in the classification of a house as 'unfit' for human habitation. 'Unfitness' may mean different things to different people and to the same people at different times.

Although it is not the purpose of this paper to examine local sources of data it has been argued that housing is increasingly becoming a local rather than a national problem. The extent to which national statistics are available for smaller areas than the nation and thus can be traced down to the local scale is therefore likely to be of considerable concern. References to regional and local housing statistics are, therefore, included in the text, but even at a local authority level, the smallest areal units generally available, statistics often require further definition for some purposes. For instance, the planning problems associated with 100 'unfit' dwellings for a local authority may well be completely different if they are concentrated in one area rather than distributed randomly over the whole district. For a short discussion of the deficiency of the available statistics on housing conditions and quality at the local level, see Duncan [B 5], pp. 51–8.

In the same way that statistics are not readily comparable if their definitions are incompatible, the comparison of figures for areas that are not similarly delimited may be largely meaningless. This is a problem common to many statistics based on administrative areas, as are housing statistics, because the boundaries are often being altered in small but significant ways and at a higher level 'the regions' of England and Wales have undergone substantial re-definition since the end of the last war. One particular set of areas, the conurbations, need very special care because their official definition in the Census was altered in some cases between 1961 and 1966 and because the new sub-divisions of the Economic Planning Regions for which many statistics are presented do not in every case coincide with the Census conurbations. These considerations apart, a particular study such as the house condition survey in W. Yorkshire (*Housing Survey Report No. 5* [QRL 32]) may wish to consider an area that suits its own purposes better than the existing conurbation or regional sub-division.

Where regular statistical series are published it is general practice to note any boundary changes and wherever possible to adjust past figures to the new areas. Elsewhere, it is of course always important to check that the statistical areas used in one publication are consistent over time, and that comparisons between publications are valid in this respect. Unfortunately in a study of this length it is only possible to point out these pitfalls and not to catalogue the myriad boundary changes and re-definitions that plague so much statistical comparison.

The statistics of housing for the inter-war years have already been described in Bowley's paper, [B 2] and since there have inevitably been limitations of space, discussion in this survey has been restricted to post-war statistics with a deliberate emphasis on those that are currently published. For this purpose the coverage of statistics is as far as possible up-to-date as at March 1972 but this date has no overall significance in so far as the periodicity and date of publication of statistics is concerned. At the time of writing, for example, the 1971 Census has been conducted but as yet no information on housing has been published. Some reference, however, will be made to this source and to other surveys that are expected to appear in the near future.

1 Stock of Dwellings

1.1 Numbers

1.1.1 The housing stock at any one time is composed of all those buildings, parts of buildings and structures which are used or are usually used as living quarters. As such, an enormously wide range of types and living arrangements is included in addition to the general picture of residential units exemplified, perhaps, by the semi-detached or terraced house. In the *1961 Censuses of England and Wales* and of *Scotland* [QRL 12] such unusual accommodation as 'chalets, huts, shacks, tents and converted railway carriages and mobile structures such as caravans, houseboats and barges' were treated as buildings if they were some person's usual residence on Census night. In England and Wales, but not in Scotland, if the non-mobile structures mentioned above were vacant but complied with certain specified constructional characteristics then they were recorded as vacant buildings and, as we shall see later, in some cases as vacant dwellings.

1.1.2 This heterogeneity should be borne in mind when the basic unit of the housing stock—the dwelling—is defined (*Sample Census 1966* [QRL 12]) as 'structurally separate accommodation with independent access to the street or to a public staircase or hall'. Apart from the basic human need for shelter, however inadequately this may be provided, the definition essentially aims at identifying that certain degree of privacy that a household or family occupying such a structure can expect. For example, structurally separate accommodation is that which is 'all contained behind its own front door; bathrooms and water closets did not count as part of the accommodation for this purpose' whilst independent access was further described in the 1966 Census [QRL 12] as the ability of the occupants to 'come and go

without having access to anyone else's living quarters'. It should be admitted that in the majority of cases this definition works very well but in some cases for various economic and social reasons the desire or the ability of a household to achieve this degree of privacy is limited. This is especially the case where the definition is applied to buildings that have been, since their initial construction, adapted to provide accommodation for several households.

1.1.3 Although too many qualifications to the definitions would create serious difficulties in evaluating the information collected in the Census an exception is made in the case of what are commonly known as 'bed-sitting-rooms'. Were a bed-sit to contain all its facilities (except a bathroom and W.C.) behind its own front door then it would be counted as a dwelling by the strict Census definition. To prevent this, however, bed-sitting-rooms in converted houses were further required to contain their own cooking facilities and bathroom before they were considered to be a 'dwelling'.

1.1.4 But anomalies still remain that can be illustrated by some hypothetical but not unlikely situations in converted buildings. Consider, for instance, a set of rooms that although self-contained (except for a bathroom and WC) have more than one means of access to a common staircase or hall. Here the accommodation will not constitute a Census dwelling. This may have repercussions in Census terms for the rest of the accommodation in that building since the 'independent access' rule has been broken and the whole building is now considered to be one 'dwelling'. Thus if there are, say, two other 'flats' in the building which fulfil the condition of structural separateness these cannot be counted and where one should reasonably expect there to be three dwellings there is only one 'dwelling'.

I.I.5   There may arise other cases where part of a building is permanently separated from the rest and has independent access to the street from outside the dwelling, e.g. by means of a staircase specially provided for the occupants of the upper part of the structure. If this is the only means of access for these occupants then the building will always be counted as containing at least two 'dwellings'. On the other hand, if there is also access to the rest of the building through some impermanently sealed opening and any other part of the building contains non-structurally separate accommodation then the whole building is again considered to be one dwelling.

I.I.6   *The accuracy of the Sample Census 1966*
It is unlikely that any Census will ever be entirely complete in its coverage but this proved to be a particular problem for the *1966 10% Sample Census* [QRL 12] because its accuracy depended fundamentally on the adequacy of the sample frame. The sample addresses in England and Wales were chosen mainly from the 1961 enumeration and from the lists of hereditaments for which a proposal for valuation had been made since the 1st April 1961. The frame was found, however, to be 'at least $1\frac{1}{4}\%$ deficient in private dwellings' and as a whole there was a shortage of about 20,000 dwellings in the sample. The deficiencies of the 1961 Census as a sample frame for the 1966 enumeration are discussed in some detail in the notes to the *1966 Sample Census* [QRL 12]. In Scotland the addresses were taken mainly from the Valuation Roll for 1964/65 and although the post-census inquiry was not as detailed as that in England and Wales it seems likely that 'the total deficiency accounts for less than 0.25% of the population of Scotland as a whole.'

Estimates for the stock of dwellings have been published in the Supplementary Tables to *Housing Statistics* [QRL 26] based on the 1966 Census for Great Britain which attempts to rectify the shortcomings of that publication in that there are adjustments 'to allow for the under-enumeration and for the tenure distribution of dwellings enumerated as vacant or with occupier absent' and, 'included in the figures is an estimate of "reasonably separate" dwellings, that is household spaces of three or more rooms which, although not separate dwellings by the strict census definition, do provide adequate accommodation with the exclusive use of bath, hot water tap, inside WC, sink and stove.' These estimates are given for regions and conurbations whereas Census figures are, of course, available at all levels down to enumeration district.

I.I.7   *Definitional changes*
Apart from the general problems of the application of the census definition to concrete housing situations and errors in enumeration, it is important to know how far it is possible to make comparisons between the results of different censuses. Post-war changes to the definition of the 'dwelling' have, however, been small, and differences between the practice in England and Wales and Scotland negligible. For the only significant break in the series one must go back to 1911 when more or less the present concept was adopted for the first time (the 'structurally separate dwelling' as such was first used in 1921). Prior to 1911 houses divided into flats and blocks of flats or tenements were counted as single 'houses' and all institutions and non-private family residences were also included under this heading.

I.2   Building and Dwelling Type
I.2.I   The Census is not merely concerned with the number of dwellings but also with the buildings in which they are located. The building-type classification, therefore, refers to the structural arrangement of the building and cannot be separated from consideration of the living quarters within the building. In 1961 the Census used the following classification:

(1) Non-residential (England and Wales only)
(2) Institutional
(3) Wholly residential building containing one dwelling
(4) Not wholly residential building containing one dwelling
(5) Permanent building containing more than one dwelling

Vertical dividing walls are taken as enclosing a building so that each unit in a row of terraced housing, for example, would be classified under (3) rather than (5). Horizontal division of a building, on the other hand, produces 'flatted' accommodation which was further sub-divided into 'purpose-built' and 'converted' types in the 1966 Sample Census.

1.2.2   Unfortunately since a census dwelling may contain more than one household the implications in terms of occupancy are not as clear-cut as they first appear. Moreover this sharing of dwellings which has often been made possible by substantial modification of the original building should not be confused with the 'converted' multi-dwelling buildings shown in the census tabulations since this latter category reflects only those conversions that have resulted in the creation of separate dwellings (as defined by the Census). Needless to say there is no reason why these 'converted' buildings should not also contain 'shared dwellings'.

1.2.3   Before considering other classifications of inhabited structures we should note that the Census does not provide an adequate guide to the nature of the structure bearing in mind the variety of forms that buildings may assume. It is true however that the *1961 Census* [QRL 12] considered dwellings as permanent or non-permanent, a non-permanent dwelling being a dwelling in a mobile or non-permanent structure of the type not counted as a building (see Section 1.1) unless it was some person's usual residence on Census night (NB: this may not be the same thing in England and Wales and Scotland). Confusion may also arise because a standard 'prefab' of the type built imme-

diately after the last war is considered to be a permanent building whilst they are generally known as 'temporary housing'. These non-permanent buildings were excluded from the *1966 Sample Census* [QRL 12] with the exception of caravans which were separately enumerated.

1.2.4   It is much more common and consistent with general usage to classify dwellings rather than buildings but since we rely on census stock figures there is no comprehensive record of the housing stock by dwelling type although [QRL 67], [QRL 68], and [QRL 60] have provided national estimates at different times. There is, however, much more information about types of new housing (see Section 3.1) and the 'Notes and Definitions' in *Housing Statistics* [QRL 26] should be consulted for the definitions of houses, bungalows, flats and maisonettes currently in use with the DOE.

1.3   Age Composition

1.3.1   There is no regular survey of the age composition of the stock of dwellings and for official purposes there seems little need for such information. Existing statistics show how poor an indicator age is of the adequacy of a building in terms of accommodation standards and structural condition. This is not altogether surprising since if a dwelling is to remain in the stock, alterations and improvements may be made to it, and beyond a certain point social valuations of the worth of a building are likely to be of increasing importance so that 'historic buildings' are less likely to deteriorate than some that are much younger. Nevertheless, however inadequate age may be as an indicator of quality it is still counted as a significant factor in, for example, building society lending policy and, *ceteris paribus*, the older a dwelling the greater one should expect the costs of maintenance to be.

1.3.2   *Age information from records*
The Housing Situation in 1960 [QRL 67] the *Housing Survey in England and Wales 1964*

[QRL 68] and *Scottish Housing in 1965* [QRL 60] give the best picture available for Great Britain but since they are based on national samples, only the broadest regional breakdown of the results is possible. Buildings with their incorporated dwellings were placed into one of the following age classes: (1) Before 1861, (2) 1861–1880, (3) 1881–1900, (4) 1901–1918, (5) 1919–1944, (6) Post 1945.

These surveys however may include sampling error which is unavoidable but more importantly error due to the estimation of the age of a building where no exact age is available. As an illustration of this latter point, [QRL 67] reports that the largest inaccuracies in its age figures are likely to be with houses built before the First World War, since accurate records of house completions have been generally kept since that date. For this reason age figures for dwellings built by local authorities should be reasonably reliable so that figures published in *Housing Statistics* (IMTA) [QRL 27]* from the issue covering the financial year 1967/68 are most valuable. It is perhaps unfortunate that the age groups are so broad, viz:
(i) completed on or before 31.3.45, (ii) completed after 31.3.45 and up to and including 31.3.64 (iii) after 31.3.64.

1.3.3   *Other estimates of age*

Information about the age of dwellings has also become available as a by-product of enquiries into the condition of the housing stock. The House Condition Survey in England and Wales 1967 reported in [QRL 20] and [QRL 44], the *Welsh House Condition Survey 1968* [QRL 72] and the *Housing Survey Reports No. 1–5* [QRL 28–32] have provided figures only for very broad age ranges—(i) Pre-1919, (ii) 1919–1944, (iii) post 1944—partly because of the problem of the relative sampling errors associated with a finer breakdown of age but also because the ages were essentially estimates made

---

* The publication referred to is one produced by the Institute of Municipal Treasurers and Accountants (IMTA) based on returns received by them from local authorities. It has no connection with the similarly named publication produced by the DOE, SDD and WO.

by the surveyors. A house condition survey undertaken by the Greater London Council (GLC) in 1967 reported in [QRL 66] also obtained age data for a slightly different definition of groupings of the year of construction but the dates of construction were still essentially estimates.

More recently the DOE has provided for the U.K. its own estimates of the age composition of the stock of dwellings by regions in *Social Trends* [QRL 63]. No indication is given of the basis on which these estimates have been made.

1.4   Amenities

1.4.1   In addition to shelter and privacy, accommodation may provide other services related essentially to sanitation and the preparation of food which are dependent on the amenities installed within the structure. Some of these facilities are mobile, e.g. cookers, washing machines, but in general they are associated with the design of the structure e.g. water systems, water closets. This means that the more permanent facilities can be usefully considered in relation to the dwelling stock, and tabulations of dwellings by amenities (see the *1961 Census* [QRL 12]) provide a rough guide to some types of housing obsolescence. On the other hand it may be desirable to know how many or which households have the use of these amenities and, therefore, all three Censuses since the War have provided these tabulations.

1.4.2   The questions on household amenities have changed at successive Censuses. The *Census of 1951* [QRL 12] collected details of households having either the shared use or lack of (i) a piped water supply within the building, (ii) a cooking stove or range, (iii) a kitchen sink, (iv) a water closet and (v) a fixed bath. (A water closet means a flush toilet that empties into a main sewer, septic tank or cesspool, and a bath was only included if it had a waste pipe that led outside the building.)

1.4.3   The *1961 Census* [QRL 12] recorded households without or sharing (i) a cold water tap within the building, (ii) a hot water tap within the building, (iii) a fixed bath, (iv) a water closet within or attached to the building. Instead of the inclusion directly of information about the availability of a cooking stove and kitchen sink a new feature was to divide households sharing dwellings into two groups: those that had exclusive use of both a sink and a stove and those that had exclusive use of neither. In fact the most significant innovation in the *1961 Census* [QRL 12] was that in order to be counted the water closet had to be within or attached to the building. However published statistics were more comprehensive in that it was possible to identify the number of households sharing or lacking various amenities and there were tabulations of dwellings by amenities.

Because of the almost universal availability of a cold water tap to households there was no question about it in the 1966 Census [QRL 12] but there were some qualifications to other amenities: a 'fixed bath' had to be connected to a water supply (as well as a waste pipe) and since, not surprisingly, the previous condition about the W.C. had been widely misunderstood in the 1961 Census, households were asked to distinguish between water closets accessible from inside and outside the building. The most important tabulations cover the availability of individual amenities and the number of households with the exclusive use of a hot water tap, a fixed bath and an inside W.C.

1.4.4 For the details of the facilities available to households or installed in dwellings to have any meaning it is necessary to have some yardstick by which to judge them. Obviously a dwelling or household with a hot water tap is better off than one that has none but how much more benefit does a household receive from the exclusive, rather than the shared, use of such a tap? Is the shared use of a fixed bath more or less desirable than the exclusive use of an inside water closet?

1.4.5 The 'Standard Amenities' described later are often taken as a guide to the amenities that should be available in every dwelling but these are not strictly comparable with the Census data because even where there is an overlap of amenities

the Census concentrates on their availability within the building and, therefore, not necessarily the dwelling. These amenities in any case do not provide guidance on the facilities that are required by households individually. Moreover, since a dwelling is so rigorously defined it is possible that it may contain several households and sufficient people to render the Standard Amenities inadequate. Even the 'shared use' in the Census does not adequately state the extent of such sharing.

1.4.6 When more specialised reports on housing conditions were required by the Government it was necessary and desirable to broaden both the scope of the amenities and the basic housing unit. Partly because rating lists were the most comprehensive sample frame available and there were no equivalent lists for households both *The Housing Situation in 1960* [QRL 67] and *The Housing Survey in England and Wales 1964* [QRL 68] were based not on the dwelling but on 'private dwelling rateable units' defined as 'any rateable unit used, or (in the case of empty accommodation) last used and likely to be used again, to provide a home for one or more private households.' 'Mobile dwellings, institutions, boarding houses and holiday accommodation' were excluded. This, of course, does not correspond to the Census 'dwelling' but each household's accommodation was classified according to whether it had a front door or not.

1.4.7 In [QRL 67] the corresponding collection of information on amenities was more comprehensive than that collected in the Census and reflected in some ways the rising living standards and demands of households, e.g. for central heating and garaging:

A. Front door; garden or yard; solid fuel store; refuse disposal facilities
B. Electricity, gas, mains water and mains drainage
C. Fixed baths, wash basins, hot water and water closet
D. Food cupboard, refrigerator, cooker, central heating

E. Standard Amenities under the House Purchase and Housing Act 1959

F. Need for garages

1.4.8 The 1964 Survey concentrated on 'Standard Amenities' as provided under the Act, namely:

(a) Fixed bath or shower
(b) Wash hand basin
(c) Hot and cold water supply; at a fixed bath or shower; at a wash hand basin; at a sink
(d) A water closet in or contiguous to the dwelling
(e) Satisfactory facilities for storing food

1.4.9 The parallel publication for Scotland *Scottish Housing in 1965* [QRL 60] commissioned by the Scottish Development Department also inquired solely about 'Standard Amenities'. Of course, in fact, the 'Standard Amenities' should only be applied to dwellings and therefore, to apply them to rateable units is to misuse them to a certain extent. The Scottish experience, however, somewhat in contrast to the English revealed that in the 'great majority of cases' the rateable unit was equivalent to the Census dwelling and that therefore this criticism is less valid.

1.4.10 The latest date for which national figures are available for the provision of standard amenities in dwellings is 1967 when as a result of the national House Condition Survey in England and Wales (reported in [QRL 20] and [QRL 44]) information was obtained about the first four amenities. The subsequent conurbation house condition surveys reported in the *Housing Survey Reports No. 1–5* [QRL 28–32] and the 1968 survey in Wales [QRL 72] were on the same basis. Dwellings were defined as in the 1966 Census but caravans, houseboats, shacks, camps and similar dwellings were excluded from the sample. If these types of dwellings are considered to be unsuitable for permanent habitation then they must be included in any calculation of the extent of the need for re-housing and their exclusion from the sample for this particular purpose is unfortunate. A special study of caravan dwellers and their caravans which is now considerably out of date was carried out by the Social Survey in 1959 to provide information for Sir Arton Wilson's report *Caravans as Homes*, Cmnd. 872, 1959. The results of the survey were also separately published in *A Survey of Residential Caravan Life* by P. G. Gray and Elizabeth A. Parr, The Social Survey, Central Office of Information, 1 July 1959 [QRL 8].

1.5 'Fitness'

1.5.1 If amenities are more usefully considered in relation to households, 'unfitness' represents an attempt to define the condition of the housing stock itself in terms of its unsuitability for habitation. However arbitrary or unsuitable one may consider the household arrangements they are generally observable, unequivocal and uniformly enumerated. Unfortunately, 'unfitness' has so far received no useful operational definition and reliance is put on the subjective judgement of an inspector with some statutory guidance in the matter. Section 4 of the Housing Act 1957 states that for determining 'whether a house is unfit for human habitation, regard shall be had to its condition in respect of the following matters, that is to say—(a) repair, (b) stability, (c) freedom from damp, (d) natural lighting, (e) ventilation, (f) water supply, (g) drainage and sanitary conveniences and (h) facilities for storage, preparation and cooking of food and for the disposal of waste water; and the house shall be deemed to be unfit for human habitation if and only if it is so far defective in one or more of the said matters that it is not reasonably suitable for occupation in that condition.' This list was subsequently amended in the Housing Act 1969 to include after (c) '(cc) internal arrangement' and the word 'storage' was deleted from (h). This means that bad internal arrangement is now grounds for considering any house unfit and, secondly, because of the availability of refrigerators, facilities for the storage of food are no longer a necessity.

1.5.2 After the war the first comprehensive record of the 'unfitness' of the housing stock was available in *Slum Clearance 1955* (Cmd. 9593) [QRL 61] for England and Wales and *Slum Clearance—Proposals in Scotland* (Cmd. 9685) [QRL 62] which were summaries of returns including proposals submitted by local authorities under Section 1 of the Housing Repairs and Rents Act, 1954. They contained tables for individual local authority areas with the estimates of the number of houses (N.B. special definition of 'house') in their areas which were unfit for human habitation and were suitable for action under Section 11 or 25 of the Housing Act, 1936. Useful though these figures were at the time, it is known that they were incomplete, and that certain authorities with particular problems, e.g. Glasgow, included only those unfit houses that could reasonably be dealt with in the next ten years.

1.5.3 Later, in *The Housing Situation in 1960* [QRL 67] rateable units were included as unfit if they had been submitted as such in the return to the Ministry, under Section 1 of the Housing Repairs and Rents Acts, 1954 or in proposals under Section 2 of the Housing Act 1957. They were also included if they had been the subject of official representation, or a report from any of the council's officers as unfit under the Housing Act 1957. *The Housing Survey in England and Wales, 1964* [QRL 68] and *Scottish Housing in 1965* [QRL 60] followed the same procedure.

1.5.4 The last publication to use a local authority's own assessment of housing conditions was No. 1 of [QRL 26] which gave a regional analysis for 1965 of the estimates of unfit houses and the number of dwellings they contained.

1.5.5 It was generally recognised that the inherent weakness of the concept such as its dependence on subjective assessment, its imprecise formulation and its 'nominal' measurement were exacerbated by geographical bias. In 1967 therefore a more realistic attempt was made in the House Condition Survey, as reported in *Economic Trends No. 175* [QRL 20] and '*Old Houses into New*

Homes' (Cmnd. 3602) [QRL 44] to provide data on the structural condition of the dwelling stock in England and Wales. Firstly, repair costs were estimated to enable some quantitative comparison between dwellings, and secondly, the inspectors' experience and judgement were checked in order to eliminate 'erratic' results, and measures were taken so that inspectors did not work in areas with which they were familiar or which were similar in character in order to reduce the problem of familiarity. This survey indicated that there were approximately one million (subject to the limitations of the sample) more unfit dwellings in the first quarter of 1967 than had been reported by the old method two years before. It must be emphasised, however, that a national sample of 6000 dwellings is not really adequate for this purpose.

1.5.6 A survey of the condition of dwellings in London was also carried out in 1967, the results of which are published in [QRL 66] and further enquiries were conducted in the other conurbations in England (reported in [QRL 28–32]) and in the sub-regions of Wales (reported in [QRL 72]). A new house condition survey in England and Wales was launched in the Autumn of 1971 and the published results are expected to appear shortly.

1.5.7 Mention should perhaps also be made here of the West Midlands Conurbation Housing Survey 1966, carried out a year before the comparable house condition survey in the conurbation, and the West Yorkshire Conurbation Housing Survey 1969 which was in the field in the months succeeding the house condition survey. The results are published by the DOE in *Housing Survey Reports* No. 6 and No. 7 (respectively) [QRL 33–34] and they present a considerable amount of information on the housing conditions in those areas complimentary to the house condition surveys in that they refer essentially to households rather than dwellings. [QRL 33], in addition, draws comparisons between the local and the national picture (as revealed by *The Housing Survey in England and Wales 1964* [QRL 68]).

1.5.8 Nevertheless, the classification of a house as 'unfit' is still rather an imprecise affair and as such still presents considerable difficulties of interpretation. In particular, doubts have been cast on the uniformity of interpretation across the country. In reply the sub-committee on standards of housing fitness in their report *Our Older Homes: A Call for Action* [B 26] conclude that although standards may be expressed more objectively, it will always be necessary for a degree of personal judgement to enter into the assessment and that in terms of the present day standard, where areas of houses are dealt with, orders have to be submitted to the Minister, whose Inspectorate provide the means of maintaining consistency in interpretation.

1.6 Size

1.6.1 In measuring the size of dwellings one of the major housing interests lies in the living space that it provides and this in turn is dependent to a large degree on the internal floor area of the dwelling and the number, size and shape of the rooms that make up the dwelling. It is true that there is considerable information about the size of local authority dwellings in terms of floor area and for both public and private sector dwellings in terms of the number of bedrooms but these relate only to new construction and are treated in Section 3.1. We must rely, therefore, on Census figures [QRL 12] for the size distribution of the total stock of dwellings and in a Census it is impracticable to gather any more information than the crude number of rooms. Even here, though, problems remain because over the last four Censuses the definition and enumeration of 'rooms' have changed somewhat.

1.6.2 In 1961 'rooms' included all rooms used for living, eating and sleeping. Kitchens were included only if meals were regularly eaten there (or in Scotland if they were slept in). Rooms available for these purposes but not so used were specifically included in the 1961 definition and this may have

resulted in rooms being recorded in 1961 that were excluded in 1951. In 1966 a kitchen (or scullery if used for cooking) was always counted as a room but to eliminate small kitchens in the 1971 count all those kitchens that were less than 6ft. wide were not to be included. Apart from the obvious danger of using width as a proxy for the floor area of a room this innovation may not be entirely successful since the census wording may be misconstrued to mean 'small' kitchens less than 6ft. wide rather than *all* kitchens less than 6ft. wide, an error that would lead to difficulties in interpreting the census data.

It appears that obtaining an accurate enumeration of 'rooms' is one of the most intractable problems in the Census and thus to wrangle over the implications of the definition is hardly appropriate but it is important to note that rooms used exclusively for business purposes have never been included as 'rooms' for Census purposes. In many cases this is a reasonable practice but is less so in the case of studies and offices in dwellings occupied more especially by people in the professions, since it understates the actual living space available to these households.

1.6.3 *The Housing Situation in 1960* [QRL 67] and the *Housing Survey in 1964* [QRL 68] followed the same definition as the 1961 Census but have, of course, a different basis. Even in these much smaller surveys it was still found impossible to measure the size of individual rooms. Instead [QRL 67] introduced a less useful measure, the gross internal floor area of the rateable unit, but since these figures were derived from the Inland Revenue and in many cases 'corrected' to correspond to the internal floor area their accuracy is open to doubt.

1.6.4 *The Use of Rooms.* A distinction between the use of rooms in dwellings would be a useful innovation but some of the problems associated with this are demonstrated by *Scottish Housing in 1965* [QRL 60]. Here an attempt was made to enumerate separately bedrooms and kitchens. The questions about bedrooms were asked first and for this purpose any room which was slept in was counted as a bedroom and thus by definition every rateable unit had a bedroom.

It was subsequently found that by asking about bedrooms first some households occupied only bedrooms since all rooms were slept in. This is mis-leading since, in fact, in many cases one of the 'bedrooms' was also used as a kitchen. It is also possible because of this multiple use of rooms, an occurrence more common in Scotland than in England, that some rooms were counted twice.

2 Occupancy and Ownership

2.1 Households

2.1.1 The organisation and distribution of the population in households is one of the basic elements of the social and economic life of the country and as a concept 'the private household' is much wider and looser than the 'family' which is perhaps the more familiar and traditional social unit. Particularly in relation to the housing of the population the household is the most useful concept because by definition members of a household share the same accommodation and make collective demands for housing whilst in some contexts the family extends beyond people in this situation. Of course, not all the population is contained within private households but these non-private groups usually receive separate consideration in terms of their housing requirements.

2.1.2 For the *1966 Sample Census* [QRL 12] a private household was defined as:

'(a) any group of persons, whether related or not, who live together and benefit from a common housekeeping; or

(b) any person living alone who is responsible for providing his or her own meals.'

In practice this definition does not indicate sufficiently clearly which people should be included within a particular household because of the way in which the Census is conducted. For the Housing Tables of the *1966 Census* [QRL 12] a private household included all those people actually in the household on Census night (this included visitors). The only people who were not in the household but who were included were those who were out on night-work and those people who arrived the next morning having spent that night travelling.

2.1.3 This is the *de facto* household which may be useful for counting heads but whose most obvious

limitation is that it does not reflect faithfully the household's normal composition and in some cases excludes altogether households who were totally absent on Census night from their accommodation. This limitation naturally becomes critical for the Household Composition Tables [QRL 12] and so the concept of usual residence has been introduced which brings together in the same household those members who are normally considered to be part of that household. Visitors are therefore excluded, being assigned to the household at their usual address, and all those people who live away during the week are excluded from the household unless the person returned as 'head' is in this position in which case his usual residence is the address of the household which he heads. There are, however, problems with two major groups of people; students and members of the Armed Forces. The usual residence of the former group is taken to be their home and not their term-time address, whilst the latter's usual residence is the place where they are stationed. In particular students in University towns will inflate the de facto household figures substantially and at least for some periods in the year will make special demands on the housing accommodation in these towns.

2.1.4 In addition to defining the members, certain rules were adopted to aid in the identification of households in general. In 1966 a household had to have exclusive use of at least one room so that two 'households' sharing a room were classified as one household and in distinguishing between private and non-private households in doubtful cases, the cut-off point was five persons contained within a household who were either boarders, patients, foster-children or employees depending upon the type of establishment. Within non-private establishments themselves, in England and Wales a person or group of people were treated as a separate household if they were either:

'(a) a family which does not normally depend on the institution for the provision of meals, or

(b) a person or group for whom the institution does not provide any daily meals.'

In Scotland, however, the only private households enumerated as such at non-private establishments were those in private dwellings appearing in the enumerators' lists of sample addresses. As a whole the treatment of households in non-private establishments appears arbitrary and, to a certain extent, must inevitably remain so.

2.1.5 An important practical limitation of the definition is the fact that it is sometimes difficult to apply and can lead especially to an under-enumeration of one-person households. For example, the 1966 Census for England and Wales reports that in addition to the deficiencies due to the sample frame, the post-Census survey showed that there was an under-enumeration of households to the extent of about 2% (30,000 in the sample) almost half of which was caused by the inclusion of single-person households in other households.

2.1.6 The 1951 and 1961 Censuses had substantially the same definition of a 'private household' as the 1966 Census but certain of the rules for identifying households were different. In 1951, in contrast to later practice, a household did not need exclusive use of one room to qualify and the division between private and non-private households in doubtful cases was on a different basis. All households with under ten people were counted as private; if however there were ten or more then the household was treated as non-private if the number of boarders exceeded the number in the family of the head of the household.

2.1.7 The practice in the 1961 Census was much the same as that in 1966 but differed in respect of the treatment of private households in non-private establishments. In this case a private household was

only counted if it satisfied the conditions applied in 1966 about the separate provision of meals *and* occupied structurally separate quarters. In 1951, of course, private households within institutions were enumerated as part of that institution.

2.1.8 A feature peculiar to Scotland was that in 1951 households in mobile and non-permanent dwellings were not included in the household tables but were shown as separate groups in the tables for non-private households. The procedure in 1961 was similar to that in England and Wales in that if such a structure was the 'usual residence' of a group of people then the household was enumerated as, and included in, the private household category.

2.1.9 *Definitional changes*

Up to and including 1911, the Census recorded 'separate occupiers', i.e. those included on a separate Census schedule which comprised, in addition to normal domestic households, 'non-private' households. This count was clearly unsatisfactory for many purposes, and when it was decided to define private dwellings in the 1911 Census it was also necessary to define the private family as occupiers of such a dwelling. From 1911, then, the Census recorded basically what is now called the 'private household' and there has been no major definitional change since that date. Before that date estimates of the number of households in England and Wales back to 1861 have been made by the Registrar General in the *1931 Census of England and Wales* Housing, Vol ii, Chapter 5 [QRL 12] and included in *Trends in Population, Housing and Occupancy Rates 1861–1961* [QRL 71].

2.2 Occupied Dwellings and Household Spaces

2.2.1 The accommodation occupied by a single household is known as a 'household space' in the Census and since there is, then, a one-to-one correspondence between households and occupied household spaces (which is not the case with 'dwellings') it is a much more useful unit for any consideration of the housing conditions of households. It should also be possible to assess the amount of vacant accommodation by reference to the number of vacant household spaces on Census night. This is not always accurate, however, because although 'vacant household spaces' excludes accommodation from which the occupier was absent on Census night by convention there can never be more than one vacant household space per dwelling and as a result of the definition of a household, one room cannot count as more than one household space. It should be noted, though, that in 1961 a few household spaces which became vacant just before Census date appear in the tables as separate vacant household spaces in dwellings which already contain one vacant space.

2.2.2 Vacant dwellings in 1961 and 1966 were counted as vacant on the same basis as household spaces but in 1951 a dwelling could be 'vacant' although the occupier was only temporarily absent on Census night. As a guide to the amount of accommodation that is available for occupation but is not so occupied 'vacant dwellings' define the situation with regard to the assumption that one dwelling should be occupied by one household and ignores the extent to which multi-occupancy varies between tenure groups. In addition, although dilapidated buildings that are uninhabitable should be excluded from the Census enumeration, no account is often taken of the quality of vacant accommodation in discussions of the effective margin of 'vacancies' needed for mobility. If, as evidence suggests (Penrice [B 14] p. xxv), there is a tendency for it to be 'older and less well provided with basic amenities than the housing stock in general' then it is a factor of some importance.

2.2.3 A possible source of error in the vacancy figures is the existence of extremely elusive householders who could not be contacted by the enumerator. To investigate this possibility the post-enumeration survey in 1966 re-visited one in ten of all dwellings recorded in the Census as 'vacant' or 'derelict', or 'household absent'. It is recorded that 'out of a national sample of 8,344

dwellings, 230 were found to have been occupied on Census night; this corresponds to about 0.15% of the population.'

2.3 Household Types

2.3.1 For housing matters in the Census the general concept of the 'household' has been found most useful but households are not homogeneous entities and they vary in their composition and social and economic attributes. This is reflected (except in 1951) in the separate publication of Housing Tables, and Household Composition Tables [QRL 12] of which the former provides more information on the housing situation of households. Nevertheless, households of different type and composition will make varying demands for accommodation and the most obvious type of household is the family because, after all, it is more common for people living together to be related than not. The 1966 Census definition of a family is either:

(a) a married couple with or without their never-married child(ren) or

(b) a mother or father together with his or her never-married child(ren).

A family could consist of grandparents and their never-married grandchildren where there were no parents.

2.3.2 As a sociological unit the family is often considered to be much more extensive than this definition would allow, although for a number of economic and social reasons the family has been assuming this restricted form. On the other hand, in time of trouble it is not unusual to find that families will extend hospitality to relatives or ancestors who will probably consider themselves to be an essential part of that family.

2.3.3 In 1951, on the basis of a one percent sample of Great Britain the Housing Tables [QRL 12] presented details of households by type in relation to the number of rooms occupied (see Section 2.3). Households were also classified by the age and marital status of the head. Two types of households were distinguished based on the inclusion of people in the household in one of the following groups:

I Head of household
II Spouse of head
III Designated children of the household
IV Near relatives of head or head's spouse
V Resident domestic servants
VI The remainder

Primary family units (PFUs) were composed of all those members of a private household who were classified into groups I to V above, and a '*PFU household*' was one that contained no persons other than those in the PFU. A '*composite household*' therefore included persons in addition to those in the PFU. In fact, the composition of a PFU may belie its name in that it may not contain a family by any criterion that one may adopt; a single-person household would constitute a PFU, for example. The division of households, themselves, into the two types appears to be somewhat arbitrary and an example may serve to highlight this difficulty. A '*PFU household*' could, for instance, contain resident domestic servants and their children but were a household to contain a married (widowed or divorced) brother or sister of the head, accompanied by his or her own children, then the household would be counted as a '*composite household*'. In particular the logic of including resident domestic servants as part of a family seems suspect unless they fall, perhaps, into the 'faithful old retainer' category. As a result, in terms of kinship the classification leaves much to be desired but in broad terms does give a guide to the extent to which housing and other economic conditions are forcing households, that might ideally want separate accommodation to amalgamate.

2.3.4   However satisfactory this might or might not be, when a similar exercise was carried out in the *1961 Census* [QRL 12] a family was re-defined (as in the *1966 Census* [QRL 12]) and a different classification of households was employed. The exact classification of households by type is rather long and complex and can be found in Appendix I to the Household Composition Tables *Census 1961* [QRL 12] but the broad types are:

(1) One-person households
(2) Other households not containing a family
(3) Households containing one family without others
(4) Households containing one family with others
(5) Households containing two or more families with or without others

These household types were further classified by the family type of the chief economic supporter. This means that it is not possible to compare directly the results of the inquiries into the living space of different households in the 1951 and 1961 Censuses (see Section 2.4).

2.3.5   An alternative classification of households has been developed by J. B. Cullingworth in '*English Housing Trends*' [B 4] and has been used extensively by the Government Social Survey in studies with which they have been associated. (See, for example, *The Housing Survey in England and Wales 1964* [QRL 68]). It is based on the size and age structure of the household and represents a rather tentative approach to a description of the life cycle of a household.

2.4   The Living Space of Households

2.4.1   *Potential households*
The Census is primarily a source of data on the number of households, the stock of occupied dwellings and rooms but it does give details of the sharing of dwellings and the 'fit' of households to their accommodation in terms of the density of occupation (number of persons per room) and in 1951 and 1961 the number of rooms in excess of persons or the number of persons in excess of rooms.

These figures, useful as they are, do not let us assess the extent to which the households are suited to their accommodation unless some assumptions are made about the desirable standards by which it is to be judged. One rather crude assumption that is sometimes adopted is that there should be one household per dwelling—a numerical surplus of households implying that there is overcrowding and a surplus of dwellings implying the opposite. A much better approach for relating households to dwellings is the concept of the 'potential' household which according to *Housing Statistics* [QRL 26] No. 14 is defined as 'families and other groups likely to want separate dwellings and their number is estimated as the total of Census type households *plus* married couple families, with or without children, not forming or heading a household, *less* three-quarters of those one-person households who share dwellings with other households.' The treatment of one-person households in shared dwellings is of course arbitrary. It is designed to make allowance for the fact that some such sharing is voluntary and is preferred to alternative arrangements. As a definition it has many arbitrary features, but probably it gives a better rough guide than does any other definition. An article explaining the definition of 'potential' households and some of the limitations of the concept, an outline of the method used in forecasting their numbers and forecasts for the regions of England and Wales and their sub-divisions was included in *Statistics for Town and Country Planning*, Series III, No. 1 [B 1]. Later projections using 1969 based population projections have now been given for England and Wales and for Scotland in *Housing Statistics* [QRL 26] No. 20 and are to be given for the regions in [QRL 26] No. 24. Comparable projections for the sub-divisions of regions are available on request from the DOE.

2.4.2 *Census Hypotheses.* The Registrar General has considered the problems of relating households to their accommodation and in Chapter VI of the *Housing Report* (1951) [QRL 12] four 'hypotheses' were considered concerning the number of rooms adequate for households of different types. These did not relate to any official standards but followed 'generally accepted principles' about the separation of the sexes for persons over the age of ten with respect to sleeping accommodation. A similar exercise was carried out in 1961 but since some new 'hypotheses' were formulated and the classification of households differed the results are not properly comparable and are now, in any case, considerably out of date. For a discussion of the 1961 results see [B 6].

2.4.3 *Overcrowding*
Official standards for 'overcrowding' were laid down in the Housing Act 1935 and later in the Housing Act 1957, where for a dwelling with a given number of habitable rooms the number of permitted 'equivalent persons' was laid down. Children under one are ignored and children aged from 1 to 10 count as half 'an equivalent person'. However, consideration must also be paid to the floor area of individual rooms so that size constraints were stipulated for the number of equivalent persons that may occupy rooms of various sizes.

The first part of this standard was used as a measure of overcrowding for England and Wales, in [QRL 67] and [QRL 68], and for Scotland in [QRL 60]. Whatever the errors of application especially in the Scottish study where there were problems in the identification of rooms, this standard has come under increasing criticism in recent years as being totally inadequate as a guide to reasonable concepts of overcrowding since the standard was first formulated in 1935. In particular the validity of the treatment of children under ten has been strongly questioned and indeed, the standard as a whole gives a very meagre allowance of living space per person. It is argued therefore that even in their time these surveys understated the extent of overcrowding in the country.

It would be useful if this official standard for 'overcrowding' could be used in relation to the Census material which is our most regular and comprehensive guide to housing conditions in the country but unfortunately this is not possible. First, the Census does not recognise 'equivalent persons' and secondly, 'rooms' in the *1966 Census* [QRL 12] density tabulations always includes kitchens whilst they may not under the 1957 Act. In the latter respect, however, the measure is equivalent to the 1951 and *1961 Census* [QRL 12] in practice. Lastly, there is no size restriction on the recording of rooms in the Census (but note the 1971 practice with 'small' kitchens).

2.4.4   *The bedroom standard*
The Government Social Survey has proposed a measure, incorporated in the 1960 and 1964 surveys of England and Wales [QRL 67] and [QRL 68], the Scottish survey of 1965 [QRL 60] and the W. Midlands conurbation Housing Survey (*Housing Survey Report No. 6*) [QRL 33], that is commonly known as the 'bedroom standard' and which assesses the extent to which a household under-occupies its accommodation. In any household:

'(a) Each married couple was given one bedroom
(b) Any other person aged 21 or over were each given a bedroom
(c) Persons aged 10–20 years inclusive of the same sex were paired off and a bedroom given to each pair
(d) Any person aged 10–20 years left over after this pairing was paired with a child under 10 of the same sex. If no pairing of the latter kind was possible, such a person was given a separate bedroom.
(e) Any remaining children under 10 years were paired and a bedroom was given to each pair. Any remaining child was given an additional bedroom.'

An excess of bedrooms was taken as evidence of under-occupation but, as with all such standards, it runs the risk of imposing unsuitable conditions on what is essentially a wide variety of individual circumstances.

2.4.5   *Second homes*
One final consideration in dealing with the living space of households which tends to be overlooked when so much attention is paid to the sharing of dwellings by households, is the extent to which one household may occupy more than one dwelling. It will present some difficulties of definition if 'holiday accommodation' is not to be included and especially if the tenure of such accommodation is considered. To take an extreme example a seaside caravan may be owned and used exclusively as a second home by a single household. Alternatively, it may be let as 'holiday accommodation' to other households when the owner does not require it. Finally, a single household may exclusively rent such accommodation. Where does one draw the line?

2.5   The Standard of Accommodation
2.5.1   At present, with one exception, there is no comprehensive method or yardstick for determining the general quality of the accommodation available to households. Indicators and statistics, as we have seen, are piecemeal, difficult to evaluate, and relate to the living-space and amenities available to households and the fitness of and amenities in dwellings.

2.5.2   The one exception is the 'Parker Morris' standards (see section 3.1) which relate to the needs of design and equipment in modern housing but we have no statistics that would enable us to judge how far present-day housing meets these standards and how far builders in the private sector are guided by them. Even these standards do not pay attention to the layout and density of housing and other environmental factors affecting housing quality. In this connection it is interesting to note that local authorities in England and Wales may now declare 'General Improvement Areas' under the Housing Act 1969 'to deal with the improvement of living conditions in predominantly residential areas' by 'improving the amenities of such areas, or dwellings therein, or both'. The progress of this work is now reported regularly in *Housing Statistics* [QRL 26].

Under the (Scotland) Act 1969 Scottish authorities do not declare general 'Improvement Areas' but 'Housing Treatment Areas' (see under Section 3.4).

2.5.3   *Improvement grants*

The rate at which improvements to the housing stock are being made by the provision of 'standard grants' and the installation of 'standard amenities' under the House Purchase and Housing Act is recorded in [QRL 26] for Great Britain and the regions. The picture at local authority level in England and Wales is provided in the Supplementary Tables to *Local Housing Statistics* [QRL 39]. These statistics are, however, more useful for judging the implementation of the Act than for actually gauging changes in the quality of housing because the most complete enumeration of household amenities, the Census, is not properly comparable with 'standard amenities' which are in any case related to dwellings and not households. In addition the considerable amount of 'do-it-yourself' improvements is nowhere recorded. 'Improvement grants' introduced in 1949 are also made at the discretion of the local authority (hence the term discretionary grant) for the provision of new dwellings by conversion (see Section 3.3) or for the improvement of existing dwellings. In both cases the dwellings after the completion of the work should normally conform with the 12-point standard, described in circular 54/69, and in the case of improvements may include the provision of missing 'standard amenities' as well as other facilities. The tabulations in *Housing Statistics* [QRL 26] do not, of course, give any indication of the type of improvements carried out in dwellings for which these grants are approved.

2.5.4   *The occupation of 'unfit' housing*

The extent to which households are occupying accommodation that is unfit for human habitation was the subject of special inquiries in [QRL 67], [QRL 68] and [QRL 60], but since they relied on local authorities' assessment of the dwellings all the problems that arise with the stock figures apply to these as well (see section 1.5).

2.5.5   *Temporary housing*

Apart from consideration of generally unfit housing, local authorities have control over a number of properties that are known collectively as 'temporary housing' which were initially intended only for short-term occupation. These are mainly composed of prefabs provided after the last war under the Housing (Temporary Accommodation) Act 1944 and old army camps that were taken over by local authorities immediately after the war to alleviate the housing shortage. The number of those that are remaining in use in Great Britain are shown regularly in the Supplementary Tables to *Housing Statistics* [QRL 26] along with such dwellings as have been declared 'unfit' by local authorities but which after some repair have been retained in use for the time being.

2.6   Tenure

2.6.1   The tenure by which a household occupies its accommodation is by any yardstick an important characteristic of that household and amongst other things the fundamental division between owner-occupation and renting reflects to a large extent social values and institutions as well as government policy. More importantly the tenure of a household has repercussions for the legal and financial rights and responsibilities of the household and this in turn helps to determine the desire and ability of households to attain any particular tenure status.

2.6.2   In reality the basis on which households occupy their accommodation includes a large number of individual circumstances but whatever the particular needs and aims of a classification of tenures the requirements of final tabulation mean that the number of categories should be fairly small but exhaustive. Under these circumstances it is almost inevitable that there will be some blurring of the differences and consequent difficulties with marginal cases. Despite the undoubted importance of such fundamental data as that relating to tenure the first Census to inquire about tenure in fact was that of 1961 which used the following classification:

Code	Tenure
0	Owner-occupied
1	By renting it with a farm, shop or other business premises
2	By virtue of employment
3	Rented from Local Authority or New Town Corporation (includes the Scottish Special Housing Association in Scotland)
4	Rented unfurnished from a private landlord or company
5	Rented furnished from a private landlord or company
	Some other way

2.6.3 In 1966 however, 1 and 2 were combined into an 'other tenures' category. As an illustration of the problem of assigning some tenures to a particular category, the instructions issued to Census staff for coding forms that did not fall into the first six types are particularly revealing (see the Housing Tables 1966 [QRL 12]. An almshouse, for example, hardly represents the popular picture of the type of accommodation rented furnished from a private landlord or company and similarly as a result of these instructions there is no implication that any rent is paid in money terms in groups 2, 4 and 5. Additional notes show that the relatively homogeneous owner-occupied group 0 also contains properties held on leasehold for which the initial granting was 21 years or longer (31 years or longer in Scotland); accommodation held on a shorter lease is assigned to one of the 'renting categories'. Leases of over 21 years are known as long leases in legal terms, but the intention in the Census is presumably to distinguish between the security offered by short-term and long-term leases.

2.6.4 *Households and tenure*

Tenure is an important 'axis for cross tabulation' in Census parlance; information can be obtained about the differences in housing conditions between different tenure groups, and in the Census this refers to the living space of households and the availability of amenities and garaging (in the *1966 Census* [QRL 12]). Information is also available in *The Housing Situation in 1960* [QRL 67], *The Housing Survey in England and Wales 1964* [QRL 68], and *Scottish Housing in 1965* [QRL 60] which use a similar classification to the Census.

2.6.5 *Dwellings and tenure*

The other side of the picture as it were, is the stock of dwellings by tenure but since there is not a complete correspondence between households and dwellings the problem of households with two different tenures occupying the same dwelling is encountered. The Census procedure is to classify the dwelling according to the tenure of the household which has the lowest coding. Thus if a dwelling were owner-occupied but one room of it was let to a lodger, then the owner-occupying household would be allocated code 0 and the lodger code 4 or 5 (depending upon whether the room was furnished or not.) The whole dwelling however, would be considered to be owner-occupied and the accommodation of the lodger is effectively ignored. A similar procedure is adopted in the tabulations of stock by tenure in the Supplementary Tables to *Housing Statistics* [QRL 26] but in this case, estimates of reasonably-separate accommodation (see 1.1) are also included so that the figures approach more closely a classification of household spaces by tenure.

Differences in the condition (and state of disrepair) of dwellings by tenure was investigated by the House Condition Survey in England and Wales 1967 (reported in [QRL 20] and [QRL 44]). Additional information for Wales is available in the *Welsh House Condition Survey 1968* [QRL 72] and for the conurbations as a result of the Conurbation House Condition Surveys [QRL 28–32] and for the GLC area in [QRL 66]. More recent figures will shortly become available when the results of the House Condition Survey in England and Wales conducted in the autumn of 1971 are published.

2.6.6 *Changes of tenure*

Changes of tenure are most commonly associated with household mobility but dwellings too may change their tenure when, for example, a house is sold to the occupying tenant. In either case we have relatively little regular statistical information and the most readily available figures relate to the sale of local authority dwellings. Notice that if we are concerned with changes from local authority ownership then strictly we should only consider those houses built under subsidy and not those built specially for sale although the latter are included under the local authority building programme. Global figures for England and Wales are given quarterly in *Housing Statistics* [QRL 26] but *Local Housing Statistics* [QRL 39] provides information annually for all local authorities in England and Wales.

One of the aims of the sample housing survey in England and Wales in 1960 [QRL 67] and 1964 [QRL 68] and in Scotland in 1965 [QRL 60] was to inquire into the mobility of households, a topic which has implications for a wide range of problems including vacancy rates, household formation and building policy, but one of the most interesting and valuable aspects of these inquiries was the extent to which they threw light on the intensity and direction of movement between tenure groups, a subject about which there is a dearth of published information.

The 'previous tenure of borrowers from building societies' based on the findings of the Sample Survey of Building Society Mortgages (between April 1968 and March 1969) and published in [QRL 26] No. 14 is an alternative guide to tenure mobility but the way in which the tabulation is presented means that it is not possible to estimate the size of the flows into owner-occupation. At best, however, mortgage statistics can only provide a partial view of such mobility.

Holmans [B 9] has used the data sources mentioned above to produce his own estimates of the flows of existing households between tenures in the year 1967.

3   Changes to the Stock of Dwellings

Changes to the stock of dwellings are brought about by new construction; conversions of existing buildings, be they residential or non-residential; and wastage, including demolition and abandonment. Of these it is the progress of new construction on which attention has been focused since the war because in a period of housing shortage this has been seen as the most effective way of increasing the stock and because totals of annual house completions have been an object of intense political rivalry. Using the Census stock figures at any one time as a base, to obtain figures for the stock of dwellings at some period after that date we must add on figures for new construction, allow for conversions of property, and subtract those dwellings that have been removed from the stock between the two dates. This hypothetical task enables us to highlight some of the more troublesome features of the available statistics.

3.1   New Construction

3.1.1   As we have seen, the stock of dwellings for Census purposes includes impermanent and improvised structures that were inhabited on Census night, as well as permanent dwellings, but since the figures published in *Housing Statistics* [QRL 26] relate solely to permanent dwellings 'which may be expected to maintain their stability indefinitely (60 years or more)' these temporary structures are not covered in the statistics. It is true that the completion of 'mobile homes' is shown under 'Temporary Housing' in the Supplementary Tables but these unfortunately are 'factory-built bungalows of a type intended for permanent use but which can easily be transferred from one site to another' and do not relate to those, not inconsiderable, number of caravans, houseboats, etc. that are built and used as dwellings.

3.1.2   *New construction: types*
Qualitative changes in the stock can be measured by comparing the type of housing being newly constructed with the characteristics of the existing stock but there are considerable difficulties in marrying the Census and DOE statistics. Fortunately, the types of dwelling distinguished in *Housing Statistics* [QRL 26]—houses, bungalows, flats and maisonettes—can be fitted into the Census Building Type Classification very easily. We, of course, cannot tell whether they are 'shared' or not.

Much further than this we cannot go. It might, for instance, be of interest to compare the size of new dwellings with statistics of dwellings in the Census but this is not really possible because *Housing Statistics* [QRL 26] uses the number of bedrooms per dwelling whilst the Census figures refer to total 'rooms' and there is no standard formula for describing a three-bedroomed house, say, as an x-roomed dwelling. For Scotland, though, new dwellings are tabulated by their number of apartments, where an apartment does not include any apartment not designed for use as a living room or bedroom.

Much as we might like them to be, the statistics presented in *Housing Statistics* [QRL 26] are not produced for the convenience of comparison with the Census so that in a way it is possibly unfair to criticise them for this deficiency. They do in fact present much interesting and useful information about the nature of new building with the greatest detail being available for the public sector. Thus quarterly figures are available for the number of dwellings contained within buildings of different storey heights included in 'tenders approved for local authorities and new towns' whilst the figures for the storey heights of private buildings are available annually in the Supplementary Tables.

3.1.3 *New construction: industrialised building, density and standards in approved tenders*

Other topics regularly covered in [QRL 26] based on the return TC2 introduced in 1964 (See p. 151 for a specimen copy) are the progress of local authority industrialised building, the residential densities of new local authority dwellings and their standards.* The standards are particularly interesting because they are based on the recommendations of the Parker Morris Committee in their report *Homes for To-day and To-morrow* [B 22] which laid down certain standards of design and equipment for new dwellings. The main recommendations concern floor space per person, a second WC and a wash basin, space heating, kitchen fittings, electric sockets and bedroom cupboards, all of which are described in detail in the 'Notes and Definitions' to *Housing Statistics* [QRL 26].

From the 1st January 1969 the standards relating to floor space, a second WC, space heating and bedroom cupboards, became mandatory for all local authority dwellings to be subsequently approved but it should be emphasised that these dwellings, and especially those incorporating the non-mandatory standards, are dwellings of a very high standard indeed. It is wrong, therefore, to consider the Parker Morris standards as defining a lower limit beneath which accommodation is unacceptable or intolerable. In particular many dwellings that would be generally deemed to provide adequate accommodation would not contain the requisite number of electric sockets or a second WC, let alone a wash-basin in the WC or in a room adjacent to it.

3.1.4 *New construction: private sector standards*

The lack of information on the standards of private sector housebuilding is an important gap in official statistics. Statistics exist for the number of bedrooms and storey heights in the private sector as

they do for local authorities but we are not able to judge how far private builders have been influenced by the Parker Morris standards and, therefore, whether local authority dwellings are better (or worse) equipped than private dwellings.

There are, however, two alternative sources of information, the first of which is available as a by-product of a survey of dwellings mortgaged in the United Kingdom to the Nationwide Building Society (NBS) which was reported in 'What Houses are People Buying?' 1970 [QRL 43]. This survey sought information about the type, size (superficial floor space) and number of bedrooms and reception rooms in dwellings mortgaged as well as the availability of central heating, garaging and the building materials used in the construction of the main walls. The major advantage of the data contained in the *Occasional Bulletin* [QRL 43] is that it is readily available and free but serious doubts do exist as to the validity of the results for the private sector as a whole. For a fuller discussion of the material available in the Nationwide's *Occasional Bulletin* [QRL 43] and the deficiencies of the sample employed see Section 6.1.

The second source, Building Statistical Services *Annual Surveys of New Housing* [QRL 6], first conducted in 1964, is based on a detailed physical survey of a statistically valid sample (some 370) of new houses and flats completed in Great Britain each year. Each report gives estimates of the total area of external walls, windows, external doors, roofs, floors, partitions, and garages. Typically, for each of these elements, the total area is divided by material or by type of construction. In addition there is invaluable information about the dwelling type, price, storey height of dwellings and of the floor areas of different types of room, the number of electric sockets, the availability of central heating and other internal equipment by type. Since these surveys are a commercial venture the reports are rather expensive (£100) and are obtainable solely from Building Statistical Services (14 Great College Street, London S.W.1) to whom reference should be made for further details of the contents.

*There is no information about the standards of local authority dwellings in Scotland.

3.1.5   *New construction: tenure distribution*
It is often assumed that assigning newly built housing to one of the Census tenure categories can be achieved by a straightforward division between housing by the private sector for owner-occupation and housing by the public sector for renting. This is, however, not the whole picture because some dwellings built for Government Departments, such as the police, are not in the normal sense 'rented' and some houses are built by local authorities specifically for sale. Precise figures for this latter category are available in the Supplementary Tables to *Local Housing Statistics* [QRL 39] and quarterly in *Housing Statistics* [QRL 26] so that we can estimate fairly accurately the tenure distribution of dwellings built by the public sector. Unfortunately, there is no information about the proportion of private sector building that is for owner-occupation and that for letting. DOE estimates of changes to the stock of dwellings by tenure in the Supplementary Tables to *Housing Statistics* [QRL 26] do show however the net effect of all changes to the stock of dwellings.

3.2   Stage of Construction
3.2.1   Although figures for dwelling completions may be the ultimate interest of new construction statistics, at times the actual progress of construction in the country is also required to gauge, for example, the current and future levels of activity in the building industry. Dwellings are relatively complicated pieces of equipment and their construction time may cover a number of months so that the 'flow' of construction can be represented by figures for dwellings started, under construction and completed.
3.2.2   These terms are explained in considerable detail in the return on housing progress (Form P.2 (Hsg) in Appendix II) and we need not elaborate on them here except to note that one of the commonest errors of interpretation (even by local authorities) is caused by confusion over the meanings of the terms 'started' and 'under construction' and that

the treatment of blocks of flats may hamper comparisons between months or quarters since it may result in anomalously high 'starts' figures in one period and subsequent low figures in succeeding periods.
3.2.3   The most up-to-date figures on housing progress in Great Britain are available in the DOE's press releases but for published figures both the *Monthly Digest of Statistics* [QRL 41] and the *Monthly Bulletin of Construction Statistics* [QRL 40] are useful sources. The former, though, restricts itself to figures for monthly completions whilst the latter shows dwellings started, under construction and completed. Seasonally adjusted figures for starts and completions are also available monthly in the *Monthly Bulletin* [QRL 40].
3.2.4   Although only published quarterly, the information available in *Housing Statistics* [QRL 26] is more detailed than that available in the *Monthly Bulletin of Construction Statistics* [QRL 40] so that housing progress is shown separately for England, Wales and Scotland*, and figures are included for Northern Ireland to enable the total U.K. performance to be assessed. A regional analysis (including Scotland) of starts and completions provides additional information about the activity of the various branches of the public sector—local authorities, new towns, housing associations and government departments—as well as of the total private sector.

3.2.5   *Regional and Local Housing Progress*
The coverage of the progress of new construction in the Supplementary Tables [QRL 26] is in general in greater regional detail than has been available elsewhere and so, for example, annual figures for housing progress in the regions and conurbations have been reported regularly and so have dwellings completed in the statistical sub-divisions of the regions of England and Wales. Much of this can be obtained independently by reference to *Local Housing Statistics* [QRL 39] which shows the housing progress for individual local authorities,

---

* Monthly figures for Scotland are estimates since information about the private sector is only available quarterly.

counties and regions in England and Wales and to the *Housing Return for Scotland* [QRL 25] a similar publication.

Local Housing Statistics [QRL 39] has another important use, namely that it provides a breakdown of the distribution of the building activities of local authorities outside their own areas. This would not be a problem but for the fact that dwellings are shown against the authority who built them and not the area in which they were constructed. This table should also be consulted in relation to the regional figures of housing progress in *Housing Statistics* [QRL 26].

3.2.6 *NHBRC construction statistics*

An independent source of house construction statistics is the National House Builders Registration Council (NHBRC) which is a private body set up by house builders to promote high standards of private building. Although some private house builders are not on the register it is estimated that at present 99% of houses built for the private sector are erected by NHBRC members but comparisons with DOE figures are not strictly possible because their definitions differ. For example, to comply with NHBRC regulations a registered builder is required to submit an application for inspection at least 14 days before he starts work on the dwellings. The receipt of the application for inspection is taken for statistical purposes to be the 'start'.

3.3 Conversions

3.3.1 Returning to our attempt to relate changes to the stock of dwellings over time, we now come up against the problems of the conversion and adaptation of existing structures. Conversions of these can take many forms and they need not all result in the creation of additional dwellings but a useful distinction for our purposes can be drawn between those that do and those that do not. Conversions of existing dwellings in the first place can result either in the creation of one 'new' dwelling from two or more others (e.g. the conversion of two country cottages into one) or the creation of

more dwellings than had existed originally (e.g. the creation of 'flats' in large Victorian houses). Secondly, a complete change of use of premises may result in gains and losses to the stock of dwellings, for example, when a dwelling is used as business premises or when a stable is converted into a flat.

3.3.2 Alterations that do not result in the creation of additional 'dwellings' may, however, result in the creation of more than one household space in the existing dwelling (as we have seen in relation to the Census data) but to preserve comparability with the Census stock these would have to be ignored, as would extensions to existing dwellings.

3.3.3 The statistics of the conversion and adaptation of existing dwellings and premises have been better developed in the past. After the war, the *Housing Return for England and Wales* [QRL 24] and that for Scotland [QRL 25] gave figures for all conversions and adaptations and also for the repair of unoccupied war-damaged dwellings, then an important source of new accommodation. Subsequently from March 1956 in the English publication and after 1960 in the Scottish publication the analysis became solely for grant-aided conversions under the various Housing Acts. This means that present-day statistics are incomplete in their coverage even of those conversions that result in a change in the number of dwellings, and what is more important, they relate solely to the total number of dwellings available after the completion of the work and not the net result of the conversions. The DOE does, however, still collect this information in the quarterly Form P.14 (Hsg) (Appendix II).

3.3.4 Whilst some buildings that are being changed to residential use will be included in the above figures there is no statistical indication of the extent of this change nor, moreover, of losses that are due to changes from residential to other use.

3.3.5 *Housing Statistics* [QRL 26] is the current publication for Great Britain dealing with the 'Improvement Grants' that may be provided for the improvement and conversion of dwellings under the various Housing Acts and a breakdown of these improvement grants by local authority in

England and Wales is provided annually in *Local Housing Statistics* [QRL 39]. Scottish figures are also still available in the *Housing Return for Scotland* [QRL 25]. A brief description of the amount that may be granted and the conditions, under which they are made may be found in the 'Notes and Definitions' to *Housing Statistics* [QRL 26].

3.4   Losses to the Stock of Dwellings

3.4.1   In the published statistics relating to losses to the stock of dwellings the most glaring deficiency is the paucity of information on private demolitions and wastage. To quote *Housing Statistics* [QRL 26] No. 21, apart from slum clearance, losses to the stock of dwellings 'include the removal of post-war prefabricated bungalows and of former service camps in temporary use for housing, loss through flood, fire or other damage, obsolescence, change to other use, and removal to make way for new developments of any kind.' Of these sources of loss, figures for the removal of 'prefabs' and the decline in the number of families housed in former service camps are included in the Supplementary Tables to [QRL 26] from time to time under 'temporary housing' whilst Scottish figures for the demolition or conversion of 'prefabs' are included quarterly in the *Housing Return for Scotland* [QRL 25]. No separate figures are given for the extent to which dwellings in the housing stock fall into disuse and are abandoned, how many dwellings change from residential use, and the number of dwellings cleared to make way, for example, for new roads and private residential or commercial development. Some indication of their extent may, however, be obtained from the summary table of the estimated annual gains and losses to the stock that is included annually in [QRL 26]. These estimates are 'educated guesses' by the DOE based on the Form P14 (Hsg) returned quarterly by local authorities (see Appendix II for a specimen).

3.4.2   Of all the ways in which losses take place, there is most information about slum clearance but these statistics reveal that their collection depends upon specific provisions of the Housing Acts under which local authorities are empowered to take action on 'unfit' housing. Many of the concepts and statistics, described in the 'Notes and Definitions' to *Housing Statistics* [QRL 26] relating to the 'mechanics' of slum clearance are of little direct interest in themselves. Moreover, the unit of slum clearance, 'the house', is inconsistent with the definition of a dwelling in the Census and that in general use with the Ministry; under Part II and III of the Housing Acts, 1936 and 1957, reference is made to structures, either temporary or permanent, that are used for human habitation. An exception is the practice in Scotland where a house is consistently used to mean a separate dwelling.

3.4.3   To achieve comparability with the Census, then, the statistics have to be provided in terms of the number of dwellings that have been cleared. Information which is at present lacking about the age, size, amenities and tenure distribution of houses cleared would also be invaluable in itself and as a way of assessing the qualitative changes in the housing stock. It is likely, though, that it would be particularly difficult to identify the tenure of and the amenities available to households who had in all probability left the housing considerably in advance of demolition work (see paragraph 3.4.9). The best guide to the probable changes to the stock as a result of slum-clearance remains the figures provided in the national [QRL 20, 44] and conurbation [QRL 28–32] house condition surveys for the tenure and amenity distribution of 'unfit' houses although not all the houses removed by slum clearance action are 'unfit'.

3.4.4   At present *Housing Statistics* [QRL 26] is the source of published slum clearance statistics for England and Wales, the regions and Scotland. Before 1966 this topic had been included in the *Housing Return for England and Wales* [QRL 24] and that for Scotland [QRL 25]. In England and Wales the number of houses demolished in or adjoining clearance areas are shown separately from those individual unfit houses that are demolished or cleared outside clearance areas. A great deal of confusion however, is often caused by lack of understanding of a 'clearance area', which comprises the unfit houses in an area. Houses 'adjoining a clearance area' are, on the other hand, those fit houses that are added to an area to enable a usable space to be provided during and after the clearance.

3.4.5 Not all houses that have been declared unfit for human habitation are in fact demolished or closed. At times, under powers provided in the Housing Acts, an unfit house may be made fit for habitation by the owner with the local authority's consent or by the local authority itself. The numbers of such houses that have been thereby improved are included in a separate table.

3.4.6 The closure rather than the demolition of a house presents some problems for the statistics especially if at a later date it is eventually demolished. The practice is to include the demolition in the demolition figures for that period but exlude it from the net total of all houses demolished or closed. Alternatively a house that is closed may be made fit for habitation but in England and Wales the figures do not take account of this.

3.4.7 Demolition and closure figures for Scotland in *Housing Statistics* [QRL 26] are, in contrast with the English figures, divided between 'specific statutory action' which includes all houses in clearance areas and unfit houses elsewhere and 'other action', the latter being estimated between 1955 and 1961. The coverage of 'unfit' houses under 'specific statutory action' in Scotland was revised in [QRL 26] No. 22, to include houses dealt with since 25th August 1969 as failing to meet the tolerable standard.

3.4.8 Slum clearance by individual local authorities is shown for England and Wales in *Local Housing Statistics* [QRL 39] and for Scotland in the *Housing Return for Scotland* [QRL 25].

3.4.9 Slum clearance action results in the displacement of the former occupants of the housing who need alternative accommodation and to assess the likely number of dwellings that are required for replacement it is important to know the number of households (or potential households) who occupied the housing. This information cannot be gleaned from the present statistics in [QRL 26] since they refer to the number of persons and families (*not* households) moved during the quarter whilst the practice in slum clearance programmes means that there is often a lag between the removal of the occupants of unfit housing and the clearance of their housing. Thus the figures of persons and families moved during any period cannot, then, be taken to represent those people whose housing has been demolished in that period.

4 The House-Building Industry

The activities of the house-building industry unfortunately lie on the border between the housing responsibilities of the old Ministry of Housing and Local Government and the interest in general construction of the former Ministry of Public Building and Works (MPBW). Naturally there are overlaps of interest in, for example, housing progress and completions but statistics have suffered perhaps from the lack of a separate and identifiable interest in the house-building industry as such which often means that it is difficult to distinguish housing from other types of construction. Improvements in this direction, wherever possible, would be most welcome. Certain other statistics by their very nature cannot be easily applied to any one form of construction work however, and here the statistics of the output of the building materials industry are particularly troublesome.

Since the wider aspects of construction are to be dealt with in a parallel study, *The Statistics of Construction* by M. C. Fleming, the coverage of statistics here will only include some of the more important statistics relating to housing and to house-building. An alternative source of information on construction statistics in general is the study (1967) commissioned by the MPBW and undertaken under the supervision of D. A. Turin which included the compilation of an extensive *Inventory of Construction Statistics* and a less detailed *Directory of Construction Statistics* [B 20] both of which are still most useful guides, although in some cases out of date. The results of the second phase of the study published in *Construction Statistics: The Opinion of the Private User* [B 18] provide a useful critique of construction statistics existing at that time although house-building as such received no special attention.

4.1. Employment

4.1.1   One of the distinctive features of the construction industry when compared with many other industries is the way in which the level of employment of workers may fluctuate quite widely from time to time. The permanent employees of any one firm may be a small proportion of the total work force and these are often the administrative, technical, professional and clerical workers who are usually excluded from consideration in the employment statistics. The casual nature of employment, therefore, and the existence of 'labour only' sub-contractors has caused doubt to be cast on the reliability of the figures for the employment of operatives by contractors in Great Britain on public and private sector housing included in the *Monthly Bulletin of Construction Statistics* [QRL 40], and the *Annual Bulletin of Construction Statistics* [QRL 2].

4.1.2   Direct labour

To the figures of operatives employed by contractors should also be added those workers employed by the public sector as 'direct labour' on housing but information about these employees is obtained only bi-annually in April and September as a result of special enquiries by the Department of the Environment. Figures in [QRL 40] relate to the direct labour operatives of local authorities and new towns but those in *Housing Statistics* [QRL 26], relating solely to the month of April in each year, include employment by government departments and estimates for the employment by public utilities.

4.1.3   Repair and maintenance

Apart from the employment of men on new construction there are also a considerable number of men who work on the repair and maintenance of existing dwellings. Quarterly figures for contractors' labour employed on this type of work are available in *Housing Statistics* [QRL 26] but the figures are not divided by client so that it is not possible to ascertain the amount of employment on public and private sector housing separately. The number of operatives employed as direct labour on repair and maintenance work is derived from the bi-annual enquiries mentioned above. In [QRL 40] the analysis of local authority and new town direct labour by type of work is also available by region, by type of authority and by size of authority (measured by the number of operatives employed). A complementary census conducted in the private sector of the construction industry* is reported in the *Supplement to the Bulletin of Construction Statistics* [QRL 65] where there is an analysis of employees by trade of firm and type of work, including repairs and maintenance on housing, and further tables covering employment on housing work by region and by size of firm. Estimates for the total public sector direct labour force for the month of April are included in [QRL 26].

Whilst we may regard employment on repairs and maintenance as an accurate reflection of the formal employment on this type of work there is also a considerable amount of 'concealed' employment in the form of private persons carrying out routine maintenance, repair and decoration to their own homes, which, of course, does not enter the official statistics. Much more significantly perhaps, the value of their output is also excluded from consideration in statistics, an omission which is regrettable though understandable in light of the extreme difficulty of finding any reliable base from which to estimate figures. However, attempts have been made to estimate the size of the do-it-yourself market in *Building Maintenance Statistics 1970* [QRL 11].

* Before 1971 a census inquiry into employment and output was held in April but this has now been combined with the former September census into the occupational breakdown of operatives, the combined inquiry being held in October.

4.1.4 *Wage rates and earnings*

Wage rates in house-building *per se* are not frequently published but those for the industry as a whole and information about earnings, hours worked and an index of the average hourly earning in construction are included in the *Monthly Bulletin of Construction Statistics* [QRL 40] based on information provided by the Department of Employment. *Building* [QRL 9] and the *Architects Journal* [QRL 7] also produce quarterly figures of the rates of wages for various categories of work but their major concern is with the production of 'measured rates' (including materials and wage costs) for various types of building work e.g. excavation or concrete work.

4.2 Output

4.2.1 Employment statistics can be of considerable interest as a measure of the capacity of the industry since house-building requires the availability of a large number of highly skilled workers. The actual finished product of the industry is as varied, if not more so, as the skills required to produce it so that although output could be measured in terms of the completions of dwellings the variations in the nature of the unit and the inclusion of siteworks as well as house construction in the statistics mean that in general the value of output is more useful. In interpreting figures for the production of the industry, though, it should always be borne in mind that there is considerable difficulty in measuring a quarter's output accurately in value terms and that further if this is expressed at constant prices seasonally adjusted the figures should only be taken to represent the broadest indication of trends.

4.2.2 Since the statistics of the value of output of the construction industry are collected in the same inquiry as those for employment by type of work, it is not surprising that deficiencies in the coverage of employment in respect to certain types of work are repeated in the output figures. Accordingly the value of output of contractors' labour is divided between new housing and non-housing work in the quarterly tables in [QRL 40] and the annual figures in [QRL 2] but the value of work done on repairs and maintenance does not distinguish between housing and non-housing work.

4.2.3 The quarterly value of the work done by the direct labour of the public sector reported in [QRL 40] is not divided by type of work nor is it directly comparable with the contractors' output since the latter contains a profit element which the former does not.

4.2.4 The greatest breakdown of the figures for the value of output is obtained, as in the case of the employment statistics, as a result of the special enquiries into the industry made by the Department of the Environment and parallel to the analysis of direct labour output by type of work and by region, type and size of authority included in the *Monthly Bulletin of Construction Statistics* [QRL 40], a similar analysis for the output of contractors' labour has been included annually in the *Supplement to the Bulletin of Construction Statistics* [QRL 65] showing the value of output by type of work and by region, type of firm and size of firm. An important point to note is that this regional breakdown is not based on the location of the work but on the region of location of the head office of the firm★ which may be misleading since many large firms work on a national rather than a regional scale. In contrast, the work of a local authority is carried out by and large within its own area (but see under Section 3.2).

4.2.5 Tabulations of the value of output at constant prices seasonally adjusted are available quarterly in the *Monthly Bulletin of Construction Statistics* [QRL 40] and *Housing Statistics* [QRL 26] and annually in the *Annual Bulletin of Construction Statistics* [QRL 2].

4.3 Industrialised Building

The progress of industrialised construction for local authorities and new towns in Great Britain is separately recorded in [QRL 26] although it is also

★ This is also, of course, true of the employment statistics.

subsumed under the more general heading of housing progress. An analysis by regions and by system is also included. There is, however, no definite and precise distinction between industrialised and traditional modes of construction and although guidance on the difference is given by paragraph 3 of Circular 76/65 it is unwise to place too much reliance on the data (see [B 8]).

4.4 Indicators of Future Levels of Activity

4.4.1 There exists a considerable number of statistics concerned with future levels of activity in the construction industry as a whole and in the house building industry in particular. From our standpoint the most important of these is the periodic enquiry conducted jointly by the former Ministries of Housing and Local Government and of Public Building and Works to obtain data about current and future levels of private sector house-building. Initially questionnaires were sent to some 10,000 speculative builders but starting from the enquiry sent out at the end of June 1970 the forms have been sent only to a sample of firms, stratified on the basis of the number of private starts in 1969. The results of these enquiries in terms of expected and actual starts are tabulated in *Housing Statistics* [QRL 26] quarterly where also an analysis is included of expected and actual starts by size of the builder's firm (i.e. by the number of houses they build for sale). A copy of the Return of Private Enterprise Housing is included, for reference, in Appendix II.

4.4.2 Another table in [QRL 26] showing for local authorities and new towns in Great Britain the number of dwellings 'approved but not started' reveals the extent of those dwellings for which a tender or estimate has been accepted but on which construction work has not yet started but is likely to start soon. Forecasts of future activity can be made by a knowledge of the time lag between approvals and starts and between starts and completions (see estimated time lag: start to completion in [QRL 26]). An article describing some of the methods of analysing short-term trends in housing progress is contained in 'Current Trends in Housing Progress' *Economic Trends*, May 1968 [B 19].

4.4.3 An even more fundamental series of statistics for future levels of activity are found in the 'design stage' statistics produced by the Royal Institute of British Architects (RIBA) and in the local authority design work statistics. The *Quarterly Statistical Bulletin* [QRL 45] of the RIBA includes details at a regional level of new commissions to private architects and the value of work entering 'production drawing stage'. To complement this the Ministry of Public Buildings and Works investigated the possibility of collecting similar statistics for the design work of local authorities and these have subsequently been included in the *Monthly Bulletin of Construction Statistics**[QRL 40]. The value of work is shown at the preliminary 'sketch plan' stage and the 'working drawing' stage preparatory to construction starting. Work in hand at the end of the period refers to the completion of design work on which construction has not yet started. *Local Authority Design Work Statistics* [QRL 36] attempted to show the relation between these statistics and the statistics of the value of new orders obtained by contractors but there is no straightforward method of relating the two series. The former are only a rough guide to the future level of the latter and, in addition, design stage statistics exclude the design work carried out by builders' own design teams and staff architects in industry.

4.4.4 The *Monthly Bulletin of Construction Statistics* [QRL 40] is the most important source of data on the value of new orders obtained by contractors for housing work. Figures are also included in [QRL 41] and annually in the *Annual Bulletin of Construction Statistics* [QRL 2]. The standardised value of new orders (i.e. seasonally adjusted at constant prices) is included in the *Monthly Bulletin of Construction Statistics* [QRL 40] as are regional

---

* Regional figures can be obtained on written application to the DOE.

---

figures and new orders analysed by their value ranges. With this series unfortunately there is no obvious way of relating it to the construction output series, that is, we do not know the time lag and what proportion of new orders are cancelled or speculative intentions thwarted.

4.5 Local Authority Contracts

The size and type of local authority contracts for housing in approved tenders are included quarterly in *Housing Statistics* [QRL 26] for Great Britain expressed in terms of the percentage of all schemes and of all dwellings in each category. Contracts are divided into three types: firm price contracts, direct labour estimates, and contracts with any fluctuation clauses. When considering the size of the contracts (schemes) figures cannot be taken to represent one particular site since there need be no correspondence between sites and schemes. Further analysis of tenders approved for local authorities and new towns in the Supplementary Tables to [QRL 26] include details of the types of tender and the type and form of contracts and the technical (i.e. professional) advice employed on schemes, that is, whether the expertise was supplied by the local authority, by a private firm or by the contractor.

4.6 Building Materials

4.6.1 It is difficult to define a building materials industry as such and it is even more of a problem given statistics of production of building materials to relate this production to any one type of work. Some work on this topic has however been carried out by the Building Research Station and an article appeared in *Building* January 27th, 1967 [B 3], prepared by B. D. Cullen, providing broad estimates of the amount of materials used in each class of building. Nevertheless the production and deliveries of these inputs to the industry and the building up or running down of stocks are useful indicators of the activity of the industry as a whole, of which house building is an important part, and relative movements allow us to assess to what extent the expectation of producers has matched the demands of the construction industry. Figures for a wide range of building materials and components production are included monthly in the *Monthly Bulletin of Construction Statistics* [QRL 40] and the *Monthly Digest of Statistics* [QRL 41] and annually in the *Annual Bulletin of Construction Statistics* [QRL 2] and the *Annual Abstract of Statistics* [QRL 1]. The Board of Trade *Census of Production* [QRL 13] is also an infrequent source of data.

4.6.2 Although the end use of total building material production remains a problem it is not, however, so much of a problem to define the mix of products that are used in house building and by weighting them appropriately to produce a price index of house building materials. Though prices of materials are produced independently by the Department of Trade and Industry, *Building* [QRL 9] and the *Architects Journal* [QRL 7] for example, the Department of Trade and Industry alone compiles a price index of house-building materials. Monthly movements are recorded in the *Monthly Digest of Statistics* [QRL 41], *Trade and Industry* [QRL 70] and the *Monthly Bulletin of Construction Statistics* [QRL 40] and annually in the *Trade and Industry* [QRL 70] and the *Annual Bulletin of Construction Statistics* [QRL 2].

4.7   The Costs of New Construction

4.7.1   The construction of a dwelling is not only a long process, but it is also a very expensive one and total costs including the costs of land and provision of services are very high in relation to the income of the average household. The most obvious interest, then, in the construction cost of new dwellings arises from the implications for the people who will have to pay for the very high capital cost of their accommodation.

4.7.2   Statistics on the actual areas of new dwellings and the costs of house-building are available

in considerable detail for construction on behalf of or by local housing authorities whose housing schemes until recently have been scrutinised closely by the Ministry in order to gain 'approval' for loan sanction or subsidy purposes. At local authority level the returns made by those authorities reporting to the Institute of Municipal Treasurers and Accountants included some detailed estimates of the individual costs of land, services, construction and professional fees for two-and three-bedroom houses, 'typical' of those erected during the year. From the issue for the financial year 1955/56 only the cost of construction was included in *Housing Statistics* (IMTA) [QRL 27] but now all statistics of this type have been discontinued in that publication.

4.7.3   When the *Annual Report of the Ministry of Housing and Local Government* [QRL 4] was regularly published statistics of areas and costs were restricted to two-storey three-bedroom houses approved during the year, and the average cost of construction by region adjusted to a standard floor area of 900 sq. ft. Now, however, *Housing Statistics* [QRL 26] is the most important source and figures for 'area and costs' cover a much wider range of local authority dwellings. As a whole, though, published statistics are of little value for detailed analysis due to the differing (and sometimes unspecified) basis on which the calculations of costs have been made and the considerable variation in individual tender prices for local authority housing. A valuable account of the difficulties of using tender prices as a guide to the pattern of regional construction costs is contained in P. A. Stone [B 16], p. 111.

4.7.4   Reference should be made to the 'Notes and Definitions' of *Housing Statistics* [QRL 26] to ascertain the various definitions of terms employed in the tables and to the specimen return TC2 for the range of information collected (Appendix II). The most important point is that from the beginning of 1968 dwellings are classified by designed bedspaces (as used in the Parker Morris report [B 22] and the Ministry's cost yardstick) rather than the number of bedrooms and no comparison is possible between the figures before and after that date although figures for both types of classification were given for a time and a rough conversion factor can be obtained from a table, provided in the 'Notes and Definitions' relating the bedroom and bedspace classifications for houses and bungalows approved during the second quarter of 1967.

4.7.5 Comparisons between English and Scottish figures are subject to severe limitations because the measure of floor area in Scotland is on a different basis from that in England and Wales and in Scotland, too, the size of a dwelling is measured in terms of its number of apartments rather than bedrooms or bedspaces. Whilst for England and Wales areas and costs are analysed by the type of dwelling (i.e. storey height for flats and bedspaces for houses) and the mode of construction (traditional or industrialised) the tabulation for Scotland applies to all types of dwellings in all areas. There is, however, a regional analysis of costs and average floor area for two-storey houses in England and Wales included in approved tenders. With regard to the analysis of costs by mode of construction it is worthwhile to keep in mind the caution given about figures for industrialised building in para 4.3.

4.7.6 A more detailed picture of the regional costs of construction was shown in the Supplementary Tables to *Housing Statistics* [QRL 26] No. 9 where for the year ending the 30th June 1967, the distribution of construction costs for three types of dwellings included in tenders approved was tabulated. Apart from the traditional two-storey three-bedroom houses figures are given for flats in buildings of six to eight storeys and twelve to fourteen storeys.

4.7.7 *Total costs per dwelling in L. A. schemes*
Although construction costs in themselves are of interest, at times it is desirable to know the total cost per dwelling in schemes approved for local authorities so that figures published annually from 1968 in the Supplementary Tables [QRL 26] are particularly useful. The total average cost is divided into three parts:

(i) estimated land acquisition costs;
(ii) dwelling construction;
(iii) estimated other costs.

At present the costs of land and other costs (e.g. ancillary buildings, site works etc.) are only very approximate and are liable to error whilst no corrections are made in the average total cost for factors that may vary from year to year such as the type and location of schemes. Great caution should be exercised in drawing conclusions, therefore, from figures for different years as these factors are unlikely to remain constant.

4.7.8 *Costs and standards*
Comparisons of the average cost of construction of local authority dwellings over time are going to be complicated if the standards to which they are built change substantially so that in effect costs are being contrasted between two quite different objects. For example, the adoption of the Parker Morris standards would almost certainly in most cases lead to higher construction costs. Some indication of the differences in cost between the dwellings with these standards and those without was provided in No. 3 of *Housing Statistics* [QRL 26] for the regions of England and Wales but too much reliance should not be placed on these figures, as pointed out in the Notes and Definitions, because the degree to which a dwelling attains or fails to attain these standards may be quite considerable.

4.7.9 A better measure of the increase in standards of 'traditionally built one- or two-storey local authority houses' in England and Wales (excluding Greater London) is provided by the 'constant standards cost index'. This was devised by the Ministry of Housing and Local Government to 'compare the change in costs with other price changes, to obtain a measure of the increase in 'real' standards of local authority dwellings by comparing changes in the index with changes in the tender price and to measure the effects on costs of regional changes in the programme.' In [QRL 26] No. 10, there is a full description of the index.

Since returns are collected from only some 340 local authorities, the index is shown only for the following broad regions of the country:

1. North—Northern; Yorkshire and Humberside, North-West.
2. Midlands and Wales—E & W. Midlands; Wales.
3. South—East Anglia; South-East (excluding GLC) South West.

4.7.10 *House-building costs: index numbers*
An account of the various methods which have been used in the measurement of construction costs and their practical limitations has been provided by Fleming [B 7]. This article also included descriptions and assessments of post-war (up to 1966) indices of general and specific construction costs (including housing). There are only three currently published indices, however: the 'constant standards cost index' mentioned above; the local authority tender price index and the Nationwide index of house-building costs. The output price index of housing work produced by Carter and included in his quarterly articles in *Building* [QRL 9] was discontinued in 1969. It has, however, been described in [B 7].

The method of construction of the Nationwide's index published in [QRL 43] requires some description since it is not written up elsewhere.* It is a conventional labour and materials index based on the nationally negotiated builders wage rates— combined in the ratio of 3 craftsmen to 2 labourers —and the index of the wholesale prices of house-building materials (calculated by the Department of Trade and Industry). Materials and wages are then combined in the ratio 60 : 40. As an index of changes in cost it suffers from the disadvantage that the nationally negotiated wage rates may not represent the actual labour costs since national rates tend to be a minimum. More importantly it fails

to allow for changes in productivity so that, *ceteris paribus*, the index will over-estimate cost changes when productivity is rising and underestimate them when it is falling.

4.7.11 *Land prices*
An important element in the total cost of a dwelling is the price of building land but there is a dearth of published information on this topic except for data on auction sales in the *Estates Gazette* [QRL 15]. Apart from the auction results published weekly there have been reviews of residential land prices in *Estates Gazette* [QRL 15], 11th April, 1970, 20th March, 1971 and 15th April, 1972 and an earlier review of land prices for the years 1960–64 using the same source is to be found in Stone [B 15]. Some doubts have been cast on the reliability of this data since it represents only a sample of land transactions, and possibly those for which the owner did not initially know the market price. Stone [B 15] has also pointed to the absence of data for Scotland and Wales and the relative paucity of details of auctions in the northern regions of England. In the articles in [QRL 15] mentioned above, the lack of data for Northern England is made good by incorporation of the results published in Rogers (Birmingham) *Under the Hammer*. Nevertheless, this meagre data should obviously be treated with caution and although it may be used to show land prices in broad concentric regions around London and Birmingham it does not, for instance, enable any detailed analysis of land prices within regions to be undertaken.

Since the last quarter of 1966, the Co-operative Permanent (now the Nationwide) Building Society has made available in [QRL 43] the surveyors' estimates of the site value of new property mortgaged to the Society. It appears that there are two methods of deriving these figures neither of which is a scientific assessment. The first is for the surveyor to give what is essentially a valuation based on his knowledge of local conditions. In this case some consideration is often given to the published information on land prices in [QRL 15] and so the valua-

* This information was kindly provided by the Planning Department of the Nationwide Building Society.

tion is in part determined by these figures. The other method, known as the residual method, consists of deducting the estimated cost of the building itself, which can be done fairly accurately, from the total sale price. It should be emphasised that the site value includes the costs of road works, drainage and other services and, in the latter case, unless an allowance is made for it, the profit of the builder. It is doubtful whether the two methods would yield the same results on the same site since it is difficult to see how the profit element could be estimated using the former method and, moreover, there is considerable scope for observer variability in the assessments.

Considerable work has been done in the Department of the Environment to produce an index of land prices for private sector builders based on Inland Revenue data. The information available so far has allowed the production of an index that shows the movement of prices per housing plot in England and Wales and the major regions from 1963 (with 1966 = 100). An article describing this

work and the production of the index appeared in *Economic Trends*, No. 208 [B 24], and the index will appear half-yearly in *Housing Statistics* [QRL 26] from May 1971. When sufficient information is available it is intended to construct a somewhat more useful index of price per plot including data for transactions in housing land outside 'pressure areas.' A further index of price per acre will help to overcome the present problems with the price per plot index that conceals the fact that where permitted development densities are higher land prices tend to be higher.

Direct comparisons between the movements of the DOE index and the changes in the average site value of the Nationwide are not possible because they attempt to measure different things and the time periods over which they are measured do not coincide. Nevertheless, bearing in mind the sophistication of the DOE index and the deficiencies of the Nationwide's sample (see section 6.2.3) it is perhaps surprising that the DOE's index appears to be the less stable.

5 Personal Expenditure on Housing

The problem of the measurement of personal expenditure on housing is a difficult topic. In the first place there is a fundamental division between those households who own and those who rent their accommodation. Some owner-occupiers own their accommodation outright and do not make any identifiable payments for their accommodation whilst others make regular mortgage or loan repayments; yet others make payments which cover only the interest on the loan or mortgage, for example, where the mortgage is linked with an endowment policy. Mortgage payments are also generally thought of as, at least partly, an investment in the sense that they represent both payments for current and future (after the loan is repaid) housing.

Amongst those households who rent, distinctions are often drawn between the conditions in the furnished, unfurnished and local-authority rented sector.* In the main, differences in the private rented sector are due to differences in the legal rights of tenants, particularly in relation to security of tenure. A review of the furnished code and rent-regulation is to be found in the *Report of the Committee on the Rent Acts* [QRL 56] to which reference should be made for further details on this aspect. Consideration of the rents of furnished accommodation is further complicated by the element in the payment for the services of the furniture and other services provided by the landlord such as heating, lighting, etc.

Apart from rents and mortgage payments there are a range of other payments that are incurred by householders by virtue of their occupation of property. In this category fall rate payments which are considered more fully in section 7.2; expenditure on repairs, maintenance and improvements of the property; and travel expenses. It is conventional to include the first two groups in housing expenditure but not the third although the location of a household within an area will have repercussions on the amount (and therefore the cost) of all trips but especially work trips. There is, however, one subsidiary item of income that certain households enjoy from the sub-letting of property that represents more of a problem in defining expenditure on housing; for some purposes in the statistics this income is deducted from the household's expenditure on housing with the result that some households may have zero (or negative) housing costs.

There are, then, considerable difficulties in standardising housing expenditure particularly between households in different tenure groups. The conventions adopted in the Family Expenditure Survey (FES) are described in Section 5.3 and the treatment of owner-occupation in the national account statistics is described in Section 8. The Cost of Living Advisory Committee have also considered the problems of owner-occupiers' housing costs in relation to the index of retail prices and the conclusions from their most recent deliberations are included in *A Report from the Cost of Living Advisory Committee*, Cmnd. 3677 [B 27] (but see also previous reports Cmd. 7077, Cmd. 8328, Cmd. 8481, Cmd. 9710 and Cmnd. 1657).

It is not only in respect to expenditure that tenure differences complicate the picture. The extent to which the Government helps and subsidises consumers of housing varies between tenure groups. At present local authority tenants are in general subsidised by exchequer and rate contributions towards the cost of local authority housing; owner-occupiers, too, can claim tax relief on the interest element in their mortgage repayments.

---

* The discussion in this section relates to the conditions as at March 1972 but considerable changes are envisaged under the proposals in the White Paper 'Fair Deal for Housing' [B 21].

5.1 The Working of the Rent Acts

5.1.1 The private renter does not receive a Government subsidy but he is protected to some extent by measures introduced by various Governments to control the level of rents. At the moment some form of rent control is applied to furnished and unfurnished lettings of a rateable value not exceeding £400 in Greater London and £200 in the rest of England and Wales under the Rent Act 1968. For unfurnished dwellings applications may be made for the registration of a 'fair' rent to a Rent Officer or subsequently if there is a disagreement, to a Rent Assessment Committee. Tabulations of the number of applications for registration of a 'fair' rent and their distribution by Rent Assessment Panel areas are shown in *Housing Statistics* [QRL 26] but obviously it is desirable to know something about the effects that such registration is having on the level of rents. We know from the other tables whether rents were increased or decreased and the percentage of rents registered that increased or decreased by various annual amounts.

5.1.2 Comparisons are also made in the tables in *Housing Statistics* [QRL 26] between the average previous and average registered rent by the gross value of the accommodation, sub-divided into houses, flats and rooms (i.e. non-structurally separate accommodation). In general this will highlight those classes of property where the differences were greatest but it is not valid to assume that this picture is totally representative of unfurnished lettings in England and Wales as a whole. It may be that only the grossest cases are brought to the Rent Officer but we have no real way of proving this since the statistics are just not available. Figures for the average expenditure on rents in the Family Expenditure Survey, which is discussed in more detail later, might prove helpful but unfortunately these payments are not analysed by the gross value of the accommodation occupied.★

5.1.3 *Housing Statistics* [QRL 26] also analyses the size and age of the accommodation by the three types of premises to provide some information about the standards of the accommodation that has been the object of rent regulation.

5.1.4 Information about the rent-regulation of unfurnished property is now included (from issue No. 18 of [QRL 26]) in the Supplementary Tables where occasionally details of the working of the rent determination of furnished dwellings, namely applications for the determination of a reasonable rent and applications for security of tenure, are produced. Statistics for the rent determination of furnished dwellings also appear annually in the *Handbook of Statistics* [QRL 19]. Two new tables are still regularly available, however, in *Housing Statistics* [QRL 26] which also include figures for Scotland and cover the number of applications for registration of a fair rent and the direction of change of these registered rents.

5.1.5 Information on the effects of Government intervention in the private rented sector has been available in the *Rent Act 1957 Report of Inquiry* [QRL 51] by P. G. Gray and Elizabeth Parr and more recently in [QRL 56]. This latter contains a considerable amount of information about the workings of the rent regulation machinery and the furnished code that has not been published elsewhere as in the case of the further analysis of rent regulation and rent tribunal statistics produced by the DOE specially for the report. On the other hand, both the Tenant and Landlord Surveys in 1970 aimed to gather a substantial amount of new background information for the report with reference to conditions in the S. Wales coastal belt, the conurbations of Greater London, the W. Midlands and central Clydeside and to particular stress areas within those conurbations.

5.1.6 The Tenant Survey was based on samples of all tenancies in these areas and gathered information about dwelling types and rents, the amenities in and condition of dwellings and the attitude of tenants to their rent, landlord, accommodation and to the Rent Act procedures (and to knowledge of the Rent Acts for tenants in unregistered accommodation). Inquiries were also made about

★ The DOE hopes to include FES tabulations by gross value ranges in their own analysis of the 1970 data.

the tenant households and their income, age, household type, social grade, origin and social adequacy.

The survey of landlords was narrower in its coverage than the Tenant Survey and was restricted to landlords owning property in Greater London and the W. Midlands, the sample frame being the list of tenancies interviewed in the Tenant Survey. No survey was made of landlords with property in 'stress areas'. Questions were asked about the attitude of landlords to their rents and to Rent Act procedures, their experience of problems in landlord/tenant relations and the characteristics of landlords, namely their age, sex, social grade, country of birth, colour and English-speaking ability.

5.1.7 The extent to which the Tenant Survey can be used as a reliable indicator of conditions in the whole of the private rented sector in Great Britain is debatable although one of the reasons for which it was instituted. Somewhat less than a half of all households renting their accommodation from private owners were enumerated in the conurbations of Great Britain at the 1966 Census, and approximately one third in the conurbations included in the Survey. It seems likely, therefore, that the report provides a reasonable picture of conditions in the large urban areas of the country but it is unsafe to draw conclusions on conditions outside these areas. On the other hand, the choice of 'stress areas' in the conurbations was essentially based on the advice of Rent Officers and Secretaries of Rent Assessment Committees and to quote the Report 'cannot be regarded as typical of the centres of conurbations, but only as illustrative of some types of areas of housing stress, not necessarily the worst.'

5.1.8 *Harassment and illegal evictions*
Statistics of the number of prosecutions undertaken in Great Britain for harassment and illegal eviction and the size of the fines imposed have been included in the Francis Report [QRL 56] for the period from the coming into force of the legislation until the end of March 1970.

5.2   Rents of local authority dwellings
5.2.1   To achieve a balanced picture of expenditure on housing it is desirable to view payments in two ways; in relation to income and other attributes of households and in relation to the standard of accommodation that a certain rent or mortgage payment will purchase. In fact, this latter aspect has received little attention outside the local authority sector but some data was published in the *Report of the Committee on Housing in Greater London* [QRL 55], the *Housing Survey in England and Wales 1964* [QRL 68] and *Scottish Housing in 1965* [QRL 60]. Unfortunately for local authority housing the picture is complicated by the operation of rent rebate schemes and by the attempt of local authorities to adjust the rent burden so that the high cost of supplying new housing is not shouldered solely by new tenants but to a certain extent by all tenants.

5.2.2   A very general picture of the level of rents charged for local authority dwellings has been provided every six months from April 1968 in *Housing Statistics* [QRL 26] where the figures are based on returns from a 'representative sample' of local authorities. The rents recorded are net rents (i.e. after deduction of rent rebates) and they do not include any element for rates or service charges. Although the average rent and the rent index are compiled separately for Greater London and the rest of England and Wales, the average rent will mask what one might expect to be significant variations between the regions and between different types of dwelling and authority. Further, as an 'average value' index it does not allow for changes in the quality of local authority housing, a point of some importance since the publication of the mandatory standards. To some extent the ageing of existing local authority dwellings works counter to this latter day improvement of standards but on balance the Cost of Living Advisory Committee in [B 27] feel that the index contains an upward bias.

5.2.3   The need for greater detail has been provided to some extent by the annual publication in

[QRL 27] of the returns made to the Institute of Municipal Treasurers and Accountants by a large number of local authorities in England and Wales starting from the financial year 1949/50. Unfortunately the coverage of local authorities has not been uniform and especially before issue No. 9 for 1957/58 there was a considerable deficiency in the number of urban and rural district councils reporting.

5.2.4 Rents were initially shown for only two- and three-bedroom houses analysed by age but later two-bedroom flats were included in the analysis. In 1968 *Housing Statistics* (IMTA) [QRL 27] was altered substantially and *Housing Rent Statistics* [QRL 23] (now known as *Housing Statistics Part I*) introduced 'in agreement with the Ministry of Housing and Local Government'. The rents now are shown for both houses and flats of one to three bedrooms and for four-bedroom dwellings but the computation of the rent figure now ignores the effect of rent rebates.*

5.2.5 For Scotland, the White Paper entitled *The Rents of Houses owned by Local Authorities in Scotland* [QRL 52] was first published after the war for the position at the 15th November 1949 in consultation with the Scottish Branch of the IMTA. It fulfilled, and still does fulfil, much the same role for Scotland as *Housing Statistics* (IMTA) [QRL 27] for England and Wales but it includes all Scottish Local Authorities and many of the tables are more detailed.

5.2.6 The form of the White Paper had to be altered in 1957 because the Valuation and Rating (Scotland) Act abolished owner's rates as at May 1957 and made reductions in rents under leases then current. Quoting from the return: 'Accordingly whereas all previous returns showed rents inclusive of owner's rates, the rents shown for 1957 are *net* rents, *exclusive of any rates*. Comparisons of rents as between different areas will be much more useful as owner's rates will no longer obscure the position.' Standard rents are equivalent to gross rents in

England and Wales, that is, rents before deduction of rebates (where applicable); net rents need no explanation.

5.3 Family Expenditure Survey and Related Statistics

5.3.1 The most comprehensive source of information on households, their income and their recorded expenditure on housing by tenure is the *Family Expenditure Survey* [QRL 16] prepared annually by the Department of Employment and Productivity. The Survey is based on returns made by a sample of households, the size of which was more than doubled in 1967 but which has not eliminated the possibility of substantial sampling error. The non-response rate among households in the sample, as the 1969 Survey admits, probably has the effect of biasing the sample itself towards those households with lower incomes. Further errors are, of course, always possible in completing the return but in general it can be assumed that rent and to a lesser extent rate payments would be fairly accurately returned since they are relatively large in amount and regular in occurrence.

For a detailed account of the survey, its assumptions and limitations, reference should be made to the Notes accompanying it and to the *Family Expenditure Survey, Handbook on the Sample, Fieldwork and Coding Procedures* by W. F. F. Kemsley, HMSO 1969 [B 10].

5.3.2 The title 'Family Expenditure Survey' is somewhat of a misnomer because it is in fact based on private households rather than on families but because of the method of record keeping over a period of fourteen consecutive days the rules for identifying the members of a household differ slightly from those in the Census and have much in common with the practice in the Government Social Survey (see [B 6]).

5.3.3 As we have seen problems arise in standardising housing expenditure between different households because of their different tenures. In the survey the types of tenure:

---

* Previously the rent figures represented the range of actual rents charged to tenants.

(1) Rented unfurnished
    Local Authority
    Other
(2) Rented furnished
(3) Rent-free
(4) Owner-occupied
    In process of purchase
    Owned outright

are the conventional ones used in the Census except that households who pay no rent are separately classified. The figures for expenditure in the case of tenure (1) and (2) relate to 'payments such as rent, rates and water *less* receipts from sub-letting' but to achieve comparability with these figures the expenditure of the rent-free and owner-occupied categories is a notional sum. In essence, mortgage payments are excluded from housing expenditure in the owner-occupied sector and they are shown separately under 'other payments recorded'. Instead a measure of the rent that would have been paid had the household not owner-occupied its accommodation (or occupied it rent-free) is deduced from the rateable value of the dwelling and is shown in the tables along with such payments as are made for rates (minus rebates), water and the insurance of the structure. Deductions are made in respect of income from letting or sub-letting where applicable.

5.3.4 For the purpose of analysing household expenditure by household income it is important to note that in the assessment of the gross income of owner-occupiers and those living in accommodation rent-free an addition is made to their incomes of an amount equivalent to that recorded as housing expenditure (see above). This addition is taken to represent the real income derived from the services provided by the accommodation.

5.3.5 Expenditure on repairs, maintenance and decorations is not analysed by tenure (but is included under the total expenditure on housing) presumably because owner-occupiers are more likely to make regular provision for these expenses than are tenants where the responsibility is decided

in agreement with the landlord. For this reason and because expenditures by individual households may be very large these figures are liable to rather high sampling error.

5.3.6 A large-scale Household Expenditure Enquiry was undertaken in the years 1953–54 but *The Family Expenditure Survey* [QRL 16] as such, has been published covering the years from 1957 onwards and some of the tabulations have been changed or augmented from year to year. A full index of the tables in the reports before 1963 are included in the 1965 Survey and the present survey for 1969 has an index of tables included from 1963 to date. Of special interest are tables in the 1963 survey comparing the old average levels of rates and rateable values with new ones introduced as a result of the revaluation of the rating lists in April of that year.

5.3.7 *DOE analysis of FES data*
The Family Expenditure Survey itself is used as a basic source for a wide range of purposes and the DOE has made use of this material to produce its own statistics on rents, mortgage payments and incomes reported in the Supplementary Tables to *Housing Statistics* [QRL 26]. These are in many ways much more useful than the Survey itself because they emphasize actual outgoings rather than notional sums and in other ways differ from the rather restrictive practices in that Survey.

In the first place the figures are in a more useful annual form and tabulations are both by total household and head of household income whereas the Survey emphasises only total household income. In the case of housing expenditure, it has been argued that comparisons or studies of, for example, income elasticity are more fruitfully made using what one should expect to be the most stable and permanent of household incomes, that of the head, rather than the total household income which may fluctuate from time to time. The most important difference is, as we have noted, the fact that the figures for rents and mortgage payments do not correspond to the housing expenditure figures in the Family Expenditure Survey. Those households that own their accommodation outright and those who live in theirs rent-free are excluded from consideration.

Rents exclude all other charges, rates and services wherever it has been possible to separate them but they do include water charges (unless these are paid separately); in some tabulations the sum available from letting or sub-letting of rooms and garages is not deducted from the household expenditure; and 'cases where rent was less than 20% of gross value have been excluded as special circumstances may apply'.

The payments of owner-occupiers are not the notional expenditure figures arrived at in the Survey but actual mortgage payments except that those cases are excluded where payments on the loan or mortgage cover interest only ('e.g. where the mortgage is linked with an endowment policy'). This exclusion is unfortunate because this type of mortgage is often associated with insurance company advances for house purchase that are particularly popular with the higher income groups.

Income figures are gross but in the case of owner-occupied households, an addition is made to the income of the household equivalent to the rateable value of the property as an estimate of the income derived from ownership. Since the last major re-valuation of rateable values in England and Wales was in 1963 (1966 in Scotland) the figure is adjusted for changes in letting values by the housing part of the retail price index.

5.3.8   *Sample survey of building society mortgages*
An alternative source of information for mortgage payments is the Sample Survey of Building Society mortgages, discussed later. At present, publication has been restricted to tabulations of the size and the ratio of the monthly mortgage payments to the income of the borrower (in Supplementary Tables to *Housing Statistics* No. 7 [QRL 26]) for borrowers in 1966.

5.3.9   *The index of retail prices*
One of the basic purposes in setting up the regular 'Family Expenditure Survey' was in connection with the 'index of retail prices' in order to provide a regular means of updating the weighting basis of the index. An explanation and description of the index is to be found in [B 25]. Changes in the in-dices for the three elements of housing expenditure —rent; rates; maintenance, repairs and improve-ments—are shown in [QRL 41] and annual changes are recorded in [QRL 1].

5.3.10   *Consumers' expenditure on housing*
The FES is also used as a basic source of data for the calculation of total national consumer expenditure on housing recorded in *National Income and Expenditure* (the Blue Book) [QRL 42] but the figures relate to the 'personal sector' which is rather more the sum of private households so that an ele-ment is included for the expenditure on land and buildings by private non-profit-making bodies. A detailed account of the elements of total expendi-ture on housing and the data sources consulted in its estimation are to be found in [B 11] and in a somewhat abridged form in [B 6].

6 Housing Loans and House Prices

6.1 Financial Institutions and the Supply of Funds

6.1.1 As we noted in the introduction it is only comparatively recently that statistics dealing with housing loans have been regularly prepared and published by the DOE (formerly MHLG) although figures for housing loans by local authorities have been published since 1959 in the *Housing Return for England and Wales* [QRL 24] and details of Exchequer advances to designated building societies under section 2 of the House Purchase and Housing Act 1959 were also included in this and the *Housing Return for Scotland* [QRL 25] during the currency of the scheme. Recent interest has been in the use of housing loan statistics as indicators of short-term trends in the private sector of the housing market (see [B 19]) but the collection of financial statistics owes much to the recommendations of the Radcliffe Report [B 28], a milestone in the history of British financial statistics, and HC246 (1966/7), Estimates Committee, *Report on Government Statistical Services* [B 29].

6.1.2 The understanding and interpretation of financial statistics, however, requires considerable expertise and many difficulties are encountered by the non-specialist user. To a large degree those problems arise because financial statistics in general are not framed for the convenience of the user interested in housing. Statistics on the number and amount of loans for house purchase, as we shall see, are relatively well developed, but, on the other hand, there is a paucity of information about loans for alterations, conversions and improvements to existing dwellings.

6.1.3 *Total lending for house purchase*
Figures for advances and net advances for house purchase in the U.K. by building societies, local authorities, insurance companies and banks are in-cluded in the quarterly table in [QRL 26], 'loans for house purchase: main institutional sources'. In some ways this title is misleading and may be misinterpreted.

In the first place it has been suggested that this table refers to loans obtained with housing as security, implying that a large element of building society advances is not for use in the owner-occupation of property. The limited significance of such advances may, however, be determined by reference to the table on advances in the U.K. by type of property. Furthermore, evidence in *The Report of the Chief Registrar of Friendly Societies* (Part II) [QRL 69] suggests that advances on 'business and other properties' by societies with assets exceeding £1m. included in many cases 'some dwelling accommodation to be occupied by the borrower'. Sums for the purchase of housing for letting by private landlords can also be seen to be small but building society advances may contain a relatively significant (approximately 2% in 1970) amount of further advances on property already mortgaged to the society.

Secondly, the figures for loans in the U.K. by local authorities include estimates for lending in Northern Ireland, Scotland and by the Birmingham Municipal Bank but the total figures may be misleading because they also include loans to private persons for the conversion and improvement of existing dwellings.

6.1.4 Estimates for building societies in *Housing Statistics* [QRL 26] are revised in the light of the definitive statistics provided in [QRL 69] and information about the intended use of the property on which the advances are secured is also available but since the report is only published annually and often considerably in arrears this places a limitation on its value in any current sense.

6.1.5 Various statistics dealing with three main types of institution are also provided in *Housing Statistics* [QRL 26] and in a number of other publications. By far the most detailed coverage is available for building societies but as we might expect the activities of local authorities, at least in England and Wales, have received substantial statistical treatment.

6.1.6 *Local authority housing loans*
The IMTA undertook a pilot survey for the year 1964/5 to gather statistics on advances for house purchase by a sample of local authorities under the Small Dwellings Acquisition Acts and the Housing Acts. The results published in *Statistics of Advances for House Purchase* [QRL 64] contained a great amount of detail on local authority lending and allied services in that year but unfortunately this very comprehensive record of local authority lending has not been published for subsequent years.

Local authorities, then, provide a number of services in the general field of housing finance for private owners and housing associations and this is reflected in the tabulations in *Housing Statistics* [QRL 26]. The number and value of loans for house purchase in England and Wales on new and existing dwellings is shown separately from those loans for conversion, alteration, repairs and improvements by private owners and housing associations. These should not be confused with 'improvement grants' that are not repayable.

On a local authority basis comparable figures for housing loans made during the financial year 1967/8 were shown in *Local Housing Statistics* [QRL 39] for England and Wales. Aggregate lending was also computed for counties and regions.

In addition to their lending activities, local authorities in Great Britain may provide under section 45(1) of the Housing (Financial Provisions) Act 1958 guarantees of repayment of advances made by building societies to their members. The number of these guarantees appears to be steadily declining from evidence in a table dealing with this subject in *Housing Statistics* [QRL 26] since the in-

tention was to enable people with low incomes to purchase their own homes. This objective has now been largely taken over by the Option Mortgage Scheme.

6.1.7 *Loans by building societies*
The financial statistics relating to building societies that appear in *Housing Statistics* [QRL 26] are the most comprehensive of all the institutions and this bears witness to the special importance of building societies in the general scheme of house purchasing. One of the most important tables covers the inflow of funds into societies in the United Kingdom in terms of the balance of receipts of principal plus interest credited to savers' accounts less withdrawals. This taken together with the repayments of mortgages will to a large extent determine the amount of advances and commitments for advances that building societies may make.

The number and value of advances by building societies on 'new' and 'other' dwellings covered regularly in another table allows us to see whether the average advance on new properties is greater than that for other properties and by comparison with similar tables for local authorities and insurance companies whether the same distribution of lending is shown by the other sources.

Similar tables to these two for building societies in *Housing Statistics* [QRL 26] are also included in the monthly publication *Financial Statistics* [QRL 17] and in the sheet produced by the Building Societies Association entitled *Building Society Statistics* [QRL 10].

6.1.8 *Insurance companies*
Figures for insurance companies in *Housing Statistics* [QRL 26] are restricted to details of the number and value of loans for house purchase for both new and existing dwellings. However, in *Financial Statistics* [QRL 17] a table shows figures for the book value of the loans for house purchase at the end of the two preceding years and net (cash value) lending for this purpose annually and quarterly.

6.1.9 *Bank lending*
In general, lending by banks to the public for house purchase is restricted to the granting of short-term bridging loans; long-term loans have been mainly made to bank employees. Apart from the estimated net advances for house purchase by banks included in the table 'loans for house purchase: main institutional sources' of *Housing Statistics* [QRL 26] monthly figures for the amounts outstanding as personal loans for house purchases are available in *Financial Statistics* [QRL 17] but, unfortunately, not for the number of such loans. There is no information about personal loans for the improvement and conversion of existing dwellings.

6.1.10 *The personal sector*
Another way of looking at loans for house purchase is in terms of the sectors of the economy used in National Account Statistics to record financial transactions. Borrowing by individuals for this purpose, then, represents an increase in the liabilities of the personal sector. Although the personal sector contains some unincorporated businesses and certain other bodies these are unlikely to have a substantial distorting effect. Annual figures are given in *National Income and Expenditure* (the Blue Book) [QRL 42] where loans for house purchase are analysed under the following headings:

(1) Local Authorities
(2) Other Public Sector
(3) Building Societies
(4) Insurance Companies
(5) Banking Sector

A similar table for quarterly transactions in financial assets for the personal sector is included in *Financial Statistics* [QRL 17].

6.2   Statistics Based on Mortgage Completions
6.2.1   Mortgage statistics can be used to answer the sort of questions posed in two recent titles from the series of *Occasional Bulletins* [QRL 43] issued by the Nationwide (formerly the Co-operative Permanent) Building Society: 'What Houses are People Buying?' and 'Who Buys Houses?' These Nationwide surveys have been particularly valuable in the past before the publication of similar information in *Housing Statistics* [QRL 26] but, as we shall see later, they suffer from serious limitations as a guide to the whole field of house purchasing or even building society activity. They do, however, provide the only published information on certain aspects of house purchase and for some purposes we are forced to rely on their figures.

6.2.2   *Nationwide data: housing*
'What Houses are People Buying'? has now been carried out in 1962, 1966 and 1970 and since the surveys are on the same basis, comparisons of the findings between these dates are possible although assumptions about trends cannot yet be made from these results. The inquiries sought information about the price, type, size, number of rooms and age of dwelling mortgaged during a fixed period in those years and further inquired about the provision of garaging and, in 1970, central heating. The 1970 survey was followed in November 1970 by 'Central Heating' No. 98 where a more detailed analysis of the same sample was presented. Significant variations were found in the incidence of full and partial central heating according to the type, price, and regional distribution of the dwelling as well as the income and age of the purchasers.

6.2.3   *Nationwide data: borrowers*
Some of the more significant social characteristics of borrowers from the Nationwide Building Society have been published in 'Newly Built Houses' 1966 and in 'Who Buys Houses?' 1963 and 1968. Details such as the age, income and occupational distribution of borrowers from the Society were collected as well as the price distribution of the dwellings mortgaged, the size of deposits and mortgages and the repayment period. So

much interest was aroused by the 1963 Survey that later, in response to general demand, a regional analysis of the results was issued. In the 1968 issue of 'Who Buys Houses'? the results of a smaller study of people borrowing under the 'Option Mortgage' scheme were also reported to show the impact that this scheme was having at that time, not long after its introduction under the Housing Subsidies Act 1967.

The availability of statistics such as those provided by the Nationwide often lead to their over-optimistic use but as is often the case, it is impossible to state accurately just what is or what is not a valid employment of them. The following points are, however, worth considering. All the results are based on samples of dwellings and borrowers in that they represent the results of only one Building Society among many and that, therefore, their general validity depends upon the extent to which the Nationwide is representative of general building society lending. To quote one example of bias, the Nationwide will only lend money on new dwellings that have a garage or garage space, and new dwellings without either are eliminated automatically from the sample. R. Wilkinson in [B 17] has compared data on price of dwellings and the income and age of borrowers for the Co-operative Permanent (now the Nationwide) Building Society and for a sample of all building societies (provided in *Building Society Statistics* Special Issue No. 6 [QRL 10]) and concluded that there were significant differences between them. All in all one might certainly expect there to be differences in policy between building societies.

Even the comparison made above may be misleading because the actual samples used in the Nationwide's analyses may be unrepresentative of even the Nationwide's activity because it is possible (though not necessarily always the case) that there are considerable variations in the actual distributions of borrowers (and housing) from one quarterly or four-monthly period to another.

A final caveat in drawing any general conclusion from these figures is that building societies are only one possible source of finance for house-purchase and that their borrowers do not represent the total house-buying population.

6.2.4   *The sample survey of building society mortgages and the survey of insurance company mortgages*

Matters of a rather similar nature to those reported by the Nationwide are also covered in *Housing Statistics* [QRL 26] and these tables are largely based on a 5% sample of the monthly mortgage completions by Building Societies in the United Kingdom, more details of which are to be found in the 'Notes and Definitions' to that publication. A copy of the Questionnaire sent out to building societies is included for reference in Appendix II. For this purpose the mortgages included in the analyses cover only those for the owner-occupation of all (or part) of a dwelling and are therefore in line with the figures in the *Occasional Bulletins* [QRL 43] of the Nationwide.

One regular table refers to the average purchase price, the average value of mortgages and the average recorded income of the borrower(s). This is not altogether satisfactory partly because figures are averages but also because the distribution of types of property and borrowers may not be constant over time and no allowance is made for this. Secondly, there is no standard calculation of income among Societies and some returns include figures referring to the basic income of the borrower whilst others count additional household income.

Further regular tables refer to the distribution of mortgages by the mortgage period; the purchase price of the property; the age of the borrower; and the age of the dwelling.

There is little information about insurance company mortgages and, apart from the value of loans on new and existing dwellings, the distribution of mortgages by the purchase price of the property is alone regularly tabulated. The figures are based however on returns received from a sample of companies representing about 60% of insurance company advances and to obtain the figures in the table a grossing-up factor has been used so that they are only approximate.

Some of the results of the continuous Sample Survey of Building Society mortgages have been included in the Supplementary Tables to *Housing Statistics* [QRL 26]. Most notable among these is some information about the mortgages, dwellings and borrowers under the Option Mortgage Scheme. This includes the distribution of borrowers by age, income, previous tenure and region and the age and price of the dwelling bought. For comparison similar distributions for all mortgages are tabulated alongside them.

The previous tenure of all borrowers, also reported in the Supplementary Tables, is particularly valuable because it reveals the extent of first-time purchasing of dwellings for owner-occupation in contrast to people negotiating a new mortgage and because it therefore provides information on the mobility of households from other sectors of the housing market.

6.2.5 The Building Societies Association who collaborate with the Department of the Environment in the preparation and collection of much of the material that forms the basis of the survey of mortgages have themselves provided in Special Issues Nos. 22 and 31 of *Building Society Statistics* [QRL 10] analyses of mortgage completions in 1967 and 1969 on much the same lines as those regularly included in *Housing Statistics* [QRL 26]. The pilot study (Special Issue No. 6) in this series has been discussed in [B 17].

6.3   House Prices

6.3.1   The price of houses is a topic about which there is very little published information but the General Register of Deeds in England and Wales and the equivalent General Register of Sasines in Scotland represent rich but generally untapped sources of data. For publication, figures based on mortgage returns have proved the most readily available but are in some ways inferior to figures based on the number of houses sold since building

society mortgages are only one means of acquiring houses, and building societies are known to discriminate against certain sectors of the market and not to attract the business of richer house purchasers. Difficulties also arise from the fact that dwellings are not homogeneous and that different types are often considered to occupy distinct housing markets. What is more, each parcel of land on which a dwelling is located is held in legal terms to be unique and, therefore, incomparable with any other.

6.3.2   The Nationwide Building Society has produced for the second and fourth quarters of each year figures of the average price of dwellings mortgaged in the United Kingdom and indices of house prices for Great Britain which have been published in [QRL 43]. Homes are classified into new houses and existing houses, the latter being divided into those that have modern design and standards and those that have not. This classification by design and standards is largely subjective since it is based on 'the opinion of the surveyor' and the index of second-hand house prices suffers from a similar disadvantage because it is based on an estimated 1939 valuation by the society's surveyors which has been adjusted to the base year. In both cases it is doubtful whether any adjustments are made for observer variability.

6.3.3   The limitations of the sample have already been discussed with respect to the Nationwide's data in the previous section (6.2.3) but the following qualifications should be kept in mind in interpreting the figures. They, firstly, relate to all houses mortgaged and there is no analysis by size or other attribute that might be expected to influence house prices; this is not eliminated by basing the price of new houses on variations in 'the average purchase price per square foot of floor space (calculated to exclude external walls, garages and outbuildings)' a figure which is itself dependent on the size of the dwelling. Secondly, the index of house prices will be affected by various factors that might be expected to fluctuate from half-year to half-year such as the size, quality, land costs and regional distribution of houses for purchase. Lastly, the regional breakdown used by the Society is one for its own purposes and bears little similarity to the Standard Regions existing at the moment.*

6.3.4 Apart from the figures published half-yearly by the Nationwide, the Society has also issued Bulletins on regional house prices based on the same dwellings used in the analysis of 'What Houses are People Buying?' 1966 and 1970. Since dwellings are classified by their number of bedrooms and their type as well as by region, the average prices are more useful than the 'raw' regional averages generally available but the considerations of validity that apply to any interpretation of 'What Houses are People Buying?' must also apply here (see section 6.2.3). Note, too, that where leasehold (or feuhold) properties are included in the Nationwide analyses of house prices, and these amounted to some 27.1% of the total dwellings in the 1970 survey, an element is added to the purchase price equal to 15 years ground rent whilst no addition is made for chief rent. The resulting figure is taken to be equivalent to the purchase price if the house were freehold. This is an arbitrary adjustment and will particularly influence the price data for Scotland where there is much feuhold property, and will affect comparability with the unadjusted DOE statistics, mentioned later.

6.3.5 To emphasise the difference in costs of house purchase in the various regions both 'A Regional Comparison of Average House Prices and Incomes' 1966 and 'Regional House Prices 1970' contain tables on the occupational and income distribution of borrowers by region and the varying size of deposits, loans and monthly repayments.

6.3.6 The index number of the average value of new dwellings mortgaged by private owners in Great Britain is published in the *Monthly Digest of Statistics* [QRL 41] under the index numbers of wholesale prices, in the *Monthly Bulletin of Construction Statistics* [QRL 40] and in *Housing Statistics*

[QRL 26] which also includes the actual average price. As an index of price changes it suffers from much the same defects as the Nationwide's index but since it is based on returns from 'a number of building societies, including most of the larger societies, whose combined assets represent about 75% of the total assets of the movement in Great Britain' it is obviously more comprehensive in its coverage of mortgages.

6.3.7 Regional house prices first included in [QRL 26] No. 5 for 1966 were based on the results of the Sample Survey of Building Society mortgages in the United Kingdom and related to the average purchase price of dwellings mortgaged. Separate figures for new and existing dwellings were given for the broad regions of England, Wales, Scotland and Northern Ireland. Subsequent regional house prices published in [QRL 26] have been based on data provided by the Valuation Office mainly about the sales of second-hand dwellings. A description of the coverage and the basic return are included in [B 14] and in the 'Notes and Definitions' to [QRL 26] but one singular feature of the primary data is that it is only obtained for those houses sold in a quarter which were also sold within the previous five years. Figures have been given from 1966 to 1970 by regions, type of area and age of property but the data does not cover Scotland, and unpublished figures for that country are still produced by the DOE from the questionnaire sent out in the Sample Survey of Building Society mortgages. The statistics are, however, available on request from the DOE but cannot be compared directly with the regional figures at present published for England and Wales since the former relates to the average price of a collection (not necessarily of constant composition) of dwellings 'mortgaged' during the year whilst the latter relate to three-bedroomed semi-detached dwellings sold.

6.3.8 Even at a regional scale the figures for house prices will mask differences in prices between what are known as 'pressure' and 'non-pressure' areas and essentially to highlight the differences sub-

* Note, for example, that Wales has been included as a separate region only since Bulletin No. 107 in February 1972.

regional analysis would be desirable. One of the most important factors that has militated against such a development is the difficulty of obtaining a sample large enough to be reliable. Nevertheless it has been possible to produce from the Valuation Office data mentioned above an analysis of house prices in the statistical sub-divisions of the South East in *Housing Statistics* [QRL 26] No. 9 where the average price of three-bedroomed semi-detached houses was cross-tabulated by age.

7   Housing Finance and Local Authorities

7.1.   The Finance of Local Authority Housing

7.1.1   The housing responsibilities of local authorities cover a wide field of activities and their finance is now one of the most significant elements in total local authority budgets. In fact, the demands are such that from the First World War local authorities have shared the burden of finance jointly with the central government.

7.1.2   *The housing accounts*

In respect to housing there is a statutory obligation under the Housing (Financial Provisions) Act 1958, section 50, as amended by section 26 of the House Purchase and Housing Act 1959 to keep a 'Housing Revenue Account' (HRA) and under the former Act, a 'Housing Repairs Account'. The Housing Revenue Account is, in general, concerned with what is known as 'council housing', described by *Housing Revenue Accounts* [B 23] as dealing with:

'(a)   The annual cost of
   (1)   The provision of dwellings for letting
   (2)   Maintaining and managing the dwellings provided
   (3)   Services or amenities provided exclusively for council tenants and not available to ratepayers generally
(b)   The annual income from Exchequer subsidies, rate fund contributions, rents and other sources.'

The main items of expenditure are loan charges incurred by the council in financing house construction, supervision and management of dwellings in the account and contributions to the Housing Repairs Account subject to a statutory minimum per dwelling. The sources of income are shown above.

Some authorities keep a 'Housing Equalisation Account' for the purpose of equalising the benefit of the 40-year pre-war Exchequer housing subsidy over the normal housing loan period of 60 years. Details of transfers to or from this account and of the Housing Revenue and Housing Repairs Accounts are to be found in *Housing Statistics Part II* [QRL 27] for a large sample of local authorities in England and Wales. These returns are available from the financial year 1949/50 whilst the equivalent publication in Scotland—the *Rating Review* [QRL 50]—has been published since the War.

Apart from summaries produced by aggregation of the returns from those local authorities who make returns to the IMTA for inclusion in *Housing Statistics (IMTA)* [QRL 27] national figures for the Housing Revenue Account and its component income and expenditure have been given in the Supplementary Tables to *Housing Statistics* (DOE) [QRL 26]. Unfortunately figures are available only as far back as 1962/63 and those before 1965/66 are estimates based partly on [QRL 27] and *Local Government Financial Statistics* [QRL 38].

7.1.3   *Maintenance and management expenditure*

Some publications produced by IMTA are related specifically to items in the Housing Revenue Account for individual local authorities. One of these is *Housing Maintenance and Management Statistics* [QRL 22] published for every year since 1965/66 in two parts. The first covers the total and average maintenance costs per dwelling for various categories of maintenance e.g. external and internal decorating or water and sanitary services. Average maintenance costs are further analysed by the age and by the storey-height of the structure. The Management section of this publication is mainly concerned with the item of expenditure in the

Revenue Account entitled 'Supervision and Management' which is further divided into general and special expenses. General expenses refer to those that are common to all local authorities (e.g. welfare, rent collection) whilst special expenses (e.g. central heating, wardens for old peoples' homes) are peculiar to individual authorities.

7.1.4 *Rent income*
The unrebated rents of local authority dwellings, as we have seen are dealt with in *Housing Rent Statistics* [QRL 23] which is now known as *Housing Statistics*, Part I. [QRL 27] covers the number and and amount of rent rebates to tenants whilst rent rebates to tenants in Scotland are shown in the *Rating Review* [QRL 50].

7.1.5 *Exchequer subsidies*
To ease the burden of local authorities in financing their housing activities the Government makes contributions to them towards the cost of providing new permanent dwellings and towards the cost of conversion and improvement of the existing stock. The total exchequer subsidy per annum in England and Wales for these two purposes has been given in the *Annual Report of the Ministry of Housing and Local Government* [QRL 4] and at intervals in the Supplementary Tables to *Housing Statistics* [QRL 26]. Separate figures for Wales and Scotland are included in the *Digest of Welsh Statistics* [QRL 14] and the *Annual Report of the Scottish Development Department* [QRL 5] respectively. It is difficult to relate the subsidies shown in these tables to subsidies specifically to the Housing Revenue Account because, firstly, contributions towards improvements and conversions are only included in that account if the improvement has been made to a dwelling in the account and, secondly, because under pre-war subsidy legislation subsidies could be provided to private enterprise whilst the contributions to private builders under post-war legislation are only under section 46 of the Housing (Financial Provisions) Act 1958 towards dwellings for the agricultural population. In addition each new piece of

subsidy legislation has been grafted on to the existing pattern of payments and this means that the total subsidy at any one time is arrived at on the basis of a number of quite different calculations.

7.1.6 *Non-statutory housing accounts*
The Housing Revenue Account of local authorities may only record transactions for certain specified housing activities as we have seen, but it is also restricted in that no 'capital' transactions can be recorded there. A Housing Capital Account may be kept by local authorities that corresponds to the HRA but the only published figures for local authorities in England and Wales are to be found in the *Return of Outstanding Debt (IMTA)* [QRL 57]. This analyses the outstanding debt for housing purposes under the headings of (1) sites, buildings, etc., (2) housing advances, improvement grants, etc., the former corresponding to construction activity for 'council housing'. Unfortunately, once again, only a sample of local authorities are covered. The *Rating Review* [QRL 50] for Scotland is in some respects more useful because it provides particulars of the net capital expenditure during the year and the net capital debt at the end; however, there is no distinction between purposes under 'Housing'.

Items that are not included in the HRA and may be in a non-statutory housing account, may include, according to [B 23]: '(1) Grants and loans to housing associations; (2) Improvement grants to private persons; (3) Grants to private persons e.g. the agricultural dwellings under section 46 of the Housing Financial Provisions Act 1958; (4) Rates, water, gas charges received from tenants; (5) Expenses in connection with demolition and closing orders and other activities under Part II of the Housing Act 1957, and in connection with clearance areas under Part III; (6) Salaries of housing staff investigating private Rent Act cases; (7) Income and expenditure relating to houses provided prior to 1919'. In addition all capital transactions in relation to the items listed above and accounts of advances for house purchase should be covered. There are no publications at a local authority level known to the author which deal with these individual items.

7.1.7 On the other hand, there exist two important annual summaries of the finance of local authority housing in Great Britain. The first, *Local Government Financial Statistics* [QRL 38] prepared by the DOE for England and Wales contains global figures of the transactions in the revenue and capital accounts relating to:

(1) Housing and land to which the HRA relate
(2) Improvement grants
(3) Other housing
(4) Slum clearance
(5) Advances under the Housing Acts.

The other, *Local Financial Returns, Scotland* [QRL 37] produced by the SDD is less detailed than its English counterpart in that accounts (2) to (4) above are aggregated into a single account. Although the returns for individual local authorities on which [QRL 38] is based are not separately published, they are available for study on application to the DOE.

7.1.8 There is very little information on the borrowing by local authorities specifically for housing purposes but the value of loans sanctioned for housing is included annually in the *Handbook of Statistics* [QRL 19]. One important specialised source of funds however is the Public Works Loans Board (PWLB) which will lend 34% (or 44% in the prosperous areas) of the amount of new capital investment expenditure (or £100,000 if greater) at rates of interest only slightly above the rate at which the Exchequer itself can borrow. The *Annual Report* [QRL 3] of the PWLB shows the advances to and repayments of loans by local authorities for housing during the previous year.

7.2. Rating Statistics

7.2.1 Rates and the rating system are of interest for a number of purposes under any general discussion of housing, and these depend to a large extent on three important characteristics of the rating system. First, the payment of rates falls almost universally on the occupiers of property in a local authority area and, second, the amount of the rate depends upon the use and the characteristics of the property. Finally, rates are a form of local taxation that contributes a major share of local authority revenue.

7.2.2 *Rate rebates*

Since the burden of the rates is so universal it is, as we have seen, an important element in the housing expenditure of households. As a tax on the occupation of property its effect is said to be regressive, unlike income tax, and may cause hardship to people with low incomes. The Allen Committee was set up, therefore, to 'assess the impact of rates on households in different income groups and in different parts of Great Britain, with special regard to any circumstances likely to give rise to hardship.' The Committee obtained information from FES and the Regular Expenditure Survey (RES) which was in the field from September to November 1963. Regression analysis was used on the data in an attempt to test and to measure the influences affecting both the rates paid by households in 1963/4 and the increase in rates over the previous year. As a result their report [QRL 54] contains a great deal of information on the influences of the physical characteristics of a dwelling on the amount of rates paid and the relationship between household characteristics (such as income) and rate-payment. This report led to the introduction of rate rebates under the Rating Act 1966 in Scotland and the General Rating Act 1967 in England and Wales for which all direct and indirect rate-payers are eligible dependent upon their income. The *Return of Rate Collection* [QRL 58] records the total and average rebate for a sample of local authorities in England and Wales but *Rate Rebates in England and Wales* [QRL 46] is more comprehensive in its coverage of details and includes all local authorities. The latter publication gives figures for the amount granted, the number of recipients and these as a percentage of all domestic hereditaments in the area. Variations in this percentage between areas may not truthfully reflect the differing proportions of low income rate-payers but rather the extent to which people have bothered to apply for or are aware of rate rebates. Other tables deal with various categories of households—(1) owner-occupied and other direct rate-payers; (2) local authority or new town tenants; (3) other indirect ratepayers—and the incidence of rate rebates between and among the different types. *Rate Rebates in Scotland* [QRL 47] does not differ substantially from the English publication but does distinguish as a separate type of household 'other direct rate-payers'.

7.2.3   *Rateable units*

The satisfactory calculation of the rate by a local authority depends on an accurate inventory of the number of rateable units, subdivided into commercial, industrial and domestic types, within its area and for this purpose valuation lists are kept and amended by local authorities. As a whole, then, the number of domestic hereditaments in an area is a reflection of the amount of residential property in that area and as such a listing of this property provides a readily accessible sample frame for housing studies, e.g. *The Housing Survey in England and Wales 1964* [QRL 68]. For this purpose, however, information in rating offices is of more value than nationally available statistics but one of the publications by IMTA the *Return of Rate Collection* [QRL 58] does include figures for the number of domestic hereditaments in the areas of those local authorities that make the return to the Institute. Equivalent figures for all local authority areas are available in *Rates and Rateable Values in England and Wales* [QRL 48] and *Rates and Rateable Values in Scotland* [QRL 49]. Nevertheless these figures need to be approached with caution because some hereditaments are mixed, i.e. they contain commercial premises as well as living accommodation and are not, therefore, included as domestic. Further there is no direct comparison between hereditaments and dwellings or even household spaces; some household spaces may be missed or

rated jointly in dwellings used for multi-occupation, agricultural and some other dwellings are de-rated whilst valuation lists are rarely kept up-to-date.

7.2.4   *Rateable values*

The rate for any particular property is given in terms of the rate in the pound payable on the rateable value of the property. The rateable value can be and often is taken as a guide to the 'quality' of the domestic hereditament and aggregate or average figures for, say, a local authority area as a general guide to the standard of housing in that area, bearing in mind, of course, that comparisons between areas will be influenced by the general level of 'commercial' rents in the respective areas.

For this purpose [QRL 48] is useful because in addition to particulars of rates and rate products it gives an analysis of rateable values by type of hereditament. The number and value of all domestic hereditaments is shown and, with the exclusion of Crown domestic hereditaments, a breakdown is shown for the following rateable value classes:

(1) £1–£100   (2) £101–£200   (3) Over £200

Crown properties are not in the normal sense 'rated' but instead the government makes contributions to the local authority in whose area the crown property is located. In this analysis agricultural dwellings and single caravan sites are included in the £1–£100 category. This publication covers all local authorities, including the GLC administrative counties and England and Wales separately. The comparable publication for Scotland is [QRL 49] but unfortunately rateable values are not analysed by value-classes, instead the domestic 'subjects' are divided between local authority-owned and other types. In the *Rating Review* [QRL 50] there is also shown for a sample of local authorities in Scotland the total rateable value for houses.

Rateable values have also been the subject of a table in the *Report of the Commissioners of Her Majesty's Inland Revenue* [QRL 53] because it is at present one of the responsibilities of that department to produce and revise the valuation lists, the latest revision coming into force in 1963. The number and value of rateable units is shown separately for England, Wales and aggregates of administrative counties and all district councils. In addition, a detailed breakdown of the distribution of domestic hereditaments over a number of rateable value classes is shown. This table is now included in *Inland Revenue Statistics* [QRL 35].

7.2.5   *The rate for housing*
In levying the rate, the authority must specify the amount of the rate for particular services and housing is an important part of these. Thus the rate poundage and the rate levied per head for local authority housing activities are shown annually in the *Return of Rates* [QRL 59] published by the IMTA for a large proportion of local authorities in England and Wales. Government grants towards 'housing' are treated similarly in the tables for comparative purposes with the local payments but, of course, the grants are shown as credits. The *Rating Review* [QRL 50] for Scotland provides details of the estimated net cost of housing *in toto* and *per capita* for a sample of local authorities in that country.

8 Housing in National Account Statistics

The national accounts of the United Kingdom are essentially just that—a balance sheet of income and expenditure—and the statistics of the national accounts are generally provided in that form. They are not, however, restricted to national aggregates and the accounts are usually presented in the form of an analysis of the transactions by broad sectors of the economy. Certain of the transactions of the 'personal sector', for example, have already been discussed in connection with housing loans, and consumers' expenditure on housing. Other groupings in the economy produce the Companies, Public Corporations, Local Authorities and Central Government Sectors.

Discussion of statistics in this section will be confined to the annual *National Income and Expenditure* (known as the Blue Book) [QRL 42] because this is the basic published source of information. Limitations of space, however, mean that any treatment of even the housing statistics contained in the Blue Book must be partial and *National Account Statistics —Sources and Methods* [B 11] remains an invaluable reference work; it contains not only a description of and a conceptual framework for the national accounts but also comprehensive descriptions and explanations of the way in which estimates are produced and assessments of their reliability. Changes in procedure since 1967 are noted in the current Blue Book.

A useful way of relating housing and the national income statistics for our purpose is to consider the particular problems presented by housing under the three headings of Income, Product and Expenditure corresponding to the three national aggregates.

8.1 Income

8.1.1 National income is a measure of the value of goods and services becoming available to the nation and includes only those incomes which arise from economic activity, described as factor incomes. The measurement of the value of the services provided by the national housing stock presents two particular problems.

8.1.2 First, a large proportion of all dwellings are owner-occupied and so a large percentage of income can only be derived by imputation. This is considered more fully in the next section.

8.1.3 Second, the provision of council housing by local authorities is counted as a trading activity which is subsidised (i.e. housing is provided at less than its cost) to the extent of the deficit on the housing revenue account. To assess the real value of the services provided by the local authority dwelling stock, then, the amount of receipts from housing rents are not taken as the sums paid by local authority tenants but are taken to be equal to the annual loan charges incurred in the provision of this housing which are the equivalent of interest on capital and depreciation. To quote *Sources and Methods* [B 11], 'Rent income from houses, is, therefore, an imputed measure related to the economic rent. However, in so far as the loan charges are related to the original cost of the houses and not to their current replacement cost, the rent income as measured here is related to less than the full economic rent and does not reflect current market values.'

8.2 Product

8.2.1 The sum of domestic factor incomes measures the total output of goods and services within the country, described as the domestic product. In the national accounts production has a wider meaning than is usually given to it and it includes essentially those goods and services which are exchanged for money.

8.2.2 In relation to housing, on the other hand, there is a case for including the provision of owner-occupied dwellings within the production boundary, though there is no exchange of money since the owner and occupier are one and the same person. The services provided by the dwelling do nevertheless have a value equivalent to the net income which could be obtained by letting the building commercially. Since there is little direct evidence on the levels of 'commercial rents' the income from owner-occupation has to be imputed from the rateable value of owner-occupied accommodation adjusted for changes since the last revaluation in light of movements in the rent component of the index of retail prices. This is necessarily an aribtrary evaluation in an economy in which rent control has existed to varying extents for over fifty years and where for this and other reasons there is a very imperfect market in housing.

8.2.3 Because of its importance, then, the ownership of dwellings is shown in the Blue Book [QRL 42] as a separate industry contributing towards the Gross Domestic Product (GDP), and this includes the rent income, actual or imputed, from the ownership of dwellings, and of property occupied by non-profit-making bodies. International comparisons, however, should be treated with reserve when other countries have a 'free' housing market and a lower proportion of owner-occupiers, enabling a more realistic assessment of market rents to be made.

8.3 Expenditure

8.3.1 The national income as a measure of the goods and services becoming available to the nation can also be measured by summing expenditures. With regard to housing, however, a difficulty is introduced by the division of expenditure between consumption and investment. Houses share the characteristics of both consumers' goods since, once completed, they are used directly by consumers, and capital goods since they last for an indefinitely long time. In the accounts statistics in general 'personal expenditure on goods and services' covers purchases for current use and also the purchase of durable goods but an exception is made in the accounts in the case of the purchase of land and dwellings and costs incurred in connection with the transfer of their ownership. These are treated as items of personal capital expenditure.

8.3.2 Dwellings, then, are the major element in fixed capital formation by the personal sector but dwellings are also provided by the companies sector and by the public sector. Fixed capital formation in dwellings includes all expenditure on the construction of new dwellings plus architects' and quantity surveyors' fees but, in fact, estimations for the private sector are based on production rather than expenditure statistics, and deficiencies in the available information (see *Sources and Methods* [B 11], pp. 377–8) mean that the absolute value of the figures is not particularly reliable. There are also further problems in defining the scope of capital expenditure. Which items of expenditure on the repair, maintenance and improvement of existing dwellings should be counted as current and which as capital expenditure? As a rule, it is impracticable for privately-owned dwellings to distinguish between the two types of work and so the convention of including only grant-aided conversions and improvements, estimated from grants paid by local authorities, in capital formation has been adopted in the Blue Book; other conversions and improvements are included under consumers' expenditure. We should note here, though, that for the public sector all works of conversion and improvement are counted as capital formation.

8.3.3 New dwellings also contain certain items of relatively immovable equipment that are generally considered to be an integral part of the building as is the case, for example, with central heating. These items are included as far as is possible in the figures for capital formation but if central heating, say, is installed in an existing dwelling then the work is included as consumers' expenditure, although still undeniably of 'capital' nature. In many ways it would be desirable to count such elements of housing expenditure as capital formation since the present practice is inconsistent and likely to be misleading but it should be remembered that if there are great difficulties in deriving a meaningful value in consumers' expenditure for the benefit of the owner-occupation of dwellings then the problems of a similar exercise with other consumer durables would be almost intractable and the figures almost completely fictitious.

8.3.4 In the same way that international comparisons of the contribution of the ownership of dwellings to the Gross National Product (GNP) may be misleading, comparisons of the proportion of GNP spent on gross domestic capital formation for housing cannot necessarily be taken to indicate the relative standards of housing in different countries; national preferences may vary but so may many other conditions. The stage of economic development, the efficiency of the house-building industry, the standards of the existing stock of dwellings and climatic conditions, all will influence the amount of expenditure on housing and it is extremely difficult to allow for these factors in such comparisons.

9 Desirable Improvements and Future Developments

9.1 The Stock of Dwellings

9.1.1 The most troublesome feature of the data relating to the stock of dwellings is the infrequency with which it is collected and published. The Census remains the most important and regular source of information but it can be expected at the most no more frequently than every five years. There appears to be a case, therefore, for instituting a regular system of surveys in relation to the stock, and this is all the more important because the 'flow' statistics discussed in Section 3 allow only the broadest indication of changes between Census dates to be charted.

9.1.2 The *General Household Survey* (GHS), described in *Statistical News No. 16* [B 12] would be a useful vehicle for the collection of much of this material. The household interview schedule for 1971, included for reference in Appendix II, has questions for instance on the amenities available to households. Useful as sample surveys are, however, they cannot replace the regular census in certain fields such as the collection of accurate data for small areas, and would probably be unsuitable for topics relating to house condition and quality.

9.1.3 Some improvements might be useful in the statistics relating to amenities, the use of rooms and housing quality. With respect to amenities available to households there seems to be a case for making the census questions in more ways comparable with 'standard amenities' and now that information has been available from the 1966 Census about garaging it seems a pity that the 1971 Census did not take the opportunity to ask about the availability of central heating in dwellings. It would help, for one thing, to bring the census data into line with modern expectations of standards.

9.1.4 The census data also tells us nothing about the use of rooms occupied by households but this information is of obvious social importance and would be welcome for comparative purposes with the statistics of new construction.

Although it is too early to know exactly the type and quality of information to be published, the GHS for 1971 does include questions on the availability of central heating and the use of rooms. These topics are perhaps better included in a sample survey because it is always difficult to introduce new questions into the census partly for fear of overloading and partly because of the errors in enumeration if the question is not simple and carefully worded. With the GHS, the forms are completed by trained interviewers, and it is to be hoped that it will be possible to obtain accurate responses to these more complex questions.

9.1.5 The present approach to the condition of dwellings is essentially a negative one with its roots in nineteenth-century housing legislation, and the fact that the inspectors' estimate in 1967 differed so widely from the assessment two years before with the same definition of unfitness gives rise to some doubt about the validity of the method. It is difficult to see how any improvement can be made within the present framework and it seems likely that a much more comprehensive approach is needed in assessing housing quality but some improvement could be achieved by indication of the relevant factors (listed in the Housing Act 1957 as amended by the Housing Act 1969) which were 'so far defective' that they rendered the houses 'unfit for human habitation'. An appraisal of some of the existing methods and approaches to assessing the physical quality of housing is contained in Duncan [B 5].

9.1.6 It would be desirable to have some up-to-date statistics on the condition of dwellings in

Scotland since the present statistics refer to 1965 and are based on local authorities' own assessments.

9.2 Occupancy and Ownership

9.2.1 With regard to statistics concerning households, occupancy and tenure, the infrequency of publication is again the most serious defect since we rely on census figures. The Family Expenditure Survey (FES) has provided limited annual data about household tenure, size and composition but there has always been the danger of overloading this survey and partly in response to this danger the GHS was introduced to obtain household and personal information on a wide range of topics (see the Household Schedule for the GHS in Appendix II).

9.2.2 Where a small-scale sample survey such as the GHS or FES is of little value is in the estimation of accurate population (and household) totals for sub-regions and regions between census dates. For many purposes, the information available from the census is hopelessly out-of-date especially since there is at present no means of measuring migration flows except in a rather uncertain and general manner. Perhaps the ideal solution would be the adoption of 'population registers' that could be regularly and speedily up-dated but there are probably overwhelming political reasons against any such move.

9.2.3 Not only do we lack precise knowledge between censuses about population mobility but we are almost completely ignorant of tenure mobility. Improvements in this direction would be invaluable in themselves and for the forecasting of trends in the housing market. In this connection it is interesting to note that a pilot study was undertaken in 1967 by the MHLG to ascertain the feasibility of collecting statistics on local authority lettings. It showed, however, that it would be difficult (see [B 14]) to obtain standardised returns from existing records. The GHS, too, includes questions on household tenure mobility and migration over the last five years, and these results will be most welcome.

In the light of changing standards since 1935, it would be desirable if some more widely acceptable standard for 'overcrowding' than the statutory one could be formulated for statistical purposes.

9.3 Changes to the Stock of Dwellings

9.3.1 Basic improvements would be most valuable in the statistics relating to losses from the stock of dwellings and conversions. There are also gaps in the basic official statistics for housing standards in the private sector and in Scotland that ought to be rectified.

9.3.2 It is interesting to note that details of many categories of loss that are not covered in the statistics except as an aggregate figure in the summary table of annual gains and losses to the housing stock, are, however, collected by the DOE on Form P. 14 (Hsg) (see Appendix II). However unreliable some of the data contained in this primary source may be, it would be helpful if the separate estimates for each category (with which the Department presumably make its own overall estimates) could be made available. In particular, figures for the *net* loss or gain to the stock of dwellings by conversion (both assisted and unassisted) would be useful and have, moreover, been published in the past.

9.3.3 With respect to the slum clearance statistics, the present practice in using the 'house' as the basic unit for tabulation is anomalous and is inconvenient for comparative purposes. Reference to Form P13 (Hsg) in Appendix II reveals that, in fact, figures for the number of 'separate dwellings' as well as 'houses' are included on the basic return, and there seems to be little reason why these should not be published along with, or perhaps in place of, the present ones.

9.3.4 With reference to housing standards, apart from the desirability of extending the analysis of the standards of local authority housing to Scotland and collecting information from the private sector, it would be useful to collect information about the total number of 'rooms' in newly built housing. Not only would this allow comparability with the census but it would also be a guide to the 'standard' of new housing in terms of the amount of freedom it allows for the separation of functions within the home.

9.4   The House-Building Industry

9.4.1   Possibly the most inconvenient feature of the statistics relating to the house-building industry is the fact that regional figures for contractors' employment on and output of housing work do not in fact relate to the region in which the work is being carried out, but to the region in which the head office of the firm is registered. This obviously makes any regional analysis of output or employment from the present statistics hazardous and is further complicated by the fact that the regional statistics for the value of new orders obtained by contractors refers to the region in which the work will be carried out. A desirable improvement would be to introduce a standard definition where regional figures related to work done within a region.

9.4.2   Another serious regional problem concerns the lack of comparability of Scottish construction cost figures with those for England and Wales. Improvements could be made by standardising the measures of floor area and by providing a breakdown of the Scottish figures by type of dwelling and mode of construction. The classification of dwellings by 'apartments' in Scotland also introduces difficulties and the adoption of the bedroom, or better the bedspace, classification would help considerably.

9.4.3   The former MPBW compiled an index of house-building costs which has not so far been published but it would be of interest since there is no published information on the costs of private-sector new construction and the most reliable indices relate to local authority housing.

Since speculative building characterises much of private sector house-building a desirable improvement in the figures, perhaps linking it to the private enterprise housing enquiry, would be to include a separate category for 'work not covered by orders' under new orders for housing. At present in [QRL 40] the value is shown for all types of work and will include an element, though probably small, of other speculative building. With this series too there is no obvious way of relating it to construction output series, that is, we do not know the time-lag, and what proportion of new orders are cancelled or speculative intentions thwarted. This information might be of interest.

9.5   Personal Expenditure on Housing

9.5.1   In the light of likely changes in the law relating to rents and rebates in the local authority and private rented sector, it is probably unwise to make any wholesale suggestions for improvement. It would, however, be useful if the coverage of statistics relating to the rent-determination of furnished lettings, the rents of unfurnished lettings and the special tabulations of FES data on housing expenditure in *Housing Statistics* [QRL 26] could be extended.

9.5.2   Information about the rent-determination of private furnished lettings might be more frequently published, as far as possible comparable with that collected for rent-regulation, namely the size, age, type and gross value of accommodation and the average previous and average registered rent. The full range of information collected on rent registration can be found in the returns RS7 and RS8 in Appendix II.

9.5.3   It is known that information about the rents of private unfurnished lettings is collected in connection with the index of retail prices, and publication of these figures would provide an interim guide to the level of rents between the annual publications of the Family Expenditure Survey. It may be noted that the index for the rents of local authority dwellings is already published in *Housing Statistics* [QRL 26].

9.5.4   The two most obvious areas into which the special FES-based tabulations in *Housing Statistics* [QRL 26] could be extended are first, data for the private rented furnished sector and, second, more regional analysis. Presumably it is limitations imposed by the size of the sample and the attendant substantial sampling error that restricts the scope for such analysis at present. The intention of the DOE to include in future an analysis of rents by gross values in its special tabulations (see section 5) is most welcome but also draws attention to the gap in statistics represented by the lack of adequate information on the rents of different types and qualities of dwellings.

9.6   Housing Loans and House Prices

9.6.1   Although the present statistics indicate that building societies are the most important source of finance for house purchase, local authorities, insurance companies and to a lesser extent banks, are of some importance. It is clearly desirable that more information should be published (or if not already collected, then collected and published) about their lending and particularly about the types of borrower and housing that are catered for by local authorities and insurance companies.

9.6.2   On the other hand, the information at present available about borrowers and their housing, chiefly in connection with building society advances, is very useful but might be usefully extended. For instance at the moment it is presumably because the majority of borrowers are males, that no details are given about their sex, but some figures for their marital status, if not of the type of household of which they are part, would be a most useful future innovation and would considerably broaden the scope of the analysis that is possible. With regard to the type of housing being purchased by building society advances, it should be noted that much more information is collected than is published (see the Monthly Questionnaire on Building Society Mortgages in Appendix II).

9.6.3   Another aspect that has received little attention is the extent of first-time purchasing of dwellings. This problem is linked to the general lack of data on tenure mobility, which is discussed in Section 2.6.6, but of importance here is the extent to which an increase in mortgage advances represents an extension of home ownership rather than increased mobility by existing owner-occupier households.

Finally, the feasibility of obtaining regional figures for mortgage completions and bank lending for improvements, alterations and conversions should be examined.

Quick Reference List

Notes to the Quick Reference List

1. The QRL key to publications includes all those mentioned in the text arranged alphabetically by title.

2. The housing statistics from the Census of Population in Northern Ireland (discussed in Appendix I) are included in the QRL but this publication does not appear in the QRL key; it does not therefore have a reference number.

3. For convenience, the QRL has been divided into sections following the major headings of the text. As a general rule the listing of the series follows the order in which they are mentioned and where one series is relevant under several headings it has been included where appropriate. However, there is no complete cross-referencing of series.

4. *Prices of Publications*
   (a) The price quoted is that of the latest copy of the publication. In the case of *ad hoc* material, the original price has been quoted where this seems appropriate but this does not necessarily imply that the publication is still in print.
   (b) All prices in £.s.d have been converted to their nearest equivalent in decimal currency.

5. *Area and Breakdown of Series*
The following abbreviations have been adopted:

LA	Local Authority
GLC	Greater London Council area
E & W	England and Wales

S	Scotland
GB	Great Britain
NI	Northern Ireland
UK	United Kingdom

6. *A Note on Census Publications*
   1. The tabulations from the *Census of Population in Gt. Britain* [QRL 12] included in the Quick Reference List are those in the 1966 Sample Census and not those from the full Census which is taken every ten years.
   2. The published County volumes of the Sample Census in Great Britain contain two levels of presentation (three in Scotland) which can be described in terms of the areas to which the tables refer:
In England and Wales *Scale A* is the fullest scale and applies to:

   (a) The administrative county as a whole with and without any associated county boroughs
   (b) Each county borough and new town
   (c) Each municipal borough and urban district expected to have more than 50,000 population on Census day
   (d) The aggregate, within the administrative county, of all municipal boroughs and urban districts combined and of all rural districts.

Scale B which is less detailed than Scale A and applies to:

   (a) Those municipal boroughs and urban districts expected to have between 15,000 and 50,000 population on Census day.
   (b) All rural districts expected to have more than 15,000 population on Census day.

In Scotland *Scale A* applies to:

(a) Each county of city
(b) Each county
(c) The county exclusive of large burgh(s)
(d) Each large burgh expected to have more than 50,000 population on Census day.

Scale B applies to:

(a) Each large burgh and small burgh expected to have a population of 15,000 or more but fewer than 50,000 on Census day
(b) Each district of county expected to have a population of 15,000 or more on Census day.

Scale C applies to:

(a) Small burghs and districts of county with expected population of less than 15,000 on Census day.

3. In the QRL reference will be made to the three scales of presentation adopted in the County volumes but unpublished Census data is also generally available at Scale B for all areas down to enumeration district and at Scale A for all local authorities in Great Britain. Further details are available on application to the Office of Population Censuses and Surveys, and the General Register Office, Scotland.

Quick Reference List—Table of Contents

QUICK REFERENCE LIST

Descriptive Title	Breakdown	Area	Frequency	Publication (See QRL Key)	Text Reference and Remarks
THE STOCK OF DWELLINGS **Numbers**					
Acreage, population, private households and dwellings	Scales A & B (plus scale C in Scotland)	GB	Decennial	County Report 1966 [QRL 12]	A description of the scales A, B and C and the practice adopted with regard to the inclusion of census tabulations in the QRL are given in *A Note on Census Publications* in the Notes to the Quick Reference list.
Area, buildings for habitation and population	County boroughs and counties	NI	„	General Report *1966 Census of Northern Ireland*	See Appendix I
Area, population, buildings for habitation, private households and valuation	County boroughs, counties, administrative areas and towns with 1000 or more population	„	„	„	„
The stock of dwellings	By regions and conurbations	GB	Half-yearly	[QRL 26]	1.1.6 Stock at annual and half-yearly intervals from 1966
Building and dwelling type					
Dwellings and household spaces by type of building	Scales A and B (see remarks to first series)	GB	Decennial	County Report 1966 [QRL 12]	1.2.3
Dwellings by type of building	E & W, regions and conurbations	E & W	„	[QRL 12]	„
Dwellings by type of building and tenure	Scotland, regions and conurbation	S	Decennial	[QRL 12]	1.2.3
Structural type		E & W	1960	[QRL 67]	1.2.4
Dwelling type		„	1964	[QRL 68]	Based on samples of rateable units
		S	1965	[QRL 60]	„ „ „
					„ „ „
Age composition					
Age composition	Greater London, other conurbations, non-conurbations	E & W	1960	[QRL 67]	1.3.2

	Greater London, rest of E & W	"	1964	[QRL 68]	"
		S	1965	[QRL 60]	"
	LA	E & W	Annual	[QRL 27]	1.3.2 Based on returns from a large sample of local authorities
		"	1967	[QRL 20], [QEL 44]	1.3.3 Secondary source: [QRL 26], Nos. 9, 10, 14
	Regions	UK	Annual	[QRL 63]	1.3.3
	Sub-regions of Wales	Wales	1968	[QRL 72]	"
	Conurbations (outside Greater London)	E & W	Various dates 1967–69	[QRL 28–32]	1.3.3 Secondary source: [QRL 26], Nos. 10, 14, 16
Age composition	Boroughs	Greater London	1967	[QRL 66]	" , "
Amenities					
Private households by availability of certain household amenities and sharing of dwellings	Scale A (see Remarks to first series)	GB	Decennial	County Report 1966 [QRL 12]	1.4.1 The types of amenity recorded have varied between censuses. The 1961 Census has been the only one to provide a tabulation of dwellings by amenities. For further census tabulations of amenities see under OCCUPANCY AND OWNERSHIP
Private households by availability of certain household amenities	Scale B (see Remarks to first series)	"	"	"	"
Household amenities	Greater London, other conurbations, non-conurbations	E & W	1960	[QRL 67]	1.4.7
Standard amenities	Greater London, rest of E & W	"	1964	[QRL 68]	1.4.8 Some reference to availability of 'standard amenities' by type of accommodation but concentrates mainly on availability to households
Standard amenities	Sub-regions of Scotland. Amenities by area, age, tenure. Relationship between amenities and fitness	S	1965	[QRL 60]	1.4.9

Descriptive Title	Breakdown	Area	Frequency	Publication (See QRL Key)	Text Reference and Remarks
Availability of standard amenities in dwellings by condition	Broad regions: (i) Northern, Yorkshire and Humberside, NW (ii) SE (iii) rest of E & W	E & W	1967	[QRL 20], [QRL 44]	1.4.10 Secondary source: [QRL 26], Nos. 9, 10,14
	Conurbations (outside Greater London)	"	Various dates 1967–69	[QRL 28–32]	1.4.10 Secondary source: [QRL 26], Nos. 10, 14, 16
	Sub-regions of Wales	Wales	1968	[QRL 72]	1.4.10
Fitness					
Number of houses 'unfit for human habitation'	LA	E & W	1955	[QRL 61]	1.5 For an explanation of the term 'house' see 3.4.2 and for the coverage of 'unfit houses' see 1.5.2
	"	S	"	[QRL 62]	"
'Fitness' and length of life of rateable units	Greater London, other conurbations, non-conurbations	E & W	1960	[QRL 67]	1.5.3 Local authorities' estimates of the fitness and length of life of rateable units included in the survey
	Greater London, rest of E & W	"	1964	[QRL 68]	"
'Unfit' houses and dwellings	Sub-regions of Scotland Regions	S	1965	[QRL 60]	"
The condition of the stock of dwellings	Broad regions: (i) Northern, Yorkshire and Humberside, NW (ii) SE (iii) rest of E and W Fitness, age, tenure, state of repair, amenities	E & W	1967	[QRL 26] No. 1 [QRL 20], [QRL 44]	1.5.4 1.5.5 Secondary source: [QRL 26], Nos. 9, 10, 14
	Boroughs Useful life, condition, type, age, tenure, number of rooms and facilities, suitability for conversion, improvement or demolition	Greater London	"	[QRL 66]	1.5.6

The condition of the stock of dwellings	Conurbations (outside Greater London) Fitness, age, state of repair, tenure, amenities Sub-regions	E & W	Various dates 1967–69	[QRL 28–32]	1.5.6 Secondary source: [QRL 26], Nos. 10, 14, 16
		Wales	1968	[QRL 72]	" " "
Size					
Dwellings and household spaces rooms	Scale A (see remarks to first series)	GB	Decennial	County Report 1966 [QRL 12]	1.6 and 2.2
	Scale B (see remarks to first series)	"	"	"	" " "
Dwellings by tenure and rooms	Scale A (see remarks to first series)	"	"	"	1.6
Distribution of dwellings and households by number of rooms, 1961 and 1966	County	"	"	"	"
Occupied dwellings by number of rooms, 1961 and 1966	E & W, regions and conurbations	E & W	"	Hsg. Tables 1966 [QRL 12]	"
	Scotland, regions and conurbation	S	"	"	"
Shared dwellings by number of rooms, 1961 and 1966	E & W, regions and conurbations	E & W	Decennial	Hsg. Tables 1966 [QRL 12]	1.6
	Scotland, regions and conurbation	S	"	"	"
Size of dwellings	Greater London, other conurbations, non-conurbations	E & W	1960	[QRL 67]	1.6.3
	Greater London, rest of E & W	"	1964	[QRL 68]	"
	Floor area of dwellings, number of rooms, use of rooms	S	1965	[QRL 60]	1.6.4
Private dwellings: inhabited dwellings by households, rooms and population	County boroughs, counties, administrative areas	NI	Decennial	General Report, *1966 Census of Northern Ireland*	See Appendix I
OCCUPANCY AND OWNERSHIP **Households** Acreage, population, private households and dwellings	See relevant series in QRL under STOCK OF DWELLINGS				
Area, population, buildings for habitation, private households and valuation	" "				

Descriptive Title	Breakdown	Area	Frequency	Publication (See QRL Key)	Text Reference and Remarks
Number of households		E & W	1861–1931	Housing, Vol. II [QRL 12], 1931	2.1.2 Figures before 1911 are the Registrar General's estimates
	Greater London, other conurbations, non-conurbations	"	1960	[QRL 67]	Estimates based on a sample of rateable units in England and Wales (6005 in 1960 and 6351 in 1964) and on a sample of 3000 rateable units in Scotland, 1965
	Greater London, rest of E & W	"	1964	[QRL 68]	"
		S	1965	[QRL 60]	"
Occupied dwellings and household spaces					
Occupied dwellings, shared dwellings and household spaces	See relevant series in QRL under STOCK OF DWELLINGS				2.2
Household types					
Households by type and size	E and W, S	GB	Decennial	Household Composition Tables 1966 [QRL 12]	2.3 Separate Household Composition Tables are published for England and Wales, Scotland
Households by type, size and dependent children	"	"	"	"	"
Households by type, size and earners	E and W, regions, conurbations; S, regions and conurbation	"	"	"	"
Households by size, dependent children and earners	E and W, S	"	"	"	"
Households by size, families, earners and dependent children	E and W, regions, conurbations, counties, county boroughs, local authority areas with populations of 50,000 or more, new towns; S, regions and conurbation, cities, counties, large boroughs with populations of 50,000 or more, new towns	"	"	"	"
Households by size	E and W, counties, local authority areas with populations of 15,000 or more,	"	"	"	"

Households by earners and dependent children	new towns; S, cities, counties, large boroughs, counties excluding large boroughs, small boroughs and districts of county with populations of 15,000 or more, new towns	,,	,,	,,	,,
Households by size, socio-economic group of chief economic supporter, by earners and dependent children	E and W, S	GB	Decennial	Household Composition Tables 1966 [QRL 12]	1. The term 'Chief Economic Supporter' requires explanation and distinguishing from 'Head of Household'. The former is chosen by a number of rules that take into account (i) employment status, (ii) family status, (iii) sex, (iv) age, in that order of precedence and does not necessarily refer to the member of the household who receives the largest income. The 'Head of Household' is by and large the person returned as such 2. Separate Household Composition Tables are published for England and Wales, Scotland
Households by size and socio-economic group of chief economic supporter	E and W, regions and conurbations; S, regions and conurbation	,,	,,	,,	Separate Household Composition Tables are published for England and Wales, Scotland
Households by socio-economic group of chief economic supporter, earners and dependent children	E and W, regions and conurbations; S, regions and conurbation	,,	,,	,,	,,
Households by families: numbers and percentages	E and W, regions, conurbations, counties, county boroughs, local authority areas with populations of 50,000 or more, new towns; S, regions and conurbation, cities, counties, counties (except large boroughs), large boroughs with populations of 50,000 or more, new towns	GB	Decennial	Household Composition Tables 1966 [QRL 12]	2.3

Descriptive Title	Breakdown	Area	Frequency	Publication (See QRL Key)	Text Reference and Remarks
Households with no family by age and sex of chief economic supporter	E and W, regions, counties, county boroughs, local authority areas with populations of 15,000 or more, new towns; S, regions and conurbation, cities, counties, large boroughs, counties (except large boroughs), small boroughs and districts of county with populations of 15,000 or more, new towns	"	"	"	"
Families by type of head	"	"	"	"	"
Families by size and type of head	E and W, regions and conurbations; S, regions and conurbation	"	"	"	"
Families by size, type of head and type of household	E and W, S	"	"	"	"
Families by size, dependent children and type of household	E and W, regions and conurbations; S, regions and conurbation	"	"	"	"
Families by type of head, dependent children and type of household	E and W, S	"	"	"	2.3 Separate Household Composition Tables are published for England and Wales, Scotland
Families by socio-economic group of head, type of head and dependent children	E and W, S	GB	Decennial	Household Composition Tables 1966 [QRL 12]	Separate Household Composition Tables are published for England and Wales, Scotland
Families by size and socio-economic group of head	E and W, regions and conurbations; S, regions and conurbation	"	"	"	"
Families by tenure and density of occupation	E and W, regions, conurbations, counties, county boroughs, local authority areas with populations of 15,000 or more, new towns; S, regions and conurbation, cities, counties, large boroughs, counties (excluding large	"	"	"	"

Subject	Area		Period	Source	
(boroughs), small boroughs and districts of county with populations of 15,000 or more, new towns					
Families by dependent children: combination of ages	E and W, S	,,	,,	,,	,,
Families and dependent children by ages of parents	,,	,,	,,	,,	,,
Married couples: husbands' and wives' ages in combination, lone parents by ages	,,	,,	,,	,,	,,
Married couples by socio-economic group of husband	,,	,,	,,	,,	,,
Married couples by socio-economic group of husband and age of wife	,,	,,	,,	,,	,,
Married couples by dependent children and age of wife	E and W, S	GB	Decennial	Household Composition Tables 1966 [QRL 12]	Separate Household Composition Tables are published for England and Wales, Scotland
Married couples with dependent children in specified age groups by age of wife	,,	,,	,,	,,	,,
Wives and mothers by economic activity and dependent children	,,	,,	,,	,,	,,
Chief economic supporter of households by sex, age and socio-economic group	,,	,,	,,	,,	,,
Chief economic supporter of households by sex, age and marital condition	E and W, regions and conurbations; S, regions and conurbation	,,	,,	,,	,,
Chief economic supporter by age, sex and type of household	E and W, S	,,	,,	,,	,,
Housewives by age and dependent children	,,	,,	,,	,,	,,
Housewives by own age and socio-economic group of chief economic supporter	E and W, regions and conurbations; S, regions and conurbation	,,	,,	,,	,,
Housewives by age, sex and marital condition	,, ,,	,,	,,	,,	,,

Descriptive Title	Breakdown	Area	Frequency	Publication (See QRL Key)	Text Reference and Remarks
One- and two-person households containing persons of pensionable age	"	"	"	"	"
Persons of pensionable age by marital condition and type of household	E and W, S	"	"	"	"
One-, two-, three-person households containing persons of pensionable age	E and W, regions and conurbations; S, regions and conurbation	"	"	"	"
Chief economic supporters from outside the British Isles by country of birth and type of household	E and W, S	GB	Decennial	Household Composition Tables 1966 [QRL 12]	Separate Household Composition Tables are published for England and Wales, Scotland
Households by size and number of visitors	"	"	"	"	"
Households by size and domestic servants by sex and marital condition	"	"	"	"	"
Household types	Tenure, net weekly rent, persons per room, bedroom standard, standard amenities	E & W	1964	[QRL 68]	2.3.5
	"	S	1965	[QRL 60]	
The living space of households Households by size, 1961 and 1966	E and W, regions and conurbations S, regions and conurbation	E & W S	1961, 1966	Hsg. Tables 1966 [QRL 12] "	
Private households by size of household	Scale B	GB	"	County Report 1966 [QRL 12]	A description of the scales A, B and C and the practice adopted with regard to the inclusion of census tabulations in the QRL are given in *A Note on Census Publications* in the Notes to the Quick Reference List
Private households by size, rooms occupied and sharing of dwellings	Scale A	GB	1961, 1966	County Report 1966 [QLR 12]	A description of the scales A, B and C and the practice adopted with regard to the inclusion of census tabulations in the QRL are given in *A Note on Census Publications* in the Notes to the Quick Reference List

Private households by rooms occupied	Scale B		"	"
Private households by density of occupation (persons per room) by size of household (see remark 1)	Scale A		"	"
Private households by density of occupation (persons per room)	Scale B		"	"
Private households by size, rooms occupied, sharing of dwellings and tenure	Scale A		"	"
Households by rooms occupied, 1961 and 1966	E and W, regions and conurbations	E & W	"	Hsg. Tables 1966 [QRL 12]
	S, regions and conurbation	S	"	"
Households in shared dwellings by rooms occupied, 1961 and 1966	E and W, regions and conurbations	E & W	"	"
Households in shared dwellings by rooms occupied, 1961 and 1966	S, regions and conurbation	S	Decennial	Hsg. Tables 1966 [QRL 12]
Households by type of building, tenure and sharing of dwelling	E & W, regions and conurbations	E & W	"	"
	S, regions and conurbation	S	"	"
Households: socio-economic group of chief economic supporter	Tenure by rooms	E & W	"	"
Households by size, rooms occupied, sharing of dwellings and tenure	E & W, regions and conurbations	S	"	"
	S, regions and conurbation	E & W	"	"
Households by tenure and density of occupation	E & W, regions and conurbations	S	"	"
	S, regions and conurbation	S	"	"

1. Note that the enumeration of all kitchens as 'rooms' in the 1966 Census means that comparisons between the density of occupation in 1961 and 1966 are not strictly valid
2. A description of the scales A, B and C and the practice adopted with regard to the inclusion of census tabulations in the QRL are given in *A Note on Census Publications* in the Notes to the Quick Reference List

Descriptive Title	Breakdown	Area	Frequency	Publication (See QRL Key)	Text Reference and Remarks
Private households; size, rooms occupied, and density of room occupation	County boroughs, counties, administrative areas	NI	,,	General Report, 1966 Census of Northern Ireland	See Appendix I
Projections of potential households	Regions (including Scotland)	GB	1971	[QRL 26], Nos. 20 and 24	2.4.1 Estimates of housing 'need'
Accommodation size and the living space of households	Greater London, other conurbations, non-conurbations, persons per room, statutory 'overcrowding' and 'the bedroom standard'	E & W	1960	[QRL 67]	2.4.3
	Greater London, rest of England and Wales	,,	1964	[QRL 68]	,,
		S	1965	[QRL 60]	,,
		W. Midlands	1966	[QRL 33]	2.4.4
The Registrar General's living space hypotheses		E & W	1961	Household Composition Tables 1961 [QRL 12]	2.4.2 Similar hypotheses were formulated and used in the 1951 Census in E and W
The standard of accommodation					
Private households by availability of certain household amenities and sharing of dwellings	See relevant series in the QRL under STOCK OF DWELLINGS				
Households by number of cars; cars by garaging arrangements and type of building	Scale A	GB	Decennial	County Report 1966 [QRL 12]	A description of the scales A, B and C and the practice adopted with regard to the inclusion of census tabulations in the QRL are given in *A Note on Census Publications* in the Notes to the Quick Reference List
Households by number of cars; cars by garaging arrangements	Scale B	,,	,,		,,
Households by tenure by amenities	E & W, regions and conurbations	E & W	,,	Hg. Tables 1966 [QRL 12]	2.5 and 1.4
	S, regions and conurbation	S	,,	,,	,,
One- and two-person households containing persons of pensionable age by tenure and amenities	E and W	E & W	,,	,,	,,
	S	S	,,	,,	,,

Subject	Detail	Area	Period	Source	Section
Households by size by amenities	E & W, regions and conurbations	E & W	"	"	"
	S, regions and conurbation	S	"	"	"
	E & W, regions and conurbations	E & W	"	"	"
	S, regions and conurbation	S	"	"	"
Households without amenities	E and W, regions and conurbations	E & W	Decennial	Hsg. Tables 1966	2.5 and 1.4
	S, regions and conurbation	S	"	"	"
Households by number of cars and socio-economic group of chief economic supporter	E and W, regions and conurbations	E & W	"	"	
	S, regions and conurbation	S	"	"	
Households by number of cars and numbers of earners	S, regions and conurbation	S	"	"	
	E and W, regions and conurbations	E & W	"	"	
Households with two or more cars; garaging arrangements for first and second cars	S, regions and conurbation	S	"	"	
	E and W, regions and conurbations	E & W	"	"	
Households by number of cars; cars by tenure and garaging arrangements	S, regions and conurbation	S	"	"	
	E and W, regions and conurbations	E & W	"	"	
Households without cars by tenure	S, regions and conurbation	S	"	"	
	E and W, regions and conurbations	E & W	"	"	
Households by number of cars and composition of household	S, regions and conurbation	S	"	"	
	E &W, regions and conurbations	E &W	"	"	
Households living in caravans	S, regions and conurbation	S	"	"	
	Sex, age, household type and composition, occupation and income of caravanners, types of caravan sites and condition of caravans	E & W	1959	[QRL 8]	
General Improvement Areas declared under Part II, Housing Act 1969		"	Quarterly	[QRL 26]	2.5.2 Figures available from 1969
Improvement grants approved for local authorities, housing associations and for private owners	E & W, development and intermediate areas, Scotland. Discretionary, standard and special grants	GB	"	"	2.5.3 Number of dwellings covered by standard grants available from 1959 annually in [QRL 26]. For annual figures 1949–59 of discretionary grants see [QRL 24] and [QRL 25]

Descriptive Title	*Breakdown*	*Area*	*Frequency*	*Publication (See QRL Key)*	*Text Reference and Remarks*
Improvement grants approved for local authorities	E & W, S. Discretionary grants for conversion/improvement, standard grants	"	"	"	Figures for England and Wales before 1967 include grants to housing associations. In Scotland all grants to housing associations are included in this table except those included in the series immediately above which are approved under the Housing (Scotland) Act 1966, Sec. 155, and the Housing (Financial Provisions) (Scotland) Act 1968, Sec. 17 2.5.3
Improvement grants for private owners	E & W, S. By tenure and type of grant	"	"	"	2.5.3
Improvement grants approved for housing associations	Discretionary grants for conversion/improvement by act under which approved, standard grants from 1970	E & W	Quarterly	[QRL 26]	2.5.3 Standard grants from 1967
Discretionary grants approved with relaxed standards	Dwellings to be improved to less than the 12-point standard; with less than 15 years of life; both divided by owner and by purpose (conversion/improvement)	"	"	"	2.5.3 Available from 1970
Standard grants; reduced standard and higher limit grants	(a) Reduced standard and higher limit grants approved for local authorities/private owners and housing associations (b) Higher limit grants: additional aided works; bathrooms/septic tanks/piped water in grants for local authorities/private owners and housing associations	"	"	"	2.5.3 From 1967
Standard improvement grants: provision of amenities	E and W, S. By owner	GB	"	"	1.4 Standard grants do not apply to local authorities in Scotland. Available

Item	Coverage	Area	Period	Reference	Section	Remarks
Improvement grants approved and paid for private owners and housing associations	E and W, S. Discretionary/ standard grants by number of dwellings and amounts of grants	"	"	"		from 1959 annually in [QRL 26] and quarterly in [QRL 25]
Improvement grants approved	Regions of E and W, S. By owner and type of grant	"	Numbers approved half-yearly	"	From 1965	
Improvement grants approved for local authorities and paid to private owners	Local authorities, regions and counties	E & W	Annual	[QRL 39]	2.5.3	
Standard improvement grants: provision of amenities	County boroughs and London boroughs	"	1967	"	"	
Number of households living in 'unfit' and substandard accommodation	Greater London, other conurbations, non-conurbations. Unfit accommodation, estimated life of accommodation, use of amenities	"	1960	[QRL 67]	2.5.4 and 1.4	
	Greater London, rest of E and W	"	1964	[QRL 68]	"	
	Sub-regions	S	1965	[QRL 60]	"	
Temporary housing	E and W, S. 'Prefabs', 'mobile homes', former camps used for housing, unfit houses in temporary use	GB	Annual	[QRL 26]	2.5.5 Terms as defined in the Housing Act 1957	
Housing conditions	Living space, tenure, amenities, housing costs and housing mobility	S	Quarterly	[QRL 25]	1.5.7	
		W. Midlands		[QRL 33]		
	Type of accommodation, rooms and bedrooms, living space, second homes, housing costs	W. Yorks		*Hsg. Surv. Rept. No. 7* (W. Yorks) [QRL 34]	"	
Tenure						
Households: socio-economic group of chief economic supporter by tenure	E and W, regions and conurbations	E & W	Decennia	Hsg. Tables 1966 [QRL 12]	2.6.3	
	Regions and conurbation	S	"	"	"	

Descriptive Title	Breakdown	Area	Frequency	Publication (See QRL Key)	Text Reference and Remarks
Housing conditions by tenure	Greater London, other conurbations, non-conurbations. Controlled tenancies; multi-occupation; age, size, area of accommodation; owner-occupiers inheriting accommodation; leasehold property, price of property, how money was raised, percentage paying mortgages	E & W	1960	[QRL 67]	2.6.4
	Greater London, rest of England and Wales. Number of households, number of controlled tenancies, household characteristics, rents, living space, standard of accommodation	"	1964	[QRL 68]	"
Stock of dwellings by tenure	E and W, S	S	1965	[QRL 60]	2.6.5
	"	GB	Annual	[QRL 26]	Estimates of reasonably separate accommodation (1.1.6) based on the 1966 Sample Census
Condition of dwellings by tenure	Broad regions: (i) Northern, Yorkshire & Humberside, NW; (ii) SE; (iii) rest of E & W; fitness, age, state of repair and amenities by tenure	E & W	1967	[QRL 20], [QRL 44]	2.6.5 Secondary source: [QRL 26], Nos. 9, 10, 14
	Conurbations (outside Greater London); fitness, age, state of repair and amenities by tenure	"	Various dates 1967–69	[QRL 28–32]	2.6.5 Secondary source: [QRL 26], Nos. 10, 14, 16
	Sub-regions; fitness, age, state of repair and amenities by tenure	Wales	1968	[QRL 72]	2.6.5
	Some information available at borough level; useful life, condition, type, age, number of rooms and facilities available, suitability for improvement/conversion	Greater London	1967	[QRL 66]	"

Item	Detail	Area	Frequency	Reference	Source	Remarks
Sale of local authority dwellings		E & W	Quarterly	[QRL 26]	2.6.6 and 3.1.5	Annual figures available back to 1960, quarterly from 1964, cumulative 1953–59
		LA			2.6.6	
Mobility of households: changes of tenure	Greater London, rest of E and W. Why households move. Tenure situation of households who had moved between August 1960 and December 1964	"	Annual 1964	[QRL 39] [QRL 68]	"	
	Households and individuals wanting to move; satisfaction with dwelling; type of tenure sought	"	1960	[QRL 67]	"	
	Changes in the tenure situation of 'continuing' households; why households move	S	1965	[QRL 60]	"	

CHANGES TO THE STOCK OF DWELLINGS
New construction

Item	Detail	Area	Frequency	Reference	Source	Remarks
Houses and flats completed	By number of bedrooms	E & W	Quarterly	[QRL 26]	3.1.2	For local authorities cumulative 1945–1960, annual from 1961, quarterly from 1965. For private owners from 1961
	"	Greater London	"	"	3.1.2	From 1961
Houses and flats approved by local authorities and completed by private owners	By number of apartments	S	"	"	3.1.2	For local authorities and private owners cumulative 1945–1960 and as for E and W (above)
Houses and flats completed	Per cent by region. Flats of 2–4 storeys/5 or more	E & W	Annual	"		From 1961
	By number of bedrooms and regions	"	"	"	3.1.2	From 1961
Houses and flats in tenders approved for local authorities and new towns	By storey height	"	Quarterly	"	3.1.2	Annual from 1953, quarterly from 1964
	"	S	"	"	3.1.2	
	Percentage of total approved by storey height	GB	"	"		Annual from 1960, quarterly from 1964
	By storey height and regions	E & W	"	"	3.1.2	Annual from 1958, quarterly from 1966
					3.1.2	Annual from 1965

Descriptive Title	Breakdown	Area	Frequency	Publication (See QRL Key)	Text References and Remarks
Types of heating in tenders approved for local authorities and new towns	Percentages of dwellings approved	"	"	"	3.1.2 Annual from 1964, quarterly from 1967
Dwellings reaching Parker Morris standards in tenders approved for local authorities and new towns	Percentage of total approved by number of bedrooms	E & W	Quarterly	[QRL 26]	3.1.3 Annual from 1964, quarterly from 1967
		"	1964–67	"	Included in the Supplementary Tables to issue No. 12
Industrialised dwelling construction for local authorities and new towns		"	Quarterly	"	3.1.3 and 4.3 From 1964
	By region	"	Half-yearly	"	3.1.3 and 4.3 From 1965, half-yearly from 1966
	By system	GB	"	"	3.1.3 and 4.3 From 1964, half-yearly from 1966
Industrialised dwellings completed by local authorities	LA	E & W	1966–1970	[QRL 39]	3.1.3 and 4.3 Included in Supplementary Tables to [QRL 39], No. 19
Industrialised dwellings completed by local authorities and new towns	By region and type of authority	"	Annual	[QRL 26]	3.1.3 From 1966
	By type of structure and main structural material	"	"	"	3.1.3 From 1964
Density of dwellings in tenders approved for local authorities and new towns	Density of dwellings and designed bedspaces per acre	"	Quarterly	"	3.1.3 The acreage is the 'net' residential density of the area of the site, that is, the area of housing land including half the width of any boundary roads (up to a maximum of 20 ft) but excluding the area of land used for non-housing purposes such as schools. Quarterly from 1965
Density of dwellings in tenders approved for local authorities and new towns	By region and type of authority	E & W	Annual	[QRL 26]	3.1.3 Annual from 1966
	Distribution of schemes, dwellings, persons	"	"	"	" "

Description	Region	Frequency	Reference	Section & remarks
Garages and parking spaces in housing schemes approved for local authorities and new towns	Region	"		3.1.3 Annual (published irregularly) from 1967
The standards of dwellings mortgaged	GB	1962, 1966, 1970	[QRL 43]	3.1.4
The standards of new dwellings	"	Annual	[QRL 6]	3.1.4 This source is produced mainly as a guide for building materials producers
Sale of local authority dwellings (built specifically for sale)	See the relevant series in OCCUPANCY AND OWNERSHIP			
Stock of dwellings by tenure	"			3.1.5 See remarks under Tenure above
Stage of construction				
Dwellings started, under construction and completed for public/private sector	E & W, S	Monthly	[QRL 40]	3.2.3 Useful since [QRL 40] is published monthly, cf. [QRL 26]. Monthly figures for the private sector in Scotland are estimated, and the balance of the quarter's total included in the quarter month when quarterly figures became available
Dwellings started, under construction and completed for local housing authorities/for private owners/others	E & W, S, NI	Quarterly	[QRL 41]	3.2.3 Local authorities include new towns (both Development Corporations and the Commission for New Towns) the Scottish Special Housing Association and the Northern Ireland Housing Trust
Houses completed for local authorities and new towns/housing associations and government departments/for private owners	E & W, S	"	[QRL 40]	3.2.3 Cumulative 1945–1955. Note that cumulative figures for E and W refer to the period from April 1945, for S from January 1945 and for NI from June 1944
Houses completed for local housing authorities/for private owners/others	E & W by houses/flats; NI, S	Monthly	[QRL 41]	3.2.3 Cumulative figures 1945–1959. See remarks to first entry in 'Stage of Construction' above for monthly Scottish figures

Descriptive Title	Breakdown	Area	Frequency	Publication (See QRL Key)	Text Reference and Remarks
Permanent dwellings started, under construction, completed for public/private sector	E & W, S, NI	UK	„	[QRL 26]	3.2.4 See remarks to first entry in 'Stage of Construction' for monthly Scottish figures
Permanent dwellings started and completed for local authorities/new towns/housing associations/government departments/private sector	Regions	GB	Quarterly	„	3.2.4
Starts and completions: actual and seasonally adjusted for public/private sector		„	Monthly	„	3.2.4 Secondary source: [QRL 40]
Dwellings completed	Post-war annual totals	UK	Annual	[QRL 26] No. 6	3.2.5 Useful for post-war performance but series for starts and under construction may be obtained directly by reference to [QRL 24] and to [QRL 25] both of which were first published in 1945. [QRL 24] is no longer published
Dwellings started and under construction	Regions & conurbations	GB	„	[QRL 26]	3.2.5 From 1964
Dwellings completed	„	„	„	„	„
Dwellings completed by local authorities and new towns	Region & type of authority	„	„	„	„
Dwellings completed	Regional sub-divisions	E & W	„	„	3.2.5 From 1968
Dwellings completed	New towns	GB	„	„	3.2.5 Annual for 1949–1960: [QRL 26], No. 3. Annual from 1961
Dwellings completed per 1000 population	Regions	„	„	„	3.2.5
Dwellings completed for the armed services		„	1966, 1967	[QRL 26] No. 9	„
New dwellings started by speculative builders on their own account		„	1968	[QRL 26] No. 15	„

Subject	Area	Period	Source	Text reference
Private sector sites with dwellings under construction at 31/1/1968	E & W exc. Greater London	1968	[QRL 26] No. 9	3.2.5 — See also [QRL 39], No. 6, for figures by local authority
Local authority and new town schemes with dwellings under construction in August 1968	E & W	1968	[QRL 26] No. 11	3.2.5 — See also [QRL 39], No. 8, for figures of schemes by size by local authority
Overspill: agreed town development schemes	,,	Annual	,,	3.2.5 — See also [QRL 39], Nos. 7 and 9
Dwellings started and completed	Statistical sub-divisions of regions	,,	,,	3.2.5
Effect of alterations in local authority areas on figures for dwellings started & completed	LA	1967, 1968, 1969	[QRL 39]	3.2.5 — For the first quarter of each year
Housing progress	LA, regions, counties. Dwellings started, under construction & completed	Quarterly	,,	3.2.5 — Quarterly figures before 1967 are available in the Appendix to [QRL 24]
Dwellings completed outside local authorities' own areas	LA	,,	,,	3.2.5
Distribution of dwellings completed for the Greater London Council	London boroughs and local authorities	,,	,,	,,
Distribution of houses demolished	London boroughs / GLC	,,	,,	,,
Housing progress	LA / S	,,	[QRL 25]	,,

Conversions

Subject	Area	Period	Source	Text reference
Conversions to the stock of dwellings	See the relevant series in OCCUPANCY AND OWNERSHIP			

Losses to the stock of dwellings

Subject	Area	Period	Source	Text reference
Temporary housing	E & W, S / GB	Position at each quarter month	[QRL 26]	3.4.1 — Back to 1945 in [QRL 24]
	S	Quarterly	[QRL 25]	3.4.1 — Back to 1945
Annual gains and losses to the stock of dwellings	E & W, S / GB	Annual	[QRL 26]	3.4.1 — Annual from 1961, annual averages from 1951-55, 1956-61
Slum clearance: houses demolished or closed	E & W	Quarterly	,,	3.4.2 et seq. — Cumulative 1945-54, 1955-59. Quarterly from 1955 in [QRL 24] and [QRL 25]

Descriptive Title	Breakdown	Area	Frequency	Publication (See QRL Key)	Text Reference and Remarks
Unfit houses known to have been made fit		"	"	"	3.4.5 Quarterly from 1965
Houses demolished or closed	Regions	"	"	"	3.4.2 et seq. Annual from 1955, quarterly from 1964
Slum clearance: houses demolished or closed		S	"	"	3.4.7 Annual from 1955, quarterly from 1964. Figures for 'other' action estimated between 1955 and 1961
Slum clearance	LA, regions, counties. Houses demolished in or adjoining clearance areas/unfit houses demolished or closed elsewhere	E & W	"	[QRL 39]	3.4.8 For figures before 1967, see the Appendix to [QRL 24]
Clearance areas submitted, orders submitted and confirmed, houses purchased by agreement	LA	S E & W	" "	[QRL 25] [QRL 26]	3.4.8 3.4.9 Annual from 1955, quarterly from 1964
THE HOUSE-BUILDING INDUSTRY **Employment**					
Operatives employed by contractors by type of work		GB	Quarterly	[QRL 40]	4.1.1 and 4.1.3 Figures for employment in quarter month
Local authorities' operatives engaged on construction work by type of work	Region	"	Half-yearly	"	4.1.2 and 4.1.3 Figures for employment in April and September
Local authorities' operatives engaged on construction work by type of work and type of authority		"	"		"
Local authorities' operatives engaged on construction work by type of work and size of authority		"	"		"
Housing labour force		"	Annual	[QRL 26]	4.1.2 and 4.1.3 Includes direct labour and employment by contractors on new work and repair and maintenance. For coverage of direct labour see 4.1.2

Description	Area / detail	Frequency	Reference	Section / Remarks
Employment of operatives by trade of firm and type of work	"	"	"	4.1.3
Employment of operatives by type of work	"	"	"	"
Employment of operatives by size of firm and type of work	"	"	"	"
Average weekly earnings: manual wage earners in the UK (October 1948 = 100)	UK	Half-yearly	[QRL 40]	4.1.3 Up to and including 1969 the figures refer to a week in April and October each year. After 1969 the enquiry is held in October only. Average earnings and index numbers in construction industry; before 1960 referred to both building and civil engineering contracting industries separately
Average hourly earnings and average hours worked: manual wage-earners in the UK	UK	Half-yearly	[QRL 40]	4.1.3 Includes the construction industry. See remarks to preceding entry
Index numbers of hourly earnings (October 1948 = 100)	"	"	"	"
Hourly wage rates in (a) building (b) civil engineering	London and Liverpool/Grade A districts, subdivided by type of labour — (a) E & W (b) GB	1 day 2 or 3 times per annum	"	4.1.3
Wages per 40 hour week	Craftsmen and labourers by region; apprentices by age; young labourers by age; lorry drivers by weight of vehicle — GB	Quarterly	[QRL 9]	4.1.4
Weekly wage rates	Wage rates—London/Liverpool/Grade A districts by type of labour — "	"	[QRL 7]	4.1.4
Output				
Value of output by type of work	GB	Quarterly	[QRL 40]	4.2.2 and 4.2.3. Annual figures in [QRL 2]. Secondary source: [QRL 26]
Local authorities: value of work done by type of work	Region	Half-yearly	"	4.2.4
Local authorities: value of work done by type of authority and type of work	E and W, S	"	"	"

Descriptive Title	Breakdown	Area	Frequency	Publication (See QRL Key)	Text Reference and Remarks
Local authorities: value of work done by size of authority and type of work		GB	Half-yearly	[QRL 40]	4.2.4
Value of work done by trade of firm and type of work		"	Annual	[QRL 65]	"
Value of work done by type of work	Region of registration	"	"	"	"
Value of work done by size of firm and type of work		"	"	"	"
Value of output at 1963 prices seasonally adjusted		"	Quarterly	[QRL 40]	4.2.1 and 4.2.5
Industrialised building Industrialised building	See relevant series in CHANGES TO THE STOCK OF DWELLINGS				See also 4.3
Indicators of future levels of activity Private enterprise housing enquiry		GB	Biennial	[QRL 26]	4.4.1 First enquiry July 1964
Permanent dwellings approved and approved but not started	E and W, S	"	Monthly	"	4.4.2 Cumulative 1945–50, annual from 1951, quarterly from 1964, monthly from 1966
Estimated time lag: start to completion	E and W, division into flats/houses; GB, division into public/private sector	"	Quarterly	"	4.4.2 Quarterly from 1951
Quarterly enquiry into architects' new building work	E & W, location of architects' offices	GB	Quarterly	[QRL 45]	4.4.3 Note that the regional analysis refers to the location of the architect's office and not to the location of the work to be carried out
Building design work carried out by local authorities: housing		"	Triennial	[QRL 40]	4.4.3 Covers only major projects valued at over £2,500. Figures for 4-month period ending January, May and September. Secondary source (1965—January 1968): [QRL 36]
Value of new orders obtained by contractors by type of work		"	Quarterly	"	4.4.4

Value of new orders obtained by contractors by type of work at 1963 prices seasonally adjusted		"	"	"	"
Value of new orders obtained by contractors by type of work		"	Monthly	"	"
New orders by value range and by type of work	Region	"	Quarterly	"	"
		"	"	"	"
Local authority contracts					
Size of local authority schemes	E and W, S	GB	Quarterly	[QRL 26]	4.5 / Annual from 1960
Types of local authority contracts	"	E & W	Annual	"	4.5
Contractors' schemes: types of tender and contract		"	"	"	4.5 / From 1966
Local authority housing schemes: technical advice employed		E & W	Annual	[QRL 26]	4.5 / From 1966
Housing schemes: distribution and average size: by urban and rural areas and by type of scheme		"	"	"	From 1960
Garage and parking spaces in housing schemes	Regions	"	"	"	From 1967
Building materials					
Building materials		GB	Monthly	[QRL 40]	4.6
Price index of house building materials (1963 = 100)		UK	"	[QRL 70]	4.6.2
The costs of new construction					
Floor area and cost of construction by type of dwelling in tenders approved for local authorities		E & W	Quarterly	[QRL 26]	4.7 / Annual from 1960, quarterly from 1965
Floor area and cost of construction of two-storey and five-bedspace houses in tenders approved for local authorities	Regions	"	"	"	4.7 / From 1968
Floor area and cost of construction: industrialised and traditional building in tenders approved for local authorities		"	"	"	4.7 / From 1965

Descriptive Title	Breakdown	Area	Frequency	Publication (See QRL Key)	Text References and Remarks
Floor area and cost of construction: by size in tenders approved for local authorities		S	”	”	4.7 Annual from 1961, quarterly from 1966
Distribution of construction costs: year ended 30 June 1967	Region	E & W	See descriptive title	[QRL 26]	4.7.6
Average cost per dwelling in LA schemes	”	”	Annual	”	4.7.7 From 1963
Parker Morris standards: costs: year ended June 1966	”	”		”	4.7.8
Constant standards costs index (1964 = 100)	”	”	Half-yearly	”	4.7.9 and 4.7.10 Index from 1964
Local authority tender cost (weighted average)		”	Annual	”	Published for comparison along with the above index
Index of house-building costs (quarter ended December 1965 = 100)		UK	Half-yearly	[QRL 43]	4.7.10 Figures refer to the quarters ended June and December each year
The price of residential building land	Counties	E	Weekly	[QRL 15]	4.7.11 An additional source is 'Under the Hammer' published by Rogers (Printers) Ltd. of 86, Aston Rd. North, Birmingham, which includes details of the auction prices of land sold with planning permission for residential development. There are ten separate editions covering groups of counties in the North, Midlands and West of England and parts of S. Wales. Most editions are published weekly.
Site value of new property mortgaged	Regions	UK	Half-yearly	[QRL 43]	4.7.11 Figures refer to the quarters ended June and December each year
Price index of private sector housing land (1966 = 100)	Broad regions: North, Midlands and Wales, S (exc. GL), Greater London	E & W	”	[QRL 26]	Index from 1963

PERSONAL EXPENDITURE ON HOUSING
The working of the Rent Acts

Subject	Area	Region	Frequency	QRL	Section and remarks
Rent Acts 1965 and 1968: applications for registration of fair rent	Greater London, rest of E and W, S	GB	Quarterly	[QRL 26]	5.1.4 From 1966
Registered rents compared with previous rents	Greater London, rest of E and W, E and W, S	"	"	"	"
Rent regulation 1967–70: applications for registration	Rent assessment panel areas	E & W	Annual	"	5.1 From 1967
Registered rents compared with previous rents: change by amount	Greater London, rest of E and W, E and W	"	"	"	"
Average previous rent and average registered rent: by gross value of dwellings: (a) houses, (b) flats, c) rooms	Greater London, E and W	"	"	"	5.1 Flats include lettings of rooms accessible to each other and with kitchen facilities within the letting. 'Rooms' means lettings of single rooms where bathroom/WC are not contained within the letting, and of two or more rooms that cannot be classified as flats
Registered rents by type of premises and number of rooms in dwelling		"	"	"	See remarks above. Rooms counted are living-rooms, bedrooms and kitchens. Figures from 1967 From 1967
Registered rents by type and size of premises		"	"	"	5.1.4 An abridged version of this table appears in [QRL 26]. Figures from 1966
Furnished dwellings: determination of reasonable rents and security of tenure		"	"	[QRL 19]	
Effects of Rent Act 1957		UK	1957 & 1959	[QRL 51]	5.1.5 Covers particularly the effects of decontrol. Historical interest: first interviews in 1957 and second round in 1959
Workings of the Rent Acts 1965 and 1968: tenant and landlord survey		UK	1970	[QRL 56]	5.1.5 and 5.1.7 Description of the report and the tenant and landlord surveys
Harassment and illegal evictions		"	Up to 1970	"	5.1.8

Descriptive Title	Breakdown	Area	Frequency	Publication (See QRL Key)	Text References and Remarks
Rents of types and standards of accommodation	Rents charged by private landlords, number of bedrooms, whether with bath, furnished or unfurnished	Greater London	1963	[QRL 55]	5.2.1
	Rents charged by private landlords, number of bedrooms, whether with bath, furnished or unfurnished; ratio of net rent to gross value	E & W	1964	[QRL 68]	,,
	Rents charged by private landlords, number of bedrooms, whether with bath, furnished or unfurnished; annual rent in relation to gross value	S	1965	[QRL 60]	,,
Rents of Local Authority Dwellings					
Average weekly rents of local authority dwellings (1962 = 100)	Greater London, rest of E & W	E & W	April & October	[QRL 26]	5.2.2 From 1957
Unrebated rents of local authority dwellings by size and by age of dwelling	LA. Age and size are cross classified	,,	Annual	[QRL 27]	5.2.3 and 5.2.4
Rents of LA housing by size	LA	S	,,	[QRL 52]	5.2.5 et seq.
Family Expenditure Survey and related statistics					
Weekly income of household by tenure		UK	Annual	[QRL 16]	5.3
Expenditure on housing by tenure and by income		,,	,,	,,	,,
Expenditure on housing by tenure, by income and by household composition		,,	,,	,,	,,
Expenditure on housing by tenure and administrative area		,,	,,	,,	,,
Expenditure on housing by household composition and administrative area		,,	,,	,,	,,
Expenditure on housing by tenure, income and occupation of the head of household		,,	,,	,,	,,

Subject	Area	Period	Source	Ref.	Notes
Expenditure on housing by tenure, income and age of head of household	"	"	"	"	
Expenditure on housing as a percentage of total weekly household expenditure	"	"	"	"	
Expenditure on housing by tenure	Regions	"	"	"	
Rent in proportion to income	GB	1967	[QRL 26]	5.3.7	
Rents and mortgage payments by income groups	"	"	"	"	
Distribution of rents	"	1967, 1969	"	"	
Income by tenure group by age of head of household	"	1969	"	"	
Income by tenure group by type of household	"	"	"	"	
Income by tenure group by size of household	"	"	"	"	
Income by tenure group by number of earners in household	E & W	1966	"	"	
Percentage distribution of income by tenure group	GB	1967, 1968, 1969	"	"	
Mortgage payments in relation to income	UK	1966	"	5.3.8	
The index of retail prices (16 January 1962 = 100)	"	Monthly	[QRL 41]	5.3.9	
Consumers' expenditure on housing at current and 1963 prices	"	Annual	[QRL 42]	5.3.10	

HOUSING LOANS AND HOUSE PRICES

Financial institutions and the supply of funds

Subject	Area	Period	Source	Ref.	Notes
Loans for house purchase: main institutional sources	UK	Quarterly	[QRL 26]	6.1.3	Annual from 1960, quarterly from 1963
Intended use of the property on which advances were secured	"	Annual	[QRL 69]	6.1.3	
Local authority lending for house purchase	LA, E & W	1964–65	[QLR 64]	6.1.6	
Loans by local authorities to private persons for house purchase	"	Quarterly	[QRL 26]	6.1.6	Annual from 1959, quarterly from 1964

Descriptive Title	Breakdown	Area	Frequency	Publication (See QRL Key)	Text Reference and Remarks
Loans by LAs for conversions, alterations, repairs or improvements		"	"	"	"
Housing loans by LAs		"	1967–1968	[QRL 39]	6.1.6
Building societies: guarantees by LAs		"	Quarterly	[QRL 26]	6.1.6
" " shares, deposits and mortgages		UK	"	"	6.1.7 Annual from 1960, quarterly from 1963
" " mortgage advances by type of property		"	Monthly	"	6.1.7 Annual from 1963, quarterly from 1965, monthly from July 1967
" " commitments for advances		"	"	"	6.1.7 Monthly from 1967
Insurance companies: loans for house purchase		"	"	"	6.1.8 Quarterly from 1966
" " distribution of mortgages by purchase price		"	Quarterly	"	6.1.8
Loans for house purchase by insurance companies		"	"	[QRL 17]	"
Personal loans by banks for house purchase		"	"	"	6.1.9
Transactions in financial assets: personal sector		"	Annual	[QRL 42]	6.1.10 Quarterly figures in [QRL 17]
Statistics based on mortgage completions					
Types of dwellings mortgaged		UK	1962, 1966, 1970	[QRL 43]	6.2.2
Characteristics of borrowers from Nationwide Building Society		"	1963, 1966, 1968	"	6.2.3
Building societies: mortgages, purchase prices and income of borrowers		"	Quarterly	[QRL 26]	6.2.4 and 6.2.5 From 1966
" " period of mortgage		"	"	"	"
" " number of mortgages by purchase price		"	"	"	"

Description	Breakdown	Area	Period	QRL	Section	Notes
" number of mortgages by age of borrowers		"	"	"	"	"
" number of mortgages by age of dwelling		"	"	"	"	"
" guarantee scheme		GB	Annual	"	6.2.4 and 6.2.5	From 1968
" option mortgages		"		"	6.2.4 and 6.2.5	
" previous tenure of borrower(s)		"	April 1968 to March 1969	"	6.2.4 and 6.2.5	From 1966
Insurance Companies: distribution of mortgages by purchase price		UK	Quarterly	"		

House prices

Description	Breakdown	Area	Period	QRL	Section	Notes
Average price of houses mortgaged to the Nationwide Building Society	Region	UK	Half-yearly	[QRL 43]	6.3.2	Figures for the second and fourth quarter of each year
Index of house prices (quarter ended 31 December 1965 = 100)		"	"	"	" "	
Average prices of houses mortgaged to the Nationwide Building Society by type of dwelling	"	"	1966, 1970	"	6.3.4	
Cost of house purchase		"	"	[QRL 26]	6.3.5	
Building societies: average price of new dwellings mortgaged by private owners	"	GB	Quarterly	"	6.3.6	Includes an 'average value' price index with 1963 = 100
Average mortgage and house prices	Region	UK	1966	"	6.3.7	
Average prices of 3-bedroom houses sold by age and type of area	"	E & W	Annual	"	6.3.7	Annual from 1966
Average prices of 3-bedroom houses sold by age	Sub-divisions of the SE region	SE region	1966	"	6.3.8	

HOUSING FINANCE AND LOCAL AUTHORITIES
The finance of local authority housing

Description	Breakdown	Area	Period	QRL	Section	Notes
Housing revenue account	LA (large sample)	E & W	Annual	[QRL 27]	7.1.2	Includes transfers from or to equalisation account
"		S	"	[QRL 50]	7.1.2	
		E & W	"	[QRL 26]	"	

Descriptive Title	Breakdown	Area	Frequency	Publication (See QRL Key)	Text Reference and Remarks
Housing repairs account	"	"	"	[QRL 27]	"
	"	S	"	[QRL 50]	"
Housing maintenance expenditure	"	E & W	"	[QRL 22]	7.1.3
Rents of local authority dwellings	See relevant series in PERSONAL EXPENDITURE ON HOUSING	E & W	Annual	[QRL 27]	7.1.4
Rent rebate schemes	LA (large sample)	E & W	Annual	[QRL 27]	7.1.4
	Number of tenants receiving rebate, average and total amount granted				
The cost of rent rebates	LA	S	"	[QRL 50]	7.1.4
Exchequer subsidies	Subsidies for provision of new dwellings, conversions and improvements	E & W	"	[QRL 4]	7.1.5
		"	"	[QRL 26]	7.1.5
	Amounts paid by subsidy legislation in respect of provision of dwellings	W		[QRL 14]	"
	"	S	"	[QRL 5]	"
Outstanding debt for housing purposes	LA Total debt; debt per head of population	E & W	"	[QRL 57]	7.1.6
Net capital expenditure on housing and net capital debt	LA	S	"	[QRL 50]	"
Revenue and capital accounts relating to housing	E & W	E & W	"	[QRL 38]	7.1.7
Local authority borrowing: loans sanctioned for housing		S	"	[QRL 37]	"
		E & W	"	[QRL 19]	7.1.8
Lending by the Public Works Loan Board	E & W, S	GB	"	[QRL 3]	"

Rating statistics

Descriptive Title	Breakdown	Area	Frequency	Publication (See QRL Key)	Text Reference and Remarks
Rate payments by households	Region	UK	1963/1964	[QRL 54]	7.2.2
Rate rebates	LA (large sample)	E & W	Annual	[QRL 58]	7.2.2
	LA	S	"	[QRL 46]	7.2.2
Number of domestic hereditaments	"	"	"	[QRL 47]	"
	LA (large sample)	E & W	"	[QRL 58]	7.2.3

Subject	Authority	Area	Frequency	Reference	Section	Remarks
Rateable values by type of hereditament	LA	S	,,	[QRL 48]	7.2.3	
	,,	,,	,,	[QRL 49]	,,	
	,,	E & W	,,	[QRL 48]	7.2.4	
Total rateable value: houses	LA (large sample)	S	,,	[QRL 49]	7.2.4	
Distribution of rateable values by value class	Aggregates of counties and district councils, E & W	,,	,,	[QRL 50]	7.2.4	
		E & W	,,	[QRL 25]		Previously published in [QRL 53]
Rates levied for housing	LA	S	,,	[QRL 59]	7.2.5	
Estimated net cost of housing	,,	,,	,,	[QRL 50]	,,	

HOUSING IN NATIONAL ACCOUNT STATISTICS

Subject	Authority	Area	Frequency	Reference	Section	Remarks
Gross national product by industry		UK	Annual	[QRL 42]	8.2	
Index numbers of output at constant factor cost (1963 = 100)		,,	,,	,,	,,	
Gross domestic product by industry and type of income		,,	,,	,,	,,	
Personal sector: capital account		,,	,,	,,	8.3.1	
Taxes on expenditure and subsidies allocated to consumers' expenditure		,,	,,	,,	,,	
Central Government current account		,,	,,	,,		Includes details of receipts from rents of temporary housing and Forces' married quarters and housing subsidies
Local authorities current account		,,	,,	,,	8.1.3	
Local authorities capital account		,,	,,	,,	,,	
Housing subsidies		,,	,,	,,		Includes housing
Analysis of public expenditure		,,	,,	,,	8.3	
Gross domestic fixed capital formation at current and 1963 prices by sector		,,	,,	,,	8.3	
Gross domestic fixed capital formation by sector and type of asset		,,	,,	,,		Includes 'dwellings'
Gross domestic fixed capital formation at current and 1963 prices by type of asset		UK	Annual	[QRL 42]	8.3	Includes 'dwellings'
Gross domestic fixed capital formation by industry group at current and 1963 prices		,,	,,	,,		,,

Descriptive Title	Breakdown	Area	Frequency	Publication (See QRL Key)	Text Reference and Remarks
Gross domestic fixed capital formation by industry and type of asset		"	"	"	"
Capital consumption by sector		"	"	"	8.3 [B 19], pp 383–387, discusses this and related concepts
Capital consumption by type of asset		"	"	"	"
Capital consumption by industry group		"	"	"	"
Net domestic fixed capital formation by sector		"	"	"	"
Net domestic fixed capital formation by type of asset		"	"	"	"
Net domestic fixed capital formation by industry group		"	"	"	"
Gross capital stock at 1963 replacement cost by industry and type of asset		"	"	"	"

QUICK REFERENCE LIST KEY TO PUBLICATIONS

Reference number	Organization responsible	Title	Publisher	Frequency or date of publication	Price* and remarks
[QRL 1]	Central Statistical Office	*Annual Abstract of Statistics*	HMSO, London	Annual	£2.10 (£2.20) (1972)
[QRL 2]	Department of the Environment, Statistics Construction Div.	*Annual Bulletin of Construction Statistics*	DOE	Annual	No longer available
[QRL 3]	Public Works Loan Board	*Annual Report of the Public Works Loan Board*	HMSO, London	Annual	£0.22p (24½p) (1971)
[QRL 4]	Ministry of Housing & Local Government	*Annual Report of the Ministry of Housing & Local Government*	HMSO, London	Annual	n/a
[QRL 5]	Scottish Development Dept.	*Annual Report of the Scottish Development Department*	HMSO, Edinburgh	Annual	90p (96p) (1972)
[QRL 6]	Building Statistical Services	*Annual Survey of New Housing*	Building Statistical Services, 14 Gt College St., London SW1P 3RZ	Annual	£100
[QRL 7]	Architectural Press Ltd.	*Architects Journal*	Architectural Press Ltd.	Weekly	15p
[QRL 8]	The Social Survey P. G. Gray & Elizabeth A. Parr	*A Survey of Residential Caravan Life*	Central Office of Information, London	1959	45p Available from OPCS
[QRL 9]	Building Ltd.	*Building*	Building Ltd., Builder House, Catherine St., London W.C.2	Weekly	15p
[QRL 10]	Building Societies Association	*Building Society Statistics*	Building Societies Assocn. 14, Park St., London W.1	Quarterly	Free
[QRL 11]	Department of the Environment (formerly Min. of Public Bldg. and Works) R. and D. Bulletin	*Building Maintenance Statistics 1970*	Research and Development Paper. Available from: Room 1643, Lunar House, 40, Wellesley Rd., Croydon CR9 2EL	1971	Free
[QRL 12]	General Register Office, London (now Office of Population Censuses and Surveys) General Register Office, Edinburgh	*Census of Population in Great Britain (Sample Census GB 1966)*	HMSO, London	Decennial	Various volumes, details of which are given in HMSO sectional lists No. 56 (OPCS) and No. 50 (miscellaneous, for Scottish census publications)

Reference number	Organization responsible	Title	Publisher	Frequency or date of publication	Price* and remarks
[QRL 13]	Department of Trade & Industry (formerly Board of Trade)	*Census of Production*	HMSO, London	Quinquennial	Various volumes
[QRL 14]	Welsh Office	*Digest of Welsh Statistics*	HMSO, Cardiff	Annual	£1.95 (£2.06) (1972)
[QRL 15]	Estates Gazette	*Estates Gazette*	Estates Gazette, 159, Wardour St, London W1V 4BN	Weekly	15p
[QRL 16]	Department of Employment and Productivity	*Family Expenditure Survey*	HMSO, London	Annual	£2.40 (£2.49) (1972)
[QRL 17]	Central Statistical Office	*Financial Statistics*	HMSO, London	Monthly	95p (1973)
[QRL 18]	Office of Population Censuses & Surveys, Social Survey Div.	*General Household Survey*	HMSO, London	Annual	£1.80 (£2.05) (1973)
[QRL 19]	Department of the Environment	*Handbook of Statistics*	HMSO, London	Annual	65p (67½p) (1971)
[QRL 20]	Ministry of Housing & Local Government	*House Condition Survey 1967 in Economic Trends* No. 175	HMSO, London	May 1968	44p
[QRL 21]	Department of the Environment	*Housing and Construction Statistics*	HMSO, London	Quarterly	75p (82½p) (1973)
[QRL 22]	Institute of Municipal Treasurers and Accountants	*Housing Maintenance and Management Statistics*	IMTA, 1 Buckingham Place, London SW1E 6HS	Annual	£1.00
[QRL 23]	Institute of Municipal Treasurers and Accountants	*Housing Rent Statistics* (now known as *Housing Statistics Part I*)	IMTA, 1 Buckingham Place, London SW1E 6HS	Annual	£1.50
[QRL 24]	Ministry of Housing and Local Government	*Housing Return for England and Wales*	HMSO, London	Quarterly	No longer published
[QRL 25]	Scottish Development Department	*Housing Return for Scotland*	HMSO, Edinburgh	Quarterly	15p
[QRL 26]	Department of the Environment Scottish Development Department Welsh Office	*Housing Statistics*	HMSO, London	Quarterly	90p
[QRL 27]	Institute of Municipal Treasurers and Accountants	*Housing Statistics* (now known as *Housing Statistics Part II*)	IMTA, 1 Buckingham Place, London SW1E 6HS	Annual	£1.50
[QRL 28]	Ministry of Housing and Local Government (now the Department of the Environment)	*Housing Survey Report No. 1* West Midlands Conurbation House Condition Survey 1967	HMSO, London	1969	25p (26½p) (1969)
[QRL 29]	Ministry of Housing and Local Government (now the Department of the Environment)	*Housing Survey Report No. 2* South East Lancashire Conurbation House Condition Survey 1967	HMSO, London	1969	25p (26½p) (1970)

	Author/Department	Title	Publisher	Date	Price
[QRL 30]	Ministry of Housing and Local Government (now the Department of the Environment)	*Housing Survey Report No. 3* Merseyside Conurbation House Condition Survey 1968	HMSO, London	1970	25p (26½p) (1970)
[QRL 31]	Ministry of Housing and Local Government (now the Department of the Environment)	*Housing Survey Report No. 4* Tyneside Conurbation House Condition Survey 1968	HMSO, London	1970	25p (26½p) (1970)
[QRL 32]	Ministry of Housing and Local Government (now the Department of the Environment)	*Housing Survey Report No. 5* West Yorkshire Conurbation House Condition Survey 1969	HMSO, London	1970	25p (26½p) (1970)
[QRL 33]	Ministry of Housing and Local Government (now the Department of the Environment)	*Housing Survey Report No. 6* West Midlands Housing Survey 1966	Department of the Environment, Printing & Stationery Section, Room 304, 83/91 Victoria St, London SW1H 0E2	1971	25p
[QRL 34]	Ministry of Housing and Local Government (now the Department of the Environment)	*Housing Survey Report No. 7* West Yorkshire Conurbation Housing Survey 1969	,,	1971	90p
[QRL 35]	Inland Revenue	*Inland Revenue Statistics*	HMSO, London	Annual	£1.75
[QRL 36]	Ministry of Public Building & Works (now the Department of the Environment) Statistics Branch, Construction Economics Division	*Local Authority Design Work Statistics*	Ministry of Public Building and Works	1968	Free No longer available. Statistics covering a similar area are now published in [QRL 21]
[QRL 37]	Scottish Development Department	*Local Financial Returns, Scotland*	HMSO, Edinburgh	Annual	35p
[QRL 38]	Department of the Environment	*Local Government Financial Statistics*	HMSO, London	Annual	70p (75p) (1972)
[QRL 39]	Department of the Environment Welsh Office	*Local Housing Statistics*	HMSO, London	Quarterly	98p (£1.04) (1972)
[QRL 40]	Department of the Environment Statistics Construction Division	*Monthly Bulletin of Construction Statistics*	Available from: Room S11/19, DOE, 2 Marsham Street, London SW1P 3EB	Monthly	Free
[QRL 41]	Central Statistical Office	*Monthly Digest of Statistics*	HMSO, London	Monthly	63p (72½p) (1971)
[QRL 42]	Central Statistical Office	*National Income and Expenditure*	HMSO, London	Annual	85p (93½p) (1972)
[QRL 43]	Nationwide Building Society	*Occasional Bulletin*	Nationwide Building Research Section, Nationwide Building Soc., New Oxford House, London WC1V 6PW	Quarterly	Free

Reference number	Organization responsible	Title	Publisher	Frequency of date of publication	Price* and remarks
[QRL 44]	Ministry of Housing and Local Government (now the Department of the Environment)	Old Houses into New Homes	HMSO, London	1968, Cmnd. 3602	13½p (1s) (1968)
[QRL 45]	Royal Institute of British Architects	Quarterly Statistical Bulletin	Royal Institute of British Architects, Research and Statistics Department, 66 Portland Place, London W1	Quarterly	£5 per annum
[QRL 46]	Department of the Environment Welsh Office	Rate Rebates in England and Wales	HMSO, London	Annual	82p (85½p) (1972)
[QRL 47]	Scottish Development Department	Rate Rebates in Scotland	HMSO, Edinburgh	Annual	26p
[QRL 48]	Department of the Environment Welsh Office	Rates and Rateable Values in England and Wales	HMSO, London	Annual	96p (£1.02) (1973)
[QRL 49]	Scottish Development Department	Rates and Rateable Values in Scotland	HMSO, Edinburgh	Annual	40p (1973)
[QRL 50]	Scottish Branch of the Institute of Municipal Treasurers and Accountants	Rating Review	IMTA, Available from: Town Chamberlain, Kirkcaldy, Fife	Annual	50p (1973)
[QRL 51]	The Social Survey P. G. Gray & Elizabeth A. Parr	Rent Act 1957 Report of Inquiry	HMSO, London	1960, Cmnd. 1246	12½p (14p) (1960)
QRL 52	Scottish Development Department	Rents of Houses owned by Local Authorities in Scotland (now known as Rents of Houses owned by Public Authorities in Scotland)	HMSO, Edinburgh	Annual	16p (18p) (1971)
[QRL 53]	Inland Revenue	Report of the Commissioners of Her Majesty's Inland Revenue	HMSO, London	Annual	68p (73½p) (1972)
[QRL 54]	Chairman: Prof. Sir Roy Allen	Report of the Committee of Enquiry into the Impact of Rates on Households	HMSO, London	1964, Cmnd. 2582	£1.52½ (£1.57½) (1965)
[QRL 55]	Chairman: Sir Milner Holland	Report of the Committee on Housing in Greater London	HMSO, London	1965, Cmnd. 2605	£1.12½ (£1.18½) (1965)
[QRL 56]	Chairman: H. E. Francis, QC	Report of the Committee on the Rent Acts	HMSO, London	1971, Cmnd. 4609	£2.85 (£3.05) (1971)
[QRL 57]	Institute of Municipal Treasurers and Accountants	Return of Outstanding Debt	IMTA, 1 Buckingham Place, London SW1E 6HS	Annual	£1.50

[QRL 58]	Institute of Municipal Treasurers and Accountants	*Return of Rate Collection*	IMTA, 1 Buckingham Place, London SW1E 6HS	Annual	£1.00
[QRL 59]	Institute of Municipal Treasurers and Accountants	*Return of Rates*	IMTA, 1 Buckingham Place, London SW1E 6HS	Annual	£1.50
[QRL 60]	Scottish Development Department (J. B. Cullingworth)	*Scottish Housing in 1965*	Government Social Survey, British Market Research Bureau on behalf of S.D.D	1967	
[QRL 61]	Ministry of Housing and Local Government (now Department of the Environment)	*Slum Clearance 1955*	HMSO, London	1955, Cmd. 9593	17½p
[QRL 62]	Department of Health for Scotland	*Slum Clearance–Proposals in Scotland*	HMSO, Edinburgh	1956, Cmd. 9685	5p
[QRL 63]	Central Statistical Office	*Social Trends*	HMSO, London	Annual	£2.90 (1972)
[QRL 64]	Institute of Municipal Treasurers	*Statistics of Advances for House Purchase*	IMTA, 1 Buckingham Place, London SW1E 6HS		
[QRL 65]	Department of the Environment, Statistics Construction Division	*Supplement to the Bulletin of Construction Statistics*	Dept. of the Environment, London	Annual	No longer available
[QRL 66]	Greater London Council, Department of Planning and Transportation Intelligence Unit	*The Condition of London's Housing—A Survey* Research Report No. 4	The Information Centre, County Hall, London SE1	1970	£1.37½
[QRL 67]	The Social Survey P. G. Gray and R. Russel	*The Housing Situation in 1960, House Survey England & Wales*	Central Office of Information, London	1962	£1.05
[QRL 68]	The Social Survey Myra Woolf	*The Housing Survey in England and Wales 1964*	HMSO, London	1967	£1.75
[QRL 69]	Chief Registrar of Friendly Societies	*The Report of the Chief Registrar of Friendly Societies Part II*	HMSO, London	Annual	50p (52½p) (1971)
[QRL 70]	Department of Trade and Industry	*Trade and Industry*	Department of Trade and Industry, London	Weekly	10p
[QRL 71]	Building Research Station, Department of the Environment W. V. Hole and M. T. Pountney	*Trends in Population, Housing and Occupancy Rates 1861–1961*	HMSO, London	1971	80p (85½p) (1971)
[QRL 72]	Welsh Office	*Welsh House Condition Survey 1968*	HMSO, Cardiff	1969	37½p (39p) (1969)

* Where a run of years is involved, the price quoted is that for the latest year traced as indicated in parenthesis

Bibliography

[B 1] Allnutt, D. E., Cox, R. T. S., and Mullock, P. J. 'The projection of households.' *Statistics for Town and Country Planning*, Series III, No. 1. Ministry of Housing and Local Government, London, 1969.

[B 2] Bowley, Marian. 'Housing Statistics.' *Sources and Nature of the Statistics of the United Kingdom*, Vol. I. Oliver and Boyd, Edinburgh, 1952.

[B 3] Cullen, B. D. 'Material usage in new building.' *Building*, 27/1/1967, p. 115. Building Ltd., London.

[B 4] Cullingworth, J. B. *English Housing Trends*. Occasional Paper on Social Administration No. 13. G. Bell and Sons, Ltd., London, 1965.

[B 5] Duncan, T. L. C. *Measuring Housing Quality*. Occasional Paper No. 20 of the Centre for Urban and Regional Studies, University of Birmingham. Research Publications Services Ltd., 11 Nelson Road, London S.E.10, 1971.

[B 6] Farthing, S. M. *A Review of British Housing Statistics*. National House-Builders Registration Council, 58, Portland Place, London W1, 1972.

[B 7] Fleming, M. C. 'The long-term measurement of construction costs in the U.K.' *Journal of the Royal Statistical Society*, Series A, Vol. 129, Part 4, p. 534.

[B 8] Fleming, M. C. 'Housing in Northern Ireland.' *Reviews of U.K. Statistical Sources*, Vol. III, No. 6. Heinemann Educational Books, London, 1974.

[B 9] Holmans, A. E. 'A forecast of effective demand for housing in Great Britain in the 1970s.' *Social Trends*, No. 1, p. 33. H.M.S.O., London, 1970.

[B 10] Kemsley, W. F. F. *Family Expenditure Survey Handbook on the Sample, Fieldwork and Coding Procedures*. H.M.S.O., London, 1969.

[B 11] Maurice, Rita (ed). *National Accounts Statistics—Sources and Methods*. H.M.S.O., London, 1968.

[B 12] Moss, Louis. 'General household survey.' *Statistical News*, No. 16, Feb 1972, p. 167.

[B 13] Nevitt, A. A. *Housing, Taxation and Subsidies*. Nelson, London, 1966.

[B 14] Penrice, G. 'Recent developments in housing statistics.' *Economic Trends*, No. 181, p. xii, 1968.

[B 15] Stone, P. A. 'The prices of building sites in Britain.'

Land Values (edited by Peter Hall). Sweet and Maxwell, London, 1965.

[B 16] Stone, P. A. Urban development in Britain. *Population Trends and Housing*, Vol. I. Cambridge University Press, Cambridge, 1970.

[B 17] Wilkinson, R. 'Building society statistics: a review article.' *Urban Studies*, Vol. 2, No. 2, p. 186. Oliver and Boyd, London, 1965.

[B 18] Ministry of Public Building and Works, Directorate of Research and Information. *Construction Statistics: the Opinion of the Private User*. H.M.S.O., London, 1968.

[B 19] Ministry of Housing and Local Government. 'Current trends in housing progress.' *Economic Trends*, May 1968, p. ix.

[B 20] Ministry of Public Building and Works, Directorate of Research and Information. *Directory of Construction Statistics*, H.M.S.O., London, 1968.

[B 21] Government White Paper. *Fair Deal for Housing*. Cmnd. 4728. H.M.S.O., London, 1971.

[B 22] Parker Morris Committee. *Homes for Today and Tomorrow*. H.M.S.O., London, 1962.

[B 23] Working Party on the Housing Revenue Account (Chairman: J. Delafons). *Housing Revenue Accounts*, H.M.S.O., London, 1969.

[B 24] Department of the Environment. 'An index of housing land prices.' *Economic Trends*, Feb. 1971, p. xiv.

[B 25] Department of Employment and Productivity. *Method of Construction and Calculation of the Index of Retail Prices*. Studies in Official Statistics, No. 6. H.M.S.O., London, 1964.

[B 26] Central Housing Advisory Committee—Sub-Committee on Standards of Housing Fitness. *Our Older Homes: a Call for Action*. H.M.S.O., London, 1966.

[B 27] Cost of Living Advisory Committee. *A Report from the Cost of Living Advisory Committee*. Cmnd 3677. H.M.S.O., London, 1968.

[B 28] Radcliffe Committee. *Report of the Committee on the Workings of the Monetary System*. Cmnd 827. H.M.S.O., London, 1960.

[B 29] Estimates Committee (1966/7). *Report on Government Statistical Services*, HC246. H.M.S.O., London, 1967.

Appendix I

Note on Housing Statistics from the Censuses of Population in Northern Ireland

The timing of the censuses in Northern Ireland since the Second World War has been in step with those conducted in Great Britain but though we shall not be concerned with them, pre-war censuses were taken in 1926 and 1937. Although the coordination of the timing of the censuses is most welcome there still remain substantial differences between the practice in Northern Ireland and that in the rest of the United Kingdom, much more important than any differences between England and Wales and Scotland. In part this may be due to special conditions and alternative requirements in that province but there are some instances, as we shall see later, where there appears to be no obvious rationale for such practices and where standardisation throughout the United Kingdom would be useful both for comparative purposes and for improving the quality of the information obtainable from the census.

The treatment of the housing statistics derived from the Census of Population for Northern Ireland will follow the lines adopted in the main text for Great Britain, and the section headings will remain the same wherever this is possible. To avoid unnecessary duplication, however, reference will be made to the numbered paragraphs of the text for Great Britain where the intention in Northern Ireland is the same though the wording may be different, and where the difficulties of interpretation are similar. Statistics other than those based on population Censuses are dealt with fully in *Housing in Northern Ireland* by M. C. Fleming, Book 6 in this series.

I The Stock of Dwellings

1.1 Numbers

For the purposes of conducting the Census for Northern Ireland in 1966, which was not sample-based as the parallel censuses in Gt. Britain were, 'buildings for habitation' included 'all buildings used wholly or partly as residential accommodation'. The treatment of non-permanent and mobile structures differs from that described in paragraph 1.1.1 in that these structures were only counted as buildings if they were occupied on census night. An exception to this exclusion, as in England and Wales in 1961, was made in the case of 'unoccupied structures of wood, asbestos, corrugated iron etc., used as casual residences, e.g. at weekends or holiday times . . . if they appeared to be of sound construction and had amenities such as piped water, sewerage facilities and electric lighting.'

As a class, though, 'buildings for habitation' do not correspond to the concept of the building in Gt. Britain since each 'private dwelling' is counted as a 'building for habitation' and as a practical definition for housing purposes, therefore, it has few merits.*

The 'private dwelling' itself is similar to the term 'dwelling' for Gt. Britain (paragraph 1.1.2) but there are some differences in the application of the definition. Bed-sitting-rooms were not counted as dwellings (c.f. 1.1.3) and other accommodation in a converted building was only counted as a dwelling if it was structurally separate, self-contained, and the kitchen, bathroom and water closet were not shared with the occupants of another unit of accommodation in the building (see later under the definition of 'a flat').

*In 1951 even buildings in the course of erection were included although tabulated separately.

1.2. Building and Dwelling Type

As we have seen, the 'building for habitation' does not correspond to the usual notion of a building or to the concept employed in the census in Great Britain so that classifications of 'buildings' have concentrated on distinguishing between 'private dwellings' and 'other buildings', i.e. institutional establishments. For some purposes, though, in 1961 and 1966 a distinction was drawn between buildings which were wholly or not wholly residential 'if part of it was used exclusively or primarily for purposes other than living accommodation' but 'Buildings such as a dentist's or a doctor's house with a room or annexe used as a surgery and a house containing a clergyman's or author's study were, however, treated as wholly residential.' For a discussion of the implications of the exclusion of such rooms for the count of rooms in a dwelling see paragraph 1.6.2.

The Census in 1961 identified various types of 'private dwelling':

'(i) *A dwelling house* means a dwelling of permanent construction which is not divided into flats and is not a farmhouse. A prefabricated bungalow provided by a local authority is included.

(ii) *A flat* means a completely self-contained dwelling on one or more floors with a separate entrance from the street or from a common landing or staircase. It must be possible to move between its rooms internally, without using a common landing or staircase used by other households. Also none of the household arrangements must be shared with the occupants of another unit of dwelling accommodation in the building. Where a building has been converted for the use of two or more households the accommodation of any part is not regarded as a flat unless each part occupied by a householder has a main door giving access to the whole of the accommodation and unless the other conditions specified above are satisfied.

(iii) *A farmhouse* means a dwelling of permanent construction from which the occupier carries on farming as a main occupation. In practice, a dwelling described as a farmhouse on the census return was classified as such only if at least one member of the household was engaged in farming.

(iv) *Some other type of dwelling* means a tent, caravan or other moveable dwelling, or such structure as a barn, out-office, hut or shed of wood, corrugated iron or similar non-traditional material and which, though fixed, is of such a temporary and unsubstantial nature that it cannot be regarded as a permanent dwelling.'

Although this classification betrays some features peculiar to Northern Ireland, as a whole the treatment of buildings and dwellings is compatible with that adopted in Great Britain (Section 1.2.1) and suffers therefore from the same limitations (see paragraph 1.2.2) with respect to the sharing of the dwellings.

1.4 Amenities

Only in 1961 were questions asked about the availability of household arrangements or amenities to private households and these were the same amenities as listed in paragraph 1.4.3. There are no tabulations of dwellings by amenities in Northern Ireland but information was given about the availability of household arrangements to private households living in different types of dwelling.

1.6 Size

In contrast to the position in Great Britain (see paragraph 1.6.2) the enumeration and inclusion of rooms in the census records has not changed since 1951 when the definition of a 'room' was parallel to that in Great Britain. Thus in 1966 the rooms counted were 'those normally used by the household for living, eating or sleeping purposes. A kitchen if so used is included, but not a scullery which is used only for washing, cleaning or cooking' but there seems to be no good reason why the definition in use in Great Britain should not be employed or, at least, that questions should be asked to enable comparisons to be made between the count of rooms using the Irish and the British definitions.

2 Occupancy and Ownership

2.1 Households

The definition of the 'private household' in Northern Ireland is similar to that given in 2.1.2 and is the *de facto* household including visitors, domestic servants, and those who spent census night travelling and arrived in the household next morning (unless they were enumerated elsewhere). It does not therefore reflect the household's normal composition, and no household composition tables where people are assigned to the household at their usual address have been given in the Censuses for Northern Ireland (c.f. 2.1.3). However, the conditions applied in Great Britain in 1961 and 1966 (see 2.1.4 and 2.1.6) about households having exclusive use of one room have always applied in Northern Ireland.

'Non-private households' include *all* persons enumerated in hotels, boarding-houses, old peoples' homes and institutions which exist for a functional purpose other than that of providing accommodation. Notice that although dwellings in 1966 were enumerated within non-private establishments if they were occupied by a private household, the private households themselves are not separately enumerated. In Northern Ireland, as in England and Wales, the rules for distinguishing private from non-private households in doubtful cases differed between 1951 and 1961. In 1951 'private dwellings' containing three or more boarders or lodgers were re-classified and the occupants described as a non-private household but in 1961 and 1966 the practice was in line with that in Great Britain (see 2.1.4).

The Census for Northern Ireland does not define or use a 'household space' (see 2.2.1) as such but private households are cross-tabulated by the number of rooms occupied. The amount of vacant accommodation cannot then be ascertained from the census tabulations except with reference to 'uninhabited' private dwellings, where 'uninhabited' is defined in the same way as 'vacant' in the 1951 Census for Great Britain (see 2.2.2) with its attendant difficulties of interpretation.

2.3 The Living Space of Households

The information provided in the Census for Northern Ireland is similar to that indicated in paragraph 2.4.1 for Great Britain, namely, the sharing of dwellings and the density of occupation for households of varying size. Reference should be made to paragraphs 2.4.3 and 2.4.4 for the difficulties of applying official and other standards for living space to the census data.

2.5 Tenure

Questions about the tenure by which households occupied their living quarters were first asked in the Census in 1961 but they were not included in the smaller scale 1966 Census. The classification of tenures was the same as that used in 1961 in Great Britain (see 2.6.2) but codes 1 and 2 were included in a residual category and code 3 was modified to suit local conditions:

'By renting from a local or public authority, including the Northern Ireland Housing Trust, the Sailors' and Soldiers' Land Trust, Housing Associations and Government Departments.'

Tabulations in 1961 covered private households by availability of household arrangements by tenure and households by tenure, rooms occupied and socio-economic group of the head of the household, the latter only in the County Reports. The procedure for allocating tenure to a dwelling in tabulations of dwellings by tenure followed that in Great Britain (see para. 2.6.5).

Appendix II

Selected Housing Returns and Specimen Forms

Statistical information on housing is obtained centrally from a variety of sources by aggregating and manipulating the data contained in individual forms or returns. Such primary data is obtained from households, either directly as in the census household schedule or from the enumerator or interviewer, and from a number of other bodies or organisations, principally local authorities, building societies and firms engaged in house-building.

The accuracy and reliability of the basic data determines the quality of the resulting statistics. Equally the type of information included in the primary data source determines the type of statistics that may be produced and the possibilities for the extraction of non-standard statistics.

Apart from the Household Schedule for the GHS the following specimen forms are those which are used extensively in the production of the tables in *Housing Statistics* [QRL 26]. In the main there are returns made to the DOE and SDD. On the other hand, some important returns on rents and local authority finance are made to IMTA by local authorities but since most of what is collected is also published copies of these forms have not been included.

In general returns received by the DOE and SDD are confidential when they relate to individuals and firms, but not usually when (as in the majority of cases) they refer to a local authority. In any case, access to some unpublished details is usually available for the use of research workers. Particular requests are treated on their merits, regard being had to the accessibility of what is requested. Sometimes, specific requests would involve a quite disproportionate amount of effort, but often there is no great difficulty.

Where the processing has been computerised (as now applies quite widely) access may well be possible to unpublished tabulations or listings, but requests for fresh computer analyses may be more difficult and expensive. For some local authority returns (covering housebuilding, slum clearance and improvement grants) much information for individual LAs is published in [QRL 39]. For rent assessment case records (forms RS 7 and RS 8) the computer print-out gives a good deal of detail beyond what is published, though it does not give a full identifiable copy of the original form. In this particular example, of course, much of the information returned is a copy of what appears in the Rent Register, which is open to public inspection locally.

In trying to meet specific requests from researchers a small charge may be made to cover the cost of the special extraction of data or of *ad hoc* computer runs. However, in many cases no charge is made.

List of Specimen Forms

1. *General Household Survey—Household Schedule for 1971*

The GHS aims to collect information by interview from a sample of approximately 15,000 households throughout Great Britain in a year. The household schedule for 1971 has been included to indicate the types of information on housing that will become available when the results are finally published. The survey is described in [B 11].

2. *Form P. 2 (Hsg)*

This form on housing progress is completed monthly by local authorities in England and Wales and returned to the DOE.

3. *Form P. 13 (Hsg)*

Is concerned basically with slum clearance and is completed quarterly by local authorities in England and Wales and returned to the DOE.

4. *Form P. 14 (Hsg)*

Deals with changes in the stock of dwellings other than those reported on Form P. 2 (Hsg) or Form P. 13 (Hsg). This is a quarterly return to the DOE made by local authorities in England and Wales.

5. *Housing Form No. 1*

For the progress of local authority housing; completed by local authorities in Scotland and returned monthly to the SDD.

6. *Housing Form No. 120*

Deals with the treatment of sub-standard houses and is completed quarterly by local authorities in Scotland and is returned to the SDD.

7. *Housing Form No. 121*

Provides quarterly information on housebuilding for private owners and advances or guarantees under Small Dwellings Acquisition Acts and Housing Acts. It is completed by local authorities in Scotland and returned to the SDD.

8. *Return of Private Enterprise Housing*

Initially this enquiry was on a census basis three times a year but from June 1970 the forms have been sent only to a sample of firms, covering about 12% of the firms known to be engaged in private enterprise housing. The sample consists of all firms starting 151 or more dwellings per year, 20% of those starting between 21 and 50 dwellings and 10% of those starting 20 or less. A census is now taken every two years. Returns are sent to the DOE.

9. *Form T.C. 2*

Provides information on costs, densities, standards and system building and is completed by local authorities in England and Wales on acceptance of a tender for the erection of dwellings.

10. *Monthly Questionnaire on Building Society Mortgages*

The survey is based on a continuous sample of the administrative records of the societies relating to the individual mortgages granted. Completed questionnaires relating to about 5% of all mortgages are despatched monthly to the DOE from nearly a hundred societies which together account for 70% of the total assets of all building societies. The sample which includes a number of societies who are not members of the BSA is stratified by size of society so as to limit the number of smaller societies making returns. The smaller societies in the panel extract details for a larger proportion of their business in order to maintain the same overall sampling ratio of accounts. A minor exception is that the very smallest societies who conduct only 1% of all building society business are excluded.

11a–b. *Forms R.S.7 and R.S.8*

Deal with the registration of rents in Great Britain under the Rent Act 1968 and the Housing Act 1969. Form R.S.7 is completed for all registrations and returned to the DOE. Form R.S.8 is completed additionally for applications supported by a 'Certificate of Fair Rent' under schedule 2 of the Housing Act 1969.

GENERAL HOUSEHOLD SURVEY   SS 457/2

HOUSEHOLD SCHEDULE

IN CONFIDENCE

Date of interview ....   No. of households at

Time Household Schedule started ....   the address ....

	AREA		SER.		H'HLD.	OFF.USE

PER. NO.	RELATIONSHIP TO HOH	OFF. USE	SEX H/W	M F	AGE LAST BIRTH-DAY	MARITAL STATUS M S W D SEP	FAM. UNIT		C W N	How many years have you lived at this address? 0 GIVE MTHS.	1-4 GIVE YRS.	5 or more GIVE YRS.
1	HOH		X	1 2		1 2 3 4 5			1 2 3			
2			X	1 2		1 2 3 4 5			1 2 3			
3			X	1 2		1 2 3 4 5			1 2 3			
4			X	1 2		1 2 3 4 5			1 2 3			
5			X	1 2		1 2 3 4 5			1 2 3			
6			X	1 2		1 2 3 4 5			1 2 3			
7			X	1 2		1 2 3 4 5			1 2 3			
8			X	1 2		1 2 3 4 5			1 2 3			
9			X	1 2		1 2 3 4 5			1 2 3			
10			X	1 2		1 2 3 4 5			1 2 3			

IF ANY CODED 0 (MONTHS ONLY), GO TO Q.1 PAGE 2

IF ANY CODED 1-4 YEARS, GO TO Q.4 PAGE 3

IF ALL CODED 5 YEARS OR MORE, GO TO PRESENT ACCOMMODATION SECTION PAGE 8

NOTE: FOR CHILDREN UNDER 5 YEARS OF AGE, FOLLOW THE SAME FILTERS AS FOR THEIR MOTHER

- 2 -

PAST MOVEMENT

TO PERSONS 0 YEARS (MONTHS ONLY) AT PRESENT ADDRESS (ASK Q's 1-3 AND Q's 4-5)

PER. NO.	1. Where did you live before you moved here? ENTER FULL ADDRESS INCLUDING COUNTY	OFF. USE	2. Was that a private residence or something different such as an hotel, for example? IF PRIVATE RESIDENCE			3. Where were you living one year ago? ENTER TOWN OR PLACE NAME AND COUNTY IF SAME AS Q.1 RING X		OFF. USE
			Private resi-dence	MOVING GROUP NO.	Hotel etc.			
1 HOH	....		Y		X	....	X	
2	....		Y		X	....	X	
3	....		Y		X	....	X	
4	....				X	....	X	
5	....				X	....	X	
6	....		Y		X	....	X	
7	....		Y		X	....	X	
8	....		Y		X	....	X	
9	....		Y		X	....	X	
10	....		Y		X	....	X	

ALLOT A NO. TO A GROUP (OR AN INDIVIDUAL) WHO MOVED FROM THE SAME PRIVATE ADDRESS.

USE NO.1 FOR FIRST GROUP
     NO.2 FOR SECOND GROUP
           etc.

THESE PEOPLE DO NOT FORM PART OF A MOVING GROUP

TO ALL 0-4 YEARS AT PRESENT ADDRESS

4. Where were you living five years ago, that is ......(MONTH) ......(YEAR)? ENTER TOWN OR PLACE NAME AND COUNTY IF SAME AS Q.3 RING X		OFF. USE	5. (May I just check) how many moves have you made in the last five years? ENTER NO. OF MOVES
....	X		....
....	X		....
....	X		....
....	X		....
....	X		....
....	X		....
....	X		....
....	X		....
....	X		....
....	X		....

IF ANY CODED 'PRIVATE RESIDENCE' (Y) AT Q.2, GO TO Q.6 PAGE 4

OTHERS, GO TO PRESENT ACCOMMODATION SECTION PAGE 8

TO EACH MOVING GROUP

Now I should like to talk about the address you lived at
immediately before moving here - that is ....
                    ADDRESS GIVEN AT Q.1

6. Just before you moved who lived in your household,
    including .... ?
                THE MOVING GROUP

    ENTER DETAILS IN APPROPRIATE BOX BELOW

MOVING GROUP 1

RELATIONSHIP TO HOH OF PREVIOUS HOUSEHOLD	OFF. USE	IF IN PRESENT HOUSEHOLD GIVE PER. NO.	IF NOT IN PRESENT HOUSEHOLD		
			RING ↓	SEX M F	AGE AT TIME OF MOVE
HOH OF PREVIOUS HOUSEHOLD			Y	1 2	
			Y	1 2	
			Y	1 2	
			Y	1 2	
			Y	1 2	
			Y	1 2	
			Y	1 2	
			Y	1 2	

MOVING GROUP 2

RELATIONSHIP TO HOH OF PREVIOUS HOUSEHOLD	OFF. USE	IF IN PRESENT HOUSEHOLD GIVE PER. NO.	IF NOT IN PRESENT HOUSEHOLD		
			RING ↓	SEX M F	AGE AT TIME OF MOVE
HOH OF PREVIOUS HOUSEHOLD			Y	1 2	
			Y	1 2	
			Y	1 2	
			Y	1 2	
			Y	1 2	
			Y	1 2	
			Y	1 2	
			Y	1 2	

7. Why did you and .... decide to move?

THE MOVING GROUP

PROBE FULLY

	CODE	CODE
	MOVING GROUP 1	MOVING GROUP 2

MOVING GROUP 1

MOVING GROUP 2

IF MORE THAN ONE REASON GIVEN AT Q.7 ASK Q.8

DNA ... RING ⟶ AND SEE Q.9	X	X

8. What was your <u>main</u> reason for moving?

MOVING GROUP 1

MOVING GROUP 2

I22

CHECK BACK TO MOVING GROUP 1 BOX AT Q.6 AND ASK Q.s 9 – 18 OF <u>CONTINUING HOH'S ONLY</u>
ie WHERE YOU HAVE ENTERED PERSON NO. 1 AGAINST HOH.

IF NO CONTINUING HOH, DNA ..... X GO TO PRESENT ACCOMMODATION
SECTION, PAGE 8

CODE

9. How long did you live at your last address?

ENTER NO. OF COMPLETED YEARS. IF LESS THAN 1 YEAR WRITE 0 ⟶ ....

10. Did you own it or rent it?

Owned/was buying	1	ASK Q.11
Rented/rented free ...	2	ASK Q.12

<u>IF OWNED/WAS BUYING</u>

11. Did you own it

leasehold?	1	
or freehold?	2	GO TO
S. (or did you pay either feu duty. or ground burdens)?	3	Q.14

<u>IF RENTED/RENTED FREE</u>

12. Was it rented (provided) furnished or unfurnished?

Furnished/partly furnished	1
Unfurnished	2

13. Who did you rent it from?
(Who was it provided by?)

Local Authority	1
New Town Corporation or Commission	2

IF SOME OTHER ORGANISATION PROBE WHETHER

Property Company (GIVE NAME)	3
....	
Housing Association or Charitable Trust .... (GIVE NAME)	4
....	
Other organisation (SPECIFY)	6
....	

IF AN INDIVIDUAL PROBE WHETHER

Relative	7
Employer	8
Other individual	9

SPECIMEN

- 7 -

CODE

14. Did you have a fixed bath or shower with hot water supply?

Yes ... 1
No 2

15. Did you have a flush toilet?

Yes ... 1 ASK (a)
No .... 2 ASK Q.16

IF YES

    (a) Was the entrance to it

RUNNING PROMPT	inside your accommodation?	1
BUT CODE ONLY	outside your accommodation but	
FIRST THAT	inside the building?	2
APPLIES	outside the building?	3

16. How many rooms were there in your last accommodation?

    PROMPT   Bedrooms, Kitchen - a room in which you cooked, Other rooms.

    EXCLUDE   Lavatories, bathrooms, garages, rooms used entirely for business.

             TOTAL NO. OF ROOMS ⟶ ....

17. (May I just check), did you let or sub-let any of these rooms?

No .... X ASK Q.18

IF YES ENTER NO. OF ROOMS LET/SUB-LET ⟶ ....

18. And did you share any of the rooms, or the bath(shower) or flush toilet with another household?

No .... X GO TO PRESENT ACCOMMODATION SECTION, PAGE 8

IF ANY ROOMS SHARED ENTER NO. SHARED ⟶ ....

        NOTE: IF A ROOM IS LET/SUB-LET AND SHARED COUNT ONCE ONLY AS SHARED

IF BATH/SHOWER/FLUSH TOILET
SHARED, RING ⟶ Bath (shower) shared ... 1
                         Flush toilet shared 2

NOW GO TO PRESENT ACCOMMODATION SECTION, PAGE 8

- 8 -

PRESENT ACCOMMODATION

TO ALL HOUSEHOLDS

IF CARAVAN RING ⟶ 1

THEN ASK ONLY Q.s 2,12-14,20, AND POTENTIAL MOVERS SECTION

1. Was this building first built

RUNNING	before 1919?	1
PROMPT	between 1919 and 1945?	2
	1945 or later?	3
	DK	4

2. Do you own or rent this .... ?
    HOUSE/FLAT ETC.

Owns/is buying	1	ASK Q.3
Rents/rent free	2	GO TO Q.5

IF OWNS/IS BUYING

3. Do you own it

leasehold? 1

or freehold? 2

S. (or do you pay either feu duty
or ground burdens)? 3

4. Do you own it

outright? .... 1 — GO TO Q.10

or are you buying it on a
mortgage or loan? .... 2 — PAGE 10

SPECIMEN

- 9 -

	CODE

IF RENTS/RENT FREE (CODED 2 AT Q.2)

5. Is it rented (provided) furnished or unfurnished?

Furnished/partly furnished 1
Unfurnished 2

6. Is the accommodation rented (provided)
    with business premises?   Yes 1
                                       No 2

    INCLUDE FARM

7. Does the accommodation go with the present
    job of anyone in your household?   Yes ... 1
                                       No 2

8. Who do you rent it from?
    (Who is it provided by?)

Local Authority 1

New Town Corporation or Commission 2

IF SOME OTHER ORGANISATION PROBE WHETHER

Property Company (GIVE NAME) 3
....

Housing Association or Charitable Trust 4
(GIVE NAME) ....
....

Other organisation (SPECIFY) 6
....

} GO TO
Q.10

IF AN INDIVIDUAL PROBE WHETHER

Relative 7
Employer 8
Other individual 9

} ASK
Q.9

IF CODED 7-9 AT Q.8

9. Does your landlord live in this building?   Yes ... 1
                                                No 2

- 10 -

		CODE		CODE LET/SUB-LET	CODE SHARED

TO ALL HOUSEHOLDS

10. Do you have a fixed bath or shower with hot water supply?

Yes ...	1			1
No	2			

11. Do you have a flush toilet?

Yes ...	1	ASK (a)	1
No	2	ASK Q.12	

(a). Is the entrance to it

RUNNING PROMPT   inside your accommodation?   3
BUT CODE ONLY   outside your accommodation but
FIRST THAT   inside the building?   4
APPLIES   outside the building?   5

12. How many bedrooms do you have, including bed sitting rooms and spare bedrooms? ENTER NO.——→ ....

(a) Are any of them used for cooking   Yes ...   1
     like a bed sitting room for example?   No ...

13. (Apart from that) do you have a kitchen – that is, a <u>room</u> in which you cook?

Yes ...	1	ASK (a)&(b)	1	1
No	2	ASK Q.14		

(a) Is it less than 6 ft wide from wall to wall?   Yes ... 1   No 2

(b) Do (any of) you ever eat meals in it or use it as a sitting room?   Yes ... 1   No 2

SPECIMEN

14. What other rooms do you have?

ENTER BELOW, INFORMANT'S NAMES FOR ROOMS BUT
EXCLUDE BATHROOMS, LAVATORIES, GARAGES AND ROOMS
USED ENTIRELY FOR BUSINESS

NAME OF ROOM   RING ——

....	1	1	1
....	2	2	2
....	3	3	3
....	4	4	4
....	5	5	5

15. May I just check, do you let or sub-let any of the rooms you have told me about?

No   X   ASK Q.16

IF YES ENTER IN APPROPRIATE COLUMN THEN ASK Q.16

16. And do you share any of the rooms or the bath (shower) or flush toilet with any other household?

No   X   ASK Q.17

IF YES ENTER IN APPROPRIATE COLUMN THEN SEE Q.17

<u>NOTE:</u> IF A ROOM IS BOTH LET/SUB-LET <u>AND</u> SHARED CODE ONLY AS SHARED

CODE

CHECK - Is the informant's accommodation the same as
the Rateable Unit?

Yes 1   ASK Q.18
No 2   ASK Q.17

NOTE: IF IN DOUBT, QUESTION 17 SHOULD BE ASKED

17. Are there any rooms in this ....
RATEABLE UNIT
in addition to the ones you have told me about?

ENTER NO. OF ADDITIONAL ROOMS ⟶ ....
IF NONE, WRITE O.

EXCLUDE Lavatories, bathrooms, ... ges,
rooms used entirely for business.

TO ALL HOUSEHOLDS

18. Do you have any electric night storage heaters?

Yes 1
No 2

19. Do you have any other form of central heating?

Yes 1
No 2

20. Is there a car or van normally available
for use by you or members of your household?

Yes 1   ASK (a)
No 2   ASK Q.21

IF YES

(a) How many?   ENTER NO. ⟶ ....

INCLUDE ANY PROVIDED BY EMPLOYERS IF NORMALLY
AVAILABLE FOR USE BY INFORMANT OR MEMBERS
OF THE HOUSEHOLD. EXCLUDE VEHICLES USED
SOLELY FOR THE CARRIAGE OF GOODS.

CODE

TO ALL HOUSEHOLDS

21. Have any of the following been installed
in this accommodation during the last 12 months?

		Yes	No	First	Addition/ Replacement
PROMPT	A fixed bath or shower	Y	X	1	2
AND CODE	A fixed sink	Y	X	1	2
ALL THAT	A fixed wash basin other th...				
APPLY	a sink	Y	X	1	2
	A flush toilet	Y	X		

Is the entrance to it

inside your accommodation? .. Y   1   2

outside? .... Y   1   2

FOR EACH INSTALLATION RINGED Y, ASK (a) AND RECORD ————

(a) Was this a replacement of an existing ..... ,
an additional one, or was it the first one in
this accommodation?

SPECIMEN

– 13 –

CODE

22. Apart from painting and decorating, have any other
    improvements, alterations or repairs been made to this
    accommodation during the last 12 months?

    EXCLUDE IMPROVEMENTS MADE TO GARDEN

Yes ...	Y	ASK (a)
No	X	GO TO POTENTIAL MOVERS SECTION PAGE 14.

    (a) Was the total cost of these <u>other</u> improvements,
        alterations or repairs

	under £10?	1
RUNNING	£10 but less than £25	2
PROMPT	£25 but less than £50?	3
	£50 or more?	4
	DK	5

    (GIVE REASON IF KNOWN)

    ....
    ....
    ....
    ....
    ....
    ....

NOW GO TO POTENTIAL MOVERS
SECTION, PAGE 14.

POTENTIAL MOVERS

ASK FOR EVERY MEMBER OF THE HOUSEHOLD		CODE	
1. At the moment, are (any of) you seriously thinking of moving from this address?	Yes ...	1	ASK (a)
	No	2	END OF HOUSEHOLD SCHEDULE ENTER TIME COMPLETED ON BACK PAGE

IF YES

(a) Will you

	all be moving to the same address? (ONE MOVING GROUP	1	ASK Q.3
RUNNING	all be moving but to different addresses? .... (TWO OR MORE MOVING GROUPS)	2	ASK Q.2
PROMPT	or will only some of you be moving? .... (ONE OR MORE MOVING GROUPS)	3	ASK Q.2

IF CODED 2 OR 3 AT Q.1(a)

	CODE	CODE
	MOVING GROUP 1	MOVING GROUP 2
2. Which of you will be moving together - that is to the same address?	....	....
ENTER PER. NOS. FOR EACH MOVING GROUP ⟶	....	....
	....	....

TO ALL MOVING GROUPS

3. Would anyone else join you who is not living here now?		
ENTER NO. OF PERSONS. IF NONE WRITE "0" ⟶	....	....

		Sp.	Pr.	Sp.	Pr.
4. What have you done about trying to find somewhere?					
ASK	Have you applied to the Council?	1	1	1	1
OPENLY THEN	Have you made enquiries with agents or landlords?				
PROMPT ANY NOT	Was this about a place to buy?..	2	2	2	2
	or to rent?..	3	3	3	3
MENTIONED SPONTAN- EOUSLY	Have you advertised or replied to advertisements?				
	Was this about a place to buy?..	4	4	4	4
	or to rent?..	5	5	5	5
	OTHER (SPECIFY)	6		6	

MOVING GROUP 1

MOVING GROUP 2

NO ACTION TAKEN	9	9	ASK Q.5

GO TO Q.6

IF CODED 9 AT Q.4

5. When do you think you might start trying to find somewhere?

MONTHS ....

NOW ASK Q.6

TO ALL MOVING GROUPS

	CODE	CODE
	MOVING GROUP 1	MOVING GROUP 2

6. Why have you and .... decided to move?

                    THE MOVING GROUP

   PROBE FULLY

   MOVING GROUP 1

   MOVING GROUP 2

IF MORE THAN ONE REASON GIVEN AT Q.6 ASK Q.7

             DNA ... RING ————————————————→   X   X

               END OF HOUSEHOLD SCHEDULE

               ENTER TIME COMPLETED ON BACK PAGE

7. What is your <u>main</u> reason for moving?

   MOVING GROUP 1

   MOVING GROUP 2

     END OF HOUSEHOLD SCHEDULE ENTER TIME COMPLETED ON BACK PAGE

CODE

COMPLETE THIS PAGE FOR ALL HOUSEHOLDS INCLUDING NON-RESPONDENTS

Type of accommodation occupied by this household

	CODE
Whole house, detached	1
" " semi-detached	2
" " terraced	3
Flat/maisonette, purpose built	4
Other flat/maisonette/rooms	5
Dwelling with business premises	6
Other (specify)	7

CODE ONE FROM OBSERVATION,
IF IN DOUBT ASK INFORMANT

....

OBTAIN FROM RATING OFFICE

(a) Gross Value of rateable unit(s) covering this household £ ....

(b) Net Rateable Value of rateable unit(s) covering this
    household   £ ....

(c)

Description (Flat, Shop with flat, etc.)	Location in Building
....	....
....	....

SPECIMEN

INTERVIEWERS COMMENTS

Time Household Schedule completed ....

RLN 25464/1/R.222 9m 8/70 X

Form P.2.(Hsg.)

Name of Local Authority_____County_____

HOUSING PROGRESS REPORT FOR THE MONTH OF DECEMBER 1973

(1)   After completion please despatch this report in the envelope provided in time TO REACH THE DEPARTMENT OF THE ENVIRONMENT 2 MARSHAM STREET, LONDON SW1P 3EB WITHIN 5 DAYS OF THE END OF THE MONTH

(2)   One copy should be retained for reference purposes.

Date_____   Signature and designation of

officer making this return_____

NOTES AND DEFINITIONS

SECTION 1

Show in the columns provided the progress of local authority schemes for the erection of new permanent houses or flats. A separate line should be used for each scheme. The scheme numbers used should be the same as those given on Form T.C.2. and in previous progress reports.

Details of individual schemes may be omitted if no progress on them has been made during the month. ALL DWELLINGS UNDER CONSTRUCTION must however be included in the totals given in the final column of Section 1.

Do not include schemes for   (i)   conversions and improvements
(ii)   hostels provided either by new building or conversion under Section 15 of the Housing (Financial Provisions) Act 1958.
(iii) dwellings provided for an authority other than the housing authority, e.g. a police or fire authority.

SECTION 3

Dwellings to be reported in this section are those provided by new construction, whether with the aid of a loan from the local authority or without, by any housing association (including alms houses, trusts, etc.) as defined in Section of 189 of the Housing Act 1957; this includes dwellings provided by cost-rent and co-ownership housing societies promoted by the Housing Corporation.

Separate figures should be given in the appropriate columns for (a) dwellings provided by housing associations under "authorised arrangements" with the local authority under Section 120 of the Housing Act 1957 and for which therefore an Exchequer subsidy is payable and (b) all other housing association dwellings. The advice of the Department should be sought if there is any uncertainty over the correct column to use:

Show in the last part of Section 3 the number of dwellings in housing association Section 120 schemes specifically for the chronically sick or disabled which were started or completed during the month. These dwellings should also be included above, with other Section 120 starts and completions. Local authorities will normally be aware of special schemes of this sort, for which additions to the housing cost yardstick will ordinarily have been claimed.

SECTIONS 1, 3 and 4

STARTS. Dwellings should be reported as started in the month in which the laying of foundations (or slabbing if applicable) begins.

The number of dwellings reported should be the number which have reached the stage defined above, which will not necessarily be the total number of dwellings to be erected on the site. All dwellings in a block of flats should be shown as started when the individual block reaches the stage defined above.

COMPLETIONS. Dwellings should be reported as completed in the month in which they become ready for occupation. This will normally be taken to be for local authority dwellings the month in which the keys are handed over to the clerk of works, and for other dwellings the month in which notice of completion or of occupation, whichever is the earlier, is given under the Building Regulations.

UNDER CONSTRUCTION. Dwellings should be shown as under construction during the whole period between start and completion, whether or not progress is made during the month.

TYPES OF DWELLING. "Houses" include bungalows. "Flats" include maisonettes. The storey height of a flat is the total number of storeys in the building containing the dwelling. (In the case of subsidised dwellings this will not necessarily be the number of storeys qualifying for subsidy). The types of dwelling reported in each local authority scheme should correspond with those given on Form T.C.2. Any variation in the original scheme should be noted.

SECTIONS 3 and 4

NEW TOWN DESIGNATED AREAS. The local authority should include in reports, progress on dwellings in any new town designated area within the authority's boundary, except dwellings provided by the New Towns Commission or a new town development corporation.

The Commission and Development Corporations are asked to report privately built dwellings on land made available by them, but arrangements exist to prevent double counting.

134

SECTION 1   LOCAL AUTHORITY NEW PERMANENT DWELLINGS UNDER THE HOUSING ACT

	INDIVIDUAL SCHEMES																	
Building scheme number																		
NAME OF SITE AND SITE NUMBER																		
No. of dwellings in scheme																		
UNDER CONSTRUCTION at the end of previous month																		
STARTED during this month:- HOUSES																		
FLATS in 2 to 4 storeys																		
FLATS in 5 or more storeys																		
TOTAL HOUSES AND FLATS:- STARTED during this month																		
COMPLETED during this month:- HOUSES with:- 1. bedroom																		
2 bedrooms																		
3 bedrooms																		
4 or more bedrooms																		
TOTAL																		
FLATS with:- 1 bedroom																		
2 bedrooms																		
3 bedrooms																		
4 or more bedrooms																		
TOTAL FLATS in 2 to 4 storeys																		
TOTAL FLATS in 5 or more „																		
TOTAL HOUSES AND FLATS:- COMPLETED during this month:-																		
UNDER CONSTRUCTION at the end of this month:- HOUSES																		
FLATS in 2 to 4 storeys																		
FLATS in 5 or more storeys																		
TOTAL																		

SECTION 2   NEW DWELLINGS (INCLUDED ABOVE) DESIGNED OR MODIFIED FOR THE CHRONICALLY SICK OR DISABLED

a) Started this month																		
b) Completed this month																		

SECTION 3   NEW DWELLINGS FOR HOUSING ASSOCIATIONS

		Sec. 120 H. Act 1957	Other

Note

INCLUDE:-

(i) dwellings provided by

cost-rent and co-ownership

associations in the column

headed 'Other'

(ii) dwellings in any new

town designated area within

the local authority boundary

DO NOT INCLUDE:

dwellings provided by

conversions

	Sec. 120 H. Act 1957	Other
STARTED during this month:-		
HOUSES		
FLATS		
TOTAL HOUSES AND FLATS STARTED during this month:-		
COMPLETED during this month:-		
HOUSES with:- 1 bedroom		
2 bedrooms		
3 bedrooms		
4 or more bedrooms		
TOTAL HOUSES		
FLATS with:- 1 bedroom		
2 bedrooms		
3 bedrooms		
4 or more bedrooms		
TOTAL FLATS		
TOTAL HOUSES AND FLATS COMPLETED during this month		
UNDER CONSTRUCTION at the end of this month HOUSES		
FLATS		
TOTAL		
Dwellings in schemes for the CHRONICALLY SICK OR DISABLED also included above (Section 120 Housing Act 1957) a) Started this month		
b) Completed this month.		

SECTION 4   NEW DWELLINGS FOR PRIVATE ENTERPRISE

Notes

INCLUDE:-

(i) agricultural cottages built for private owners with assistance under Section 46 of the Housing (Financial Provisions) Act 1958

(ii) all privately built dwellings in any new town designated area within the local authority boundary.

DO NOT INCLUDE:-

(i) dwellings provided by Government Depts. police, fire. or other public authorities.

(ii) dwellings provided by conversions.

(iii) dwellings built by Commission for the New Towns or a new town development corporation for sale to private owners.

	Sec. 120 H. Act 1957	Other
STARTED during this month:-		
HOUSES		
FLATS in 2 to 4 storeys		
FLATS in 5 or more storeys		
TOTAL HOUSES AND FLATS STARTED during this month		
COMPLETED during this month:-		
HOUSES with:- 1 bedroom		
2 bedrooms		
3 bedrooms		
4 or more bedrooms		
TOTAL HOUSES		
FLATS with:- 1 bedroom		
2 bedrooms		
3 bedrooms		
4 or more bedrooms		
TOTAL FLATS in 2 or 4 storeys		
TOTAL FLATS in 5 or more storeys		
TOTAL HOUSES AND FLATS COMPLETED during this month		
UNDER CONSTRUCTION at the end of this month HOUSES		
FLATS in 2 to 4 storeys		
FLATS in 5 or more storeys		
TOTAL		

SECTION 5   HOUSES PROVIDED UNDER THE HOUSING (TEMPORARY ACCOMMODATION) ACT 1944

Number removed or destroyed during this month		

(left margin) OTALS   Please leave blank here no figure s to be nserted

SPECIMEN

E			
UNFIT HOUSES MADE FIT	After informal action by local authority		by owner
	After formal notice under Sections 9 (1) and 16 (1), Housing Act 1957		(a) by owner
			(b) by local authority
	After formal notice under Public Health Acts		
	Previously included in a clearance order which has been or will be modified or revoked under Section 24 Housing Act 1961.		
	Previously included in a demolition order which has been or will be revoked under Section 24 Housing Act 1957		
	Previously included in a closing order which has been or will be determined under Section 27 Housing Act 1957		

F			
OTHER HOUSES IN WHICH DEFECTS WERE REMEDIED	After formal notice under Public Health Acts		
	After formal action under Section 9 (1A), Housing Act 1957		(a) by owner
			(b) by local authority
	After informal action by local authority		

G			
UNFIT HOUSES IN TEMPORARY USE (Housing Act, 1957)	POSITION AT END OF QUARTER	Retained for temporary accommodation	Under Section 48 — Number of houses / Number of separate dwellings contained therein
			Under Section 17 (2) — Number of houses / Number of separate dwellings contained therein
			Under Section 46 — Number of houses / Number of separate dwellings contained therein

H		
PURCHASE OF HOUSES BY AGREEMENT	Houses in clearance areas other than those included in confirmed orders or compulsory purchase orders.	Number of houses
		Number of occupants

Signature and designation of officer making this return.

Date

Please ensure that the name of your authority has been inserted on the front of the form.

Form P13 (Hsg)

After completion please despatch one copy in the envelope provided to the Department of the Environment

WITHIN 7 DAYS OF THE END OF THE MONTH The other copy should be retained for reference purposes.

Local authority _____

County _____

SLUM CLEARANCE: REPAIR OF HOUSES
Return for the quarter ended 31st DECEMBER 1973

A				
HOUSES	IN OR ADJOINING CLEARANCE AREAS declared under Section 42 of the Hsg. Act 1957	Unfit for human habitation	Number of houses / Number of separate dwellings contained therein	
		included by reason of bad arrangement	Number of houses / Number of separate dwellings contained therein	
		On land acquired under Section 43 (2) Housing Act 1957	Number of houses / Number of separate dwellings contained therein	
			for official use	
DEMOLISHED during the quarter	NOT IN OR ADJOINING CLEARANCE AREAS	As a result of formal or informal procedure under Section 16 or Section 17 (1) Housing Act 1957	Number of houses / Number of separate dwellings contained therein	
		Local authority owned houses certified unfit by the Medical Officer of Health	Number of houses / Number of separate dwellings contained therein	
		Houses unfit for human habitation where action has been taken under local Acts	Number of houses / Number of separate dwellings contained therein	
		Houses included in unfitness orders made under para 2 of the Second Schedule to the Land Compensation Act 1961	Number of houses / Number of separate dwellings contained therein	
			for official use	
		Number of houses included above which were previously reported as closed in pursuance of closing orders or undertakings.	In or adjoining clearance areas / Not in or adjoining clearance areas	

B			
UNFIT HOUSES CLOSED during the quarter in pursuance of closing orders or undertakings	Under Sections, 16 (4), 17 (1) and 35 (1) Housing Act 1957 and Section 26 Housing Act 1961	Number of houses / Number of separate dwellings contained therein	
	Under Sections 17 (3) and 26 Housing Act 1957	Number of houses / Number of separate dwellings contained therein	
	PARTS OF BUILDINGS CLOSED under Section 18 Housing Act 1957	Number of dwellings	
		for official use	

C		
Number of **PERSONS DISPLACED** during quarter	From houses to be demolished in or adjoining clearance areas	
	From houses to be demolished not in or adjoining clearance areas	
	From houses to be closed	
	From parts of buildings to be closed	
	for official use	

D		
Number of **FAMILIES DISPLACED** during quarter	From houses to be demolished in or adjoining clearance areas	
	From houses to be demolished not in or adjoining clearance areas	
	From houses to be closed	
	From parts of buildings to be closed	
	for official use	

NOTES

1. SEPARATE DWELLINGS. For this purpose a house may consist of two or more separate dwellings according to the number of families occupying it. For separate occupation a family must have accommodation for living and sleeping under its exclusive control with facilities (not necessarily under its exclusive control) to do its own cooking.

2. PERSONS AND FAMILIES DISPLACED. Occupants are sometimes displaced well in advance of the demolition or closure of a house. The families and persons shown as displaced in this return should be those moved during the quarter and not necessarily the occupants of the houses shown in part A or B. They should be included whether or not they have been re-housed by the authority.

Dd. 945455 8/73

SPECIMEN

138

FORM P.14 (Hsg.)

Local Authority_____

County_____

CHANGES IN THE STOCK OF DWELLINGS

OTHER THAN THOSE REPORTED ON THE MONTHLY PROGRESS REPORT FORM P.2. (Hsg.)
AND THE SLUM CLEARANCE RETURN FORM P.13 (Hsg.)

Return for the quarter ended 1st DECEMBER 1973

(For explanatory notes see overleaf)

		Number of dwellings
1. Changes resulting from conversions (See note 3)	a) Gains _____ +	
	b) Losses _____ —	
2. Dwellings that have become permanently disused through obsolescence. dereliction or similar causes (See note 4)_____	—	
3. Lost through fire, flood, subsidence or like damage _____	—	
4. Changed from housing to other use (See note 5)_____	—	
5. a) Removed to make way for other development _____	—	
b) How many of the dwellings shown at item 5a) were thought to have been unfit for habitation _____ on the basis of Section 4 Housing Act 1957 ? (See note 6) _____		
6. Added or lost through other causes		
a) Gains (Specify cause) _____	+	
b) Losses (Specify cause) _____	—	

Signature and designation of
officer making this return _____

Date_____

Please ensure that the name of your authority has been inserted at the top of the form

Dd. 945454 8/73

NOTES ON FORM P.14

1. This return covers all dwellings whether privately or publicly owned.

2. Dwelling means a structurally separate dwelling and generally comprises any room or suite of rooms intended or used for habitation by persons living in private households having separate access to the street or to a common landing or staircase Bed-sitting rooms without kitchens and bathrooms do not qualify as separate dwellings.

3. Conversions with or without financial assistance under the Housing Act should be reported on this form. The figure to be inserted under "gains" should be the total number of dwellings after completion of the work. Under "losses" please show the original number of dwellings before conversion (e.g. a single large dwelling converted into four is regarded as 4 gains and 1 loss while two small dwellings converted into a single dwelling represents 1 gain and 2 losses).

4. Derelict houses and other dwellings that become permanently disused should not be reported on this form if they are likely to become subject to slum clearance procedures.

5. Unfit houses used for other purposes in accordance with undertakings under Section 16 of the Housing Act 1957 should not be included.

6. Old houses may be removed by private developers or under local authority (e.g. Highway) powers which might otherwise have been dealt with under slum clearance powers. It would be helpful if an estimate could be made of the number of dwellings included in 5a) which might have been considered to be unfit. Houses the subject of unfitness orders made under Schedule 2 of the Land Compensation Act 1961 should not be included on this Form.

SCOTTISH
DEVELOPMENT
DEPARTMENT

This form should be
submitted to:

SDD
Housing Statistics Branch
83 Princes Street
EDINBURGH EH2 2HH

within 7 days of the end of
the month to which it relates.

HOUSING PROGRESS REPORT

Local Authority _____   Month _____ 19 ____

PLEASE READ "NOTES FOR GUIDANCE" ON REVERSE BEFORE COMPLETING THIS FORM

NAME OF SCHEME AND DEVELOPMENT (1)	ACTION DURING MONTH			POSITION AT END OF MONTH			
	Tenders Accepted (No of houses) (2)	Houses Started (3)	Houses Completed (4)	Houses in Tenders Accepted Awaiting Start (5)	Houses Under Construction (6)	Total Houses Completed (Cumulative) (7)	Total "Tender accepted" houses in development (8)
TOTALS							

Signature _____   Date _____

Housing Form No 1
(Revise 1973)

RE 22827/3 TBL

140

NOTES FOR GUIDANCE

1.   "Scheme" includes one or more "developments". A separate line should be used for each development and, if the development comprises both multi-storey and low-rise blocks, separate lines should be used for the multi-storey blocks and the low-rise blocks.

2.   The starting of the construction of a block may be taken as the starting of all the houses in that block. Blocks not started should not be included in Column 3 or Column 6.

3.   The term "Under Construction" covers the period from the date work begins on the foundations of the block of which a house will form part to the date the house is completed. (It does not cover piling work which is regarded as site preparation).

4.   A house should be counted as completed from the date it is ready for occupation, whether it is in fact occupied or not.

5.   Houses provided by the authority other than as housing authority (eg as agent) for a police authority) should be excluded. Houses provided by the SSHA (unless provided at the authority's expense) should also be excluded.

6.   When completion of all houses in a particular development has been reported the development should be dropped from subsequent returns.

7.   The last two columns should show respectively the total number of houses so far completed in the development and the total number of houses accepted for building in the development. Column (8) is required as a continuing cross check on columns (5), (6) and (7).

Local Authority _____   Quarter Ended _____ 19 ___

TREATMENT OF SUBSTANDARD HOUSES

SPECIMEN

This form should be completed and returned to

Scottish Development Department
Housing Statistics Branch
83 Princes Street
EDINBURGH
EH 2 2HH

as soon as possible after the end of the quarter to which it relates

Housing Form No 120
(Revise 1973)

TREATMENT OF SUBSTANDARD HOUSES[2]

THIS RETURN SHOULD SHOW THE NUMBER OF HOUSES ACTUALLY CLOSED OR DEMOLISHED IN THE QUARTER – NOT THE NUMBER MADE THE SUBJECT OF STATUTORY ORDERS DURING THE QUARTER

A. HOUSES IN OR ADJOINING CLEARANCE OR HOUSING TREATMENT AREAS (dealt with under Part III of the 1966 Act or Part I of the 1969 Act)

Where substandard houses have been entered in your records as subject to closing or demolition orders under Part II of the 1966 Act and are subsequently demolished as a result of action taken under Part I of the 1969 Act the demolition should be recorded only in this Section.

	No.
1. Substandard houses demolished –	
(a) formerly returned as closed or otherwise taken out of use	____
(b) Others	____
2. Houses other than substandard demolished.	____
3. Substandard houses brought up to tolerable standard.	____

B. HOUSES NOT IN OR ADJOINING CLEARANCE OR HOUSING TREATMENT AREAS (dealt with under the 1966 Act)

Houses which, subject to demolition orders, have ceased to be used for human habitation (a) following acceptance of undertakings under Section 15(4) of the 1966 Act or (b) following approval of reconstruction for non-housing purposes in terms of Section 208(3) of that Act, should be recorded at 2. of this Section.

	Under Part II	Following Acquisition Under Part VII
1. Substandard houses demolished –		
(a) formerly returned as closed or otherwise taken out of use	____	____
(b) Others	____	____
2. Substandard houses closed or otherwise taken out of use but not yet demolished.		____
3. Houses other than substandard demolished.		____
4. Substandard houses formerly returned as closed or otherwise taken out of use but now brought up to tolerable standard.	____	

C. HOUSES DEMOLISHED UNDER PLANNING, HIGHWAY, EDUCATION, OR OTHER STATUTORY POWERS

This Section should relate strictly to the Local Housing Authority area and the necessary information should be obtained from the Local Planning, Highway etc Authority as appropriate.

	In Comprehensive Development Areas	Not in Comprehensive Development Areas
1. Substandard houses demolished		
(a) formerly returned as closed or otherwise taken out of use	____	____
(b) Others	____	____
2. Houses other than substandard demolished		____

D. SUBSTANDARD HOUSES DEMOLISHED UNDER THE BUILDING (SCOTLAND) ACT 1959 OR SIMILAR POWERS

	No.
1. Substandard houses demolished	
(a) formerly returned as closed or otherwise taken out of use	____

E. SUBSTANDARD HOUSES CLOSED OR DEMOLISHED OTHERWISE THAN BY FORMAL PROCEDURES (eg as a result of arrangements between local authorities and private owners for voluntary demolition, or by reason of a change of use of houses, with planning permission, to purposes other than housing).

Any houses previously returned as closed in Section B above should be excluded.

NOTES

1. "the 1966 Act" means the Housing (Scotland) Act 1966; "the 1969 Act" means the Housing (Scotland) Act 1969; references to the 1966 Act include, where appropriate, references to that Act as amended by the 1969 Act.

2. "Substandard houses" means primarily houses in respect of which statutory action has been taken on the grounds that they fail to meet the tolerable standard as defined in Section 2 of the 1969 Act but houses against which action was initiated on the basis that they were unfit in terms of Section 5 of the 1966 Act should also be included.

Signature ―――――――――――

Date ―――――――――――

RE 22828 2500 7/73 TCL

144

SCOTTISH
DEVELOPMENT
DEPARTMENT

THIS FORM TO BE
SUBMITTED TO:-

SDD
HOUSING STATISTICS BRANCH
83 PRINCES STREET
EDINBURGH EH2 2HH

WITHIN 7 DAYS OF THE END
OF THE QUARTER TO WHICH
IT RELATES

HOUSE BUILDING FOR PRIVATE OWNERS and
ADVANCES UNDER HOUSING ACTS AND SMALL DWELLINGS ACQUISITION ACTS

Local Authority _____ Quarter Ended _____ 19___

PART I: PROVISION OF NEW HOUSES (note 3)

NUMBER OF HOUSES	BUILDING FOR PRIVATE OWNERS (Note 1)	ANALYSIS OF HOUSES COMPLETED DURING QUARTER.				
1. Under construction at end of previous quarter						
2. Started during this quarter		Number of Apartments (Note 2)				
3. Completed during this quarter		2 or less	3	4	5	6 or more
(a) For sale						
(b) For letting						
(c) Total						
4. Under construction at end of this quarter $[1 + 2 - 3(c)]$						

SPECIMEN

Note 1   Houses for owner occupation should be included with houses for sale, and houses built by firms or corporation for their employees with houses for letting.

Note 2   Apartments include bedrooms, living rooms and kitchens used as living rooms but not kitchens used only for cooking, sculleries or bathrooms.

Note 3   Houses built by housing associations or housing societies should not be included in Part I of this return.

PART II. ADVANCES MADE UNDER HOUSING ACTS AND SMALL DWELLINGS ACQUISITION ACTS

1. Total amount of advances to Private Persons
    (a) For house purchase   £ _____
    (b) For house improvements, conversions   £ _____

2. Total amount of advances to Housing Associations
    (a) For new house building   £ _____
    (b) For acquisition of existing houses   £ _____
    (c) For house improvements, conversions   £ _____

Signature _____   Date _____
            (   )

Housing Form No 121
  (Revise 1973)

RE 22827/2 2500 7/73 TBL

DEPARTMENT OF THE ENVIRONMENT

RETURN OF PRIVATE ENTERPRISE HOUSING

CARRIED OUT BY PROPERTY DEVELOPERS

	Reference Number	These numbers should be quoted in correspondence

Department of the Environment
Statistics Directorate
Room 602, 2 Queen Anne's Gate Buildings
Dartmouth Street
London SW1H 9BP

Telephone No 01-839 7848 Extn. 229

Dear Sir(s)   28 March 1973

As you probably know regular inquiries are made of builders and property developers as a basis for estimates of the future level of housing activity.

I understand that your firm is in this business and I should be grateful if you would complete the return overleaf and send it to the above address by 13 April. If you have any queries about the inquiry we shall be very ready to help at the address or telephone number above.

Your return will be seen only by staff involved in producing summarised statistics, which will be so arranged that no information about your business can be derived from them.

Yours faithfully

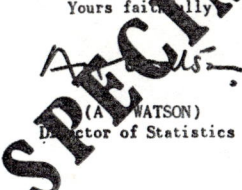

(A WATSON)
Director of Statistics

NOTES FOR GUIDANCE

1. *Please include ONLY new dwellings (i.e. houses, bungalows, flats or maisonettes) which you have had built or intend to have built in Great Britain for eventual sale or lease to other persons or companies or for your own occupation.*

2. *In the case of new flats or maisonettes please include the number of separate dwellings to be provided in the building.*

3. *Dwellings should be regarded as ''started'' when work starts on the foundations of the building.*

4. *A dwelling should be counted as ''sold or leased'' if a contract has been exchanged or completed with the purchaser or lessee otherwise it should be counted as ''not sold or leased''.*

5. *Include as ''leased'' or ''not leased'' only new dwellings intended for lease for 7 years or more or which have been leased for 7 years or more.*

6. *''Virtually completed'' means a dwelling which is not a ''completed dwelling'', but which requires only decorative finishes, minor fittings such as curtain tracks, or rectification of minor defects which may be found by the local authority building inspector. The outbuildings and site works need not be completed.*

7. *''Completed'' means a dwelling for which notice of completion or of occupation, whichever is earlier, has been given to the local authority.*

SR 33 PD

Fold here

Fold here

RETURN OF PRIVATE ENTERPRISE HOUSING

CARRIED OUT BY PROPERTY DEVELOPERS

PLEASE READ THE NOTES OVERLEAF BEFORE YOU ANSWER THE QUESTIONS
ENTER NIL IF APPROPRIATE

STARTS

Question 1	How many new dwellings were started for you: (a) in the year 1972	
	(b) between 1 January and 31 March 1973	
Question 2	How many new dwellings do you expect to have started for you: (a) between 1 April and 30 June 1973	
	(b) between 1 July and 31 December 1973	

COMPLETIONS

Question 3	How many new dwellings were completed for you: (a) in the year 1972	
	(b) between 1 January and 31 March 1973	
Question 4	How many new dwellings do you expect to have completed for you: (a) between 1 April and 30 June 1973	
	(b) between 1 July and 31 December 1973	

SALES

Question 5   Please give the following information in respect of new dwellings (irrespective of starting date) built or being built for you AT 31 MARCH 1973

(a) New dwellings virtually completed (see notes 5 and 6)	(i) Number NOT SOLD or LEASED	
	(ii) Number SOLD or LEASED	
(b) New dwellings completed but NOT SOLD or LEASED (see notes 5 and 7)		

Signed ....   Date 1973

Trading Name of Undertaking ....)

Full Postal Address (including ....)
Town and County) to which
correspondence should be sent ....)

....)

Telephone Number ....

If your name
and address is
correctly given
overleaf, you
need only state
''as over''

S.R. 33 P.D.

BIM/SR38H/S

IN CONFIDENCE

DEPARTMENT OF THE ENVIRONMENT

Please insert the completed form in the return envelope so that this address appears in the window.

Return of Private Enterprise Housing

Dear Sir(s)   29 October 1973

The regular enquiries into private housebuilding have been conducted on a sample basis since March 1970 but we have recently revised the sampling procedure using information from the 1970 annual returns to this Department. Most firms will be included in the sample for only one of the six enquiries planned for 1973 and 1974, in your case the sample for the present enquiry.

Your co-operation in the enquiry is entirely voluntary, but I would emphasise that the results, which are published in the trade press and in Housing and Construction Statistics, are used in making estimates of the future level of housing activity as a guide to government policy. I should be grateful therefore if you would complete this form and send it to the above address by 14 November. If we are to make good and timely estimates using sampling methods it is most important that firms make their returns promptly when they are selected.

If you have any queries about the enquiry we shall be very ready to help at the address or telephone number above. Your return will be seen only by staff involved in producing summarised statistics, which will be so arranged that no information about your business can be deduced from them.

Yours faithfully

(G Penrice)
Director of Statistics

Notes for Guidance

1   Please include ONLY new dwellings (ie houses, bungalows, flats or maisonettes) which were started or are to be started on sites in Great Britain owned or leased by you or your subsidiary or associated companies. Please do not include dwellings built under contract (other than a contract of house purchase) for any other party such as a property developer or local authority.

2.   If it is your practice to sell plots of land and to obtain from the purchaser a contract to build, please include such dwellings in your return where appropriate.

3   In the case of new flats or maisonettes please include the number of separate dwellings to be provided in the building.

4   Dwellings should be regarded as "started" when work starts on the foundations of the building.

5   A dwelling should be counted as "sold" if a contract has been exchanged or completed with the purchaser or if a contract to build has been received from the purchaser. Otherwise it should be counted as "not sold".

6   "Virtually completed" means a dwelling which is not a "completed dwelling", but which requires only decorative finishes, minor fittings such as curtain tracks, or rectification of minor defects which may be found by the local authority building inspector. The outbuildings and site works need not be completed.

7   "Completed" means a dwelling for which notice of completion or of occupation, whichever is earlier, has been given to the local authority.

BIM/SR 38H/S

Fold | Here (margin, left)
Fold | Here (margin, right)

IN CONFIDENCE

Return of Private Enterprise Housing

Please read the notes overleaf before you answer the questions

Enter Nil if appropriate

STARTS

Question 1	How many new dwellings did you start between 1 July and 30 September 1973	
Question 2	How many new dwellings do you expect to start between:- (a) 1 October and 31 December 1973 (Please include those already started in October)	
	(b) 1 January and 30 June 1974	
	(c) 1 July and 31 December 1974	

COMPLETIONS

Question 3	How many new dwellings did you complete between 1 July and 30 September 1973	
Question 4	How many new dwellings do you expect to complete between:- (a) 1 October and 31 December 1973 (Please include those already completed in October)	
	(b) 1 January and 30 June 1974	
	(c) 1 July and 31 December 1974	

SALES

Question 5   Please give the following information in respect of new dwellings (irrespective of starting date) built or being built AT 31 OCTOBER 1973

(a) New dwellings virtually completed (see notes 5 and 6)	(i) Number NOT SOLD	
	(ii) Number SOLD	
(b) New dwellings completed but NOT SOLD (see notes 5 and 7)		

Signed .... Date...1973

Telephone Number ....

BIM/SR 36H/S

BIM/SR 38H/L

IN CONFIDENCE

DEPARTMENT OF THE ENVIRONMENT

*Please insert the completed form in ·
the return envelope so that this
address appears in the window.*

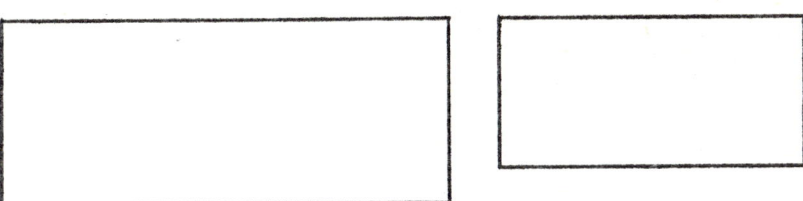

Return of Private Enterprise Housing

Dear Sir(s)   29 October 1973

Although the regular enquiry into private housebuilding activity is now being conducted on a sample basis, you will
recall that we still ask all the largest housebuilding firms, including yours, to make returns in every enquiry.

Your co-operation in the enquiry is entirely voluntary, but I would emphasise that the results, which are published in the
trade press and in Housing and Construction Statistics, are used in making estimates of the future level of housing
activity as a guide to government policy. I should be grateful therefore if you would complete this form and send it to
the above address by 14 November. If you have any queries about this enquiry we shall be very ready to help at the address
or telephone number above.

Your return will be seen only be staff involved in producing the summarised statistics, which will be so arranged that
no information about your business can be deduced from them.

Yours faithfully

(G Penrice)
Director of Statistics

NOTES FOR GUIDANCE

1   Please include ONLY new dwellings (ie houses, bungalows, flats or maisonettes) which were started or are to be
started on sites in Great Britain owned or leased by you or your subsidiary or associated companies. Please do not
include dwellings built under contract (other than a contract of house purchase) for any other party such as a property
developer or local authority.

2   If it is your practice to sell plots of land and to obtain from the purchaser a contract to build, please include such
dwellings in your return where appropriate.

3   In the case of new flats or maisonettes please include the number of separate dwellings to be provided in the building.

4   Dwellings should be regarded as "started" when work starts on the foundations of the buildings.

5   A dwelling should be counted as "sold" if a contract has been exchanged or completed with the purchaser or if a
contract to build has been received from the purchaser. Otherwise it should be counted as "not sold".

6   "Virtually completed" means a dwelling which is not a "completed dwelling", but which requires only decorative
finishes, minor fittings such as curtain tracks, or rectification of minor defects which may be found by the local authority
building inspector. The outbuildings and site works need not be completed.

7   "Completed" means a dwelling for which notice of completion or of occupation, whichever is earlier, has been given
to the local authority.

BIM/SR38H/L

IN CONFIDENCE

Return of Private Enterprise Housing

Please read the notes overleaf before you answer the questions

Enter Nil if appropriate

STARTS

Question 1	How many new dwellings did you start between 1 July and 30 September 1973	
Question 2	How many new dwellings do you expect to start between:- (a) 1 October and 31 December 1973 (Please include those already started in October)	
	(b) 1 January and 30 June 1974	
	(c) 1 July and 31 December 1974	

COMPLETIONS

Question 3	How many new dwellings did you complete between 1 July and 30 September 1973	
Question 4	How many new dwellings do you expect to complete between:- (a) 1 October and 31 December 1973 (Please include those already completed in October)	
	(b) 1 January and 30 June 1974	
	(c) 1 July and 31 December 1974	

SALES

Question 5   Please give the following information in respect of new dwellings (irrespective of starting date) built or being built AT 31 OCTOBER 1973

(a) New dwellings virtually completed (see notes 5 and 6)	(i) Number NOT SOLD	
	(ii) Number SOLD	
(b) New dwellings completed but NOT SOLD (see notes 5 and 7)		

Signed...   Date... 1973

Telephone Number ....

BIM/SR38H/L

Ministry of Housing and Local Government

HOUSING PROPOSALS (*Please submit this Form in triplicate, i.e. the white, blue and yellow sheets*). **Form T.C.2**

Local Authority : }
New Town : } ....

Site : (*Add particulars if situated in another local authority's area*)

....

....

Scheme category : **L** * (*Note 1*) *The Notes are attached* Scheme No.....................
—————— *to each pad of Forms.* (*To be used on Form P2 (Hsg.).*)
T

*Delete inappropriate words or symbol

IMPORTANT : If Firm Price tender, state the final date for acceptance ....

(*Space for Ministry use*)

PART A General particulars

TENDER

1. Type (*Note 2*) : *CO/CS/N/PD
2. Date :..
3. No. of tenders received : ....
4. Is proposed tender the lowest ? : *YES/NO
5. Are priced BQ (for buildings) attached ? (*Note 3*) *YES/NO
6. Contractor (name) : ....

CONTRACT

7. Form of contract (*Note 4*) : *A/B/C
8. Fluctuations clauses (*Note 4*) : *S/LO/MO/FP

DESIGN

9. Architect for layout (*Note 5*) : *HA/P/CA
10. Architect for buildings (*Note 5*) : *HA/P/CA
11. Quantity surveyor (*Note 5*) : *HA/P

*Delete inappropriate symbols

PART B Particulars of dwellings and costs (*Note 6*)

DWELLING TYPES

12. Authority's type symbol
13. B, H, F, M or OPF (*Note 7*)
14. Height of block in storeys (*Note 8*)
15. No. of bedrooms per dwelling (*Note 9*)
16. No. of persons per dwelling (*Note 10*)
17. Area per dwelling in sq. ft. (*Note 11*)
18. Average ditto. where appropriate (*Note 11*)

COSTS AS TENDER (*Note 12*)

19. Superstructure per dwelling
20. Substructure per dwelling
21. External works per dwelling
22. Total (Items 19+20+21) per dwelling
23. No. of dwellings of each type
24. Total cost of all dwellings (22×23) £

(*If additional columns are required, continue Items 12 to 24 on another Form, completing Items 25 to 29 and the whole of PARTS C, D and E on the last Form*)

GRAND TOTALS

= Dw.

=

25. Shops (*State number.................................*) £
26. Garages (a) With or incorporated in dwellings (*State number..............................*) £
    (b) Grouped in separate structures (*State number..............................*) £
27. Other works (*Describe*)..
    .... } £
    ....

28. **TENDER** .... £

29. (*Where applicable*) The following are included in superstructure costs (Item 19) :—
    No. .... Cookers at a total cost of £ ....
    No. .... Refrigerators at a total cost of £ ....

PART C Density and cost per person (*Note 10*)

† *Insert appropriate Yardstick figures for Category T (Note 1) schemes only.*

DENSITY

30. Total number of persons housed
    (Aggregate of 16×23) ....P
31. Avge. No. of persons per dwelling
    (30÷Grand total of 23) ....P/Dw.
32. Site area in acres (*Note 13*)....................Acres
33. Density in persons per acre
    (30÷32)................P/Acre
34. No. of cars accommodated
    (*Note 14*)................Cars

COSTS OF ALL DWELLINGS

35. Superstructures
    (Aggregate of 19×23)
36. Substructures
    (Aggregate of 20×23)
37. External works
    (Aggregate of 21×23)
38. TOTAL (=Grand total of 24)

Avge. cost per person

	TENDER (÷ Item 30)	As HOUSING COST YARDSTICK† (Circ. 40/63)
£	£	£
35.	=	
36.	=	
37.	=	
38.	=	

(*Continued on reverse side*)

PART D System building, i.e. building by industrialised methods, prefabrication, etc.
            (Where applicable)

39. Name of system and of originating firm (if different)..

40. Brief description of main principles of system..

41. Main elements *(e.g. walls, floors, staircases, plumbing, etc. indicating briefly whether finishes are included)* produced by:—
    (a) System building methods ....
    ....
    ....
    ....
    ....

    (b) Traditional or conventional methods..
    ....

42. Numbers of dwellings embodying system building, identifying types as entered in PART B.
    ....

PART E Standards

43. *(Where applicable)*   The improved standards recommended by HOMES FOR TODAY AND TOMORROW are incorporated in this scheme in respect of :—
    *(a) Floor space (including general storage)..
    *(b) Washbasin and second W.C. where appropriate.......................................
    *(c) Space heating..
    *(d) Kitchen fittings...
    *(e) Electric socket outlets...
    *(f) Bedroom cupboards...

                                                                         Please state numbers and types of dwellings affected

    Complete appropriate items

44. *(In all cases)* The main space heating installations provided in the dwellings in this scheme are as follows:—

No. of dwellings	B, H, F, M, or OPF (Note 7)	Heating installation *(Describe briefly, e.g. central heating, open fire, open fire with radiators, openable stove, closed stove, underfloor; impelled air, block storage, panel, skirting, etc.)*	†Fuel	Tenant controlled ? (YES or NO)

    † *Please enter SF (Solid fuel), SSF (Smokeless solid fuel), G (Gas), E (Electricity) or O (Oil) as appropriate.*

PART F *(For use in Ministry)*

153

PRIVATE – IN CONFIDENCE   DOE 25606

Monthly Questionnaire
on
Building Society Mortgages

SPECIMEN

154

Where boxes are provided, place a tick in the appropriate one, thus: ☑

Where the answer is not known, please write N.K. beside the question.

If there are any queries relating to this questionnaire, please refer to:

> Department of the Environment,
> Statistics Directorate (BSM Survey),
> 2 Queen Anne's Gate Buildings,
> Dartmouth Street
> London, SW1H 9BP
> Phone 01-212 8258

Building Society Code No. ....

	Office use only
	1, 2, 3

BASIC INFORMATION

1 Account No. ....*....................

2 Mortgage completed during the year 197   Month (Tick below)

Jan.	Feb.	Mar.	Apr.	May	June	July	Aug.	Sep.	Oct.	Nov.	Dec.
1	2	3	4	5	6	7	8	9	10	11	12

Office use only: 4, 5, 6

3 Is the dwelling: to be wholly occupied by the borrower? ☐ 1

to be partly occupied by the borrower? ☐ 2

not to be occupied by the borrower?

DOE 7, 8, 9

10

NOTE: WHERE THE MORTGAGE CONSISTS OF A FURTHER ADVANCE, OR THE APPLICANT ALREADY OWNS THE PROPERTY, OR THE PROPERTY IS NOT WHOLLY OR PARTLY FOR OWNER OCCUPATION, QUESTIONS 4–24 SHOULD NOT BE ANSWERED.

THE MORTGAGE

4 Amount of mortgage £..................... (If advanced in instalments, total amount approved to be shown)

11, 12, 13, 14, 15

5 Is the advance to be used wholly for the purchase of the property? Yes ☐ 1 No ☐ 2

16

6, Is it an Option Mortgage?   Yes ☐ 1   No ☐ 2

17

7 If it is, has the mortgage been arranged under the Government's Option Mortgage Guarantee Scheme?

Yes, for 100% of valuation ☐ 1   Yes, for less than 100% of valuation ☐ 2

No ☐ 3

18

8 Period for which mortgage is granted .... years .... months

19, 20   21, 22

9 Gross rate of interest to be charged ....% per annum. (ie before deducting any option mortgage subsidy)

23, 24, 25, 26

10 Repayments on the amount shown in answer to question 4 will be £..................... ....

every calendar month ☐ 1   every 4 weeks ☐ 2

27, 28, 29, 30, 31

32

(In endowment policy cases, the amount of the insurance premium should be included) (Option Mortgages: show borrower's payment to the Society)

11 Repayment method:

normal mortgage repayments ☐ 1

endowment policy ☐ 2

combination of above or any other method ☐ 3

33

THE DWELLING

		Office use only

12 Purchase price £..

Office use only
34, 35, 36, 37, 38, 39
L.A.

13 Location of the dwelling ....
(In England and Wales, from April 1974 give the London borough, Metropolitan district, or Non-Metropolitan county. Until March 1974 give the London borough, county borough or administrative county. See the "Notes for guidance" for a list of locations including those in Scotland and Northern Ireland.)

40, 41, 42, 43, 44

14 a. Is the dwelling new? ☐1   or not new? ☐2

45

14 b. If the dwelling is not new was it built

Pre 1919? ☐1   1919-1939? ☐2

1940-1960? ☐3   Post 1960? ☐4

46

15 Type of dwelling: Bungalow ☐1   Detached house ☐2

Semi-detached house ☐3   Terrace house (including end-terrace) ☐4

Flat or maisonette in converted house ☐5   Purpose built flat or maisonette ☐6

Other types (specify) .... ☐7

47

16 Is the dwelling freehold (or feuhold) with vacant possession? ☐1 No ☐2

48

17 Number of habitable rooms (including kitchen) ....

49, 50

18 With bathroom ☐1   Without bathroom ☐2

51

19 With garage ☐1   With space to build garage ☐2   No space or garage ☐3

52

20 Rateable value (net) £..

53, 54, 55, 56

THE APPLICANT

21 Sex of main (or first named) applicant   male ☐1   female ☐2

57

22 Age of main applicant........................years.

58, 59

23 Basic income (before tax) of main applicant £........................per annum

60, 61, 62, 63, 64

24 Any other income on which mortgage is based £........................per annum

65, 66, 67, 68, 69

TOTAL £ _____ per annum

70, 71, 72, 73, 74

24 a. Was the applicant previously an owner occupier?   Yes ☐1 No ☐2

75

24 b. If he was not an owner occupier was he

(a) renting privately? ☐1

(b) renting from a local authority or new town corporation? ☐2

(c) living with relatives, boarding or in an institution? ☐3

(d) in other accommodation? ☐4

76

(Specify ....

Questionnaire completed by ....(initials)

Coder........................

Checker........................

SPECIMEN

DEPARTMENT OF THE ENVIRONMENT   RS 7

RENT ACT 1968 — HOUSING ACT 1969

RENT ASSESSMENT CASE RECORD

FOR ALL REGISTRATIONS

Please complete this form in
accordance with EXPLANATORY NOTES-RS7A

	For DOE use only
Where a box is provided please tick thus ☑	1—3 8 0 1

1. DOE code number (*Note* 1) .... 4—8 ☐☐☐☐☐

2a. Postal address of premises ....

....

2b. Rent Register entry Reference Number (*Note* 2)............................ 9—13 ☐☐☐☐☐
    (*For block registrations give only the first of the consecutive Reference Numbers covered by
    this form and the address relating to that Ref. No.*)   14   ☐ 1

3. Date of application for this registration............................ Y Y M M D D
    15—20 ☐☐☐☐☐☐

4. Application made by? (*Note* 3)
        Landlord ☐ 1   Tenant ☐ 2   Joint ☐ 3   21   ☐

5. Application supported by Certificate of Fair Rent?
        Yes ☐ 1   No ☐ 2   22   ☐

6. First registration?
        Yes ☐ 1   No ☐ 2   23   ☐
    (*If 'Yes' do not complete Q.7 or Q.33.*) (*If 'No' do not complete Qs. 8—12*)

7   Reference Number of previous Rent Register entry (*Notes* 4, 30)............ 24—28 ☐☐☐☐☐

8. Premises formerly rent controlled? (*Note* 5)
        Yes ☐ 1   No ☐ 2   29   ☐

9a. Housing Act 1969, Schedule 2 registration?
        Yes ☐ 1   No ☐ 2   30   ☐
    (*If 'Yes' complete also Qs. 9 b, c, and d.*)

9b. Code number of Certificate of Fair Rent (*Note* 6)............ 31—35 ☐☐☐☐☐
    (*For block registrations give only the first of the consecutive Code Nos. involved*)

9c. "Differences"-Section 46(4)-specified in Qualification Certificate? (*Note* 6)
        Yes ☐ 1   No ☐ 2   36   ☐

9d. Notices issued under Paragraph 9 of Schedule 2? (*Note* 6)
        Yes ☐ 1   No ☐ 2   37   ☐

10. Housing Act 1969, Section 44(1) registration? (*Note* 7)
        Yes ☐ 1   No ☐ 2   38   ☐

11. Date of issue of Qualification Certificate, if any (*Note* 8)............ Y Y M M
    (*Complete only if answer to Q9a or Q10 is "Yes"*)   39—42 ☐☐☐☐

12. Tenancy held by virtue of employment? (*Note* 9)
        Yes ☐ 1   No ☐ 2   43   ☐

SPECIMEN

1

Where a box is provided please tick thus ☑

For DOE use only

13. Age of building? (*Note* 10)

| Pre-1875 ☐ 1 | 1875-1889 ☐ 2 | 1890-1918 ☐ 3 |

44 ☐

| 1919-1939 ☐ 4 | Post-1939 ☐ 5 | New ☐ 6 |

14. Type of premises let? (*Note* 11)

| Bungalow ☐ 1 | Detached house ☐ 2 |

| Semi-detached house ☐ 3 | Terrace house ☐ 4 |

45 ☐

| Flat in converted house ☐ 5 | Purpose-built flat ☐ 6 |

| Flat/rooms in house not converted ☐ 7 | Any other type of premises ☐ 8 |

15. Superficial area of premises let—either...square feet
(*Note* 12)
—or...square metres

46—50 ☐☐☐☐☐

16. Number of habitable rooms (*including kitchen*) of which tenant has sole use..............................
(*Note* 13)

51—52 ☐☐

17. General state of repair?

Good ☐ 1   Satisfactory ☐ 2   Poor ☐ 3

53 ☐

18. Has tenant the use of? (*Note* 14)

	Sole use	Shared	None	
Cold water supply from tap within the building	☐ 1	☐ 2	☐ 3	54 ☐
Hot water supply from tap within the building	☐ 1	☐ 2	☐ 3	55 ☐
Fixed bath or shower within the building	☐ 1	☐ 2	☐ 3	56 ☐
WC within the building or attached to it	☐ 1	☐ 2	☐ 3	57 ☐
Kitchen	☐ 1	☐ 2	☐ 3	58 ☐
Garage	☐ 1	☐ 2	☐ 3	59 ☐
Garden	☐ 1	☐ 2	☐ 3	60 ☐

SPECIMEN

19. Furniture provided by landlord?

Some furniture ☐ 1   No furniture ☐ 2

61 ☐

20. Services provided by landlord? (*Note* 15)

All or most ☐ 1   Some ☐ 2   None ☐ 3

62 ☐

21. External repairs responsibility of landlord?

All ☐ 1   Some ☐ 2   None ☐ 3

63 ☐

22. Internal repairs reponsibility of landlord?

All ☐ 1   Some ☐ 2   None ☐ 3

64 ☐

23. Internal decoration responsibility of landlord? (*Note* 16)

All ☐ 1   Some ☐ 2   None ☐ 3

65 ☐

Y Y Q

78—80   7 ☐ ☐

2

158

Where a box is provided please tick thus ☑

For DOE use only

Repeat 1—13 of Card 1

14   **2**

24. Are the condition of the premises and the terms of the tenancy on which the registered rent is based effectively the same as those on which the previous rent was based? *(Note 17)*

Yes ☐ 1   No ☐ 2   15 ☐

25. Net Rateable Value of premises let *(estimated if necessary)* £............... *(Note 18)*   16—18 ☐☐☐

26. Previous rent *(excluding rates)* *(Note 19)*

(For first registrations = rent paid prior to registration)
(For re-registrations = previously registered rent)

£............per   Week ☐ 1   Month ☐ 2   Q'ter ☐ 3   Year ☐ 4   19—25 ☐☐☐☐☐☐☐

27. Rent proposed by applicant *(excluding rates)* *(Note 20)*

(Complete only for applications NOT supported by Certificate of Fair Rent)

£............per   Week ☐ 1   Month ☐ 2   Q'ter ☐ 3   Year ☐ 4   26—32 ☐☐☐☐☐☐☐

REGISTRATION OF RENT

28. Date of Rent Officer's determination *(i.e. date of registration)*

....   Y Y M M   33—36 ☐☐☐☐

29a. Rent Officer's determination of rent

£............per   Week ☐ 1   Month ☐ 2   Q'ter ☐ 3   Year ☐ 4   37—43 ☐☐☐☐☐☐☐

29b. Amount, if any, specifically attributed by Rent Officer. *(Note 21)*

in respect of furniture £............per   Week ☐ 1   Month ☐ 2   Q'ter ☐ 3   Year ☐ 4   44—49 ☐☐☐☐☐☐

in respect of services £............per   Week ☐ 1   Month ☐ 2   Q'ter ☐ 3   Year ☐ 4   50—55 ☐☐☐☐☐☐

29c. Amount, if any, apportioned to services by Rent Officer. *(Note 21)*

£............per   Week ☐ 1   Month ☐ 2   Q'ter ☐ 3   Year ☐ 4   56—61 ☐☐☐☐☐☐

30. Appeal to Rent Assessment Committee? *(Note 22)*

By landlord ☐ 1   By tenant ☐ 2   No appeal ☐ 3   62 ☐

(If 'No appeal' do not complete Q.31 and Q.32)

Y Y Q   78—80   **7** ☐☐

3

Where a box is provided please tick thus ✓

31. Date of Rent Assessment Committee's determination (*Note* 23)
    (*i.e. date of registration*)

Y Y M M
15—18 ☐☐☐☐

32a. Rent Assessment Committee's determination of rent

£...per Week ☐ 1 Month ☐ 2 Q'ter ☐ 3 Year ☐ 4

19—25 ☐☐☐☐☐☐☐

32b. Amount, if any, specifically attributed by Rent Assessment Committee

in respect of furniture £.................................per Week ☐ 1 Month ☐ 2 Q'ter ☐ 3 Year ☐ 4

26—31 ☐☐☐☐☐☐

in respect of services £.................................per Week ☐ 1 Month ☐ 2 Q'ter ☐ 3 Year ☐ 4

32—37 ☐☐☐☐☐☐

32c. Amount, if any, apportioned to services by Rent Assessment Committee

£...per Week ☐ 1 Month ☐ 2 Q'ter ☐ 3 Year ☐ 4

38—43 ☐☐☐☐☐☐

33. Effective date of last registration (*Note* 24)
    (*Complete only for re-registrations*)

Y Y M M D D
44—49 ☐☐☐☐☐☐

BLOCK REGISTRATIONS ONLY (*Notes* 25-29)

34. Number of consecutive Rent Register entry Reference Numbers covered by this form

50—52 ☐☐☐

35. Rent Register entry Reference Number of the LAST of the consecutive Reference
    Numbers covered by this form..

53—57 ☐☐☐☐☐

36. Certificate of Fair Rent Code Number of the LAST of the consecutive Code Numbers
    involved. (*Complete only for block Schedule 2 registrations*)

58—62 ☐☐☐☐☐

Y Y Q
78—80 ☐☐☐

Coder ....

Checker ....

7478 642770 300m 7/71 WPLtd Gp709

DEPARTMENT OF THE ENVIRONMENT   RS 8

HOUSING ACT, 1969

RENT ASSESSMENT CASE RECORD

For Certificates of Fair Rent Issued under Schedule 2

Please complete this form in accordance with Explanatory Notes—RS8A

Where a box is provided please tick thus ✓

For DOE use only

1—3 | 8 | 0 | 1

1. D O E code number...   4—8 ☐☐☐☐☐

2a. Postal address of premises...

2b. Code number of Certificate..   9—13 ☐☐☐☐☐
(For a block of Certificates give only the first of the consecutive CFR Code Nos. covered by this form and the address relating to that Code No.)   14 | 4 |

SPECIMEN

Y Y M M

3. Date of issue of CFR(C) or CFR(CHS) ....   15—18 ☐☐☐☐

4. Age of building ?   19 ☐

    Pre-1875 ☐ 1   1875-1889 ☑ 2   1890-1918 ☐ 3

    1919-1939 ☐ 4   Post-1939 ☐ 5

5. Type of premises let ?

    Bungalow ☐ 1   Detached House ☐ 2

    Semi-detached house ☐ 3   Terrace house ☐ 4   20 ☐

    Flat in converted house ☐ 5   Purpose-built flat ☐ 6

    Flat/rooms in house not converted ☐ 7   Any other type of premises ☐ 8

6. Number of habitable rooms (including kitchen) of which tenant will have sole use   21—22 ☐☐
    after the improvements are made..

7. Net Rateable Value of premises let (estimated if necessary) £.......................   23—25 ☐☐☐

8. Controlled rent (excluding rates) at time of application for certificate

    £..per   Week ☐ 1   Month ☐ 2   Q'ter ☐ 3   Year ☐ 4   26—32 ☐☐☐☐☐☐☐

1.

Where a box is provided please tick thus ☑   For DOE use only

CERTIFICATION OF RENT

9. Date of Rent Officer's proposal

.... 33—36 Y Y M M ☐☐☐☐

10. Rent Officer's proposal

£.......................................per Week ☐1 Month ☐2 Q'ter ☐3 Year ☐4 37—43 ☐☐☐☐☐☐☐

11. Appeal to Rent Assessment Committee ?

By landlord ☐1   By tenant ☐2   No appeal ☐3   44 ☐

(if 'no appeal' do not complete Q.12 and Q.13)

12. Date of Rent Assessment Committee's determination

.... 45—48 Y Y M M ☐☐☐☐

13. Rent Assessment Committee's determination

£.......................................per Week ☐1 Month ☐2 Q'ter ☐3 Year ☐4 49—55 ☐☐☐☐☐☐☐

BLOCK ISSUES OF "CFR's" ONLY

14. Number of consecutive CFR Code Numbers covered by this form   .... 56—58 ☐☐☐

15. CFR Code Number of the LAST of the consecutive Code Numbers covered by this form   .... 59—63 ☐☐☐☐☐

78—80 Y Y Q 7 ☐☐

Coder ....

Checker ....

H5/785/19 (5/71)　　　2.　　　7444 642769 202,300 6/71 WPLtd Gp709

Subject Index

6   Housing in Northern Ireland

by

M. C. FLEMING

Senior Lecturer in Economics, Loughborough University of Technology

Contents

Reference Date of Sources Reviewed

This review is believed to represent the position, broadly speaking, as it obtained at December 1971. Later revisions have been inserted up to the proof-reading stage [May 1974] taking account, as far as possible, of any major changes in the situation—see Addenda.

Addenda*

Housing Statistics and the Re-organization of Government in Northern Ireland
Major changes have taken place since this study was written in the organization of government in Northern Ireland. Their relevance to this study are twofold. First, the names and functions of government departments have changed and second, the publication of government publications has been affected.

Government Departments
The names and functions of government departments were changed following the re-organization that took place with effect from 1st January 1974 when direct rule from Westminster, introduced in the Spring of 1972, ended. The changes relevant to this study are shown below. In the case of housing the functions of the Ministry formerly responsible have been sub-divided between two new departments. As a consequence there is now a Department of the Environment in Belfast as well as one of the same name in London, but while the British Department does exercise housing functions the Northern Ireland Department does not. All references in this study to the Department of the Environment, therefore, should be taken as referring to the British Department.

Former Department	*New Department*
Ministry of Development	{ Department of Housing, Local Government and Planning
	Department of the Environment
Ministry of Commerce	Department of Commerce
Ministry of Health and Social Services†	{ Department of Health and Social Services
	Department of Manpower Services
Ministry of Finance	Department of Finance

Government Publications
The change here relates to all serial publications listed as Northern Ireland House of Commons papers in the Quick Reference List Key and the Bibliography. This series terminated with the suspension of the

---

* These addenda were written at the proof-reading stage in early May 1974 and are meant to bring up to date those parts of the main text where major changes or additions to the information available have taken place since it was prepared.

† The functions of this Ministry referred to in this study are now performed by the Department of Manpower Services.

Northern Ireland Parliament. Publications which formerly appeared as House of Commons papers now appear as Departmental papers. The publication of Command Papers with serial numbering separate from the British series has continued.

Section 2.1.2   Characteristics of New Housing

Private sector houses
An official analysis of the sizes (superficial area) of private subsidized houses built over the period 1959–70 is to be found in a paper published by the Centre for Environmental Studies, *Housing in Northern Ireland*, p. 260 [1]—see *Additional References* below. This shows the numbers completed annually over the period, for owner-occupation and letting separately, according to five size categories.

Section 3.1   Size and Characteristics of the Housing Stock

Size of the housing stock
Information about the number of houses owned by local authorities, the Development Commissions and the Housing Trust was collected by the Ministry of Development in April 1971 and April 1972 incidentally in connection with surveys of rents at these dates. For further details of these surveys see below under the heading *Section 4.2*. The information has not been published but may be made available by the Ministry on request. Information about the number of houses in the public sector as a whole and their locations throughout the Province is now published in the Annual Reports of the Northern Ireland Housing Executive [2]—*Additional References* below—which gradually took over the functions of all public housing agencies in the period 1971 to 1973.

Age of the housing stock
Information about age will be obtained in a House Condition Survey to be made by the Northern Ireland Housing Executive in 1974 (see below for further details). In addition information of some interest in this context, inasmuch as it distinguished the number of pre-war from post-war houses owned by local authorities, was obtained in the two rent surveys described below (Section 4.2—Addenda) as well as in the similar surveys of 1956 and 1966 referred to in the main text.

Condition of the Housing Stock—House Condition Survey 1974*

This survey is to be carried out by the Northern Ireland Housing Executive in the period March to June 1974. It is aimed at providing a comprehensive and detailed assessment of housing conditions throughout the Province and will thus fill the major gap in the statistical information available in an area which we suggested earlier was the one where improvement was most desirable (see Sections 3.4 and 7). The survey is to follow the guidelines laid down by the British Department of the Environment in sample surveys of England and Wales made from 1967 onwards. The data are to be collected by personal inspection and interview by Public Health Inspectors from a sample of 25,000 dwellings, about 5 per cent of the total

* The account of this survey given here is based on information kindly supplied to the author by the Northern Ireland Housing Executive.

stock, drawn from a central computer file of domestic rated units held by the Central Rating Authority using a stratified systematic sampling technique. All dwellings are to be covered regardless of tenure, except institutions, student residences etc. Information is to be collected on the following matters:—

Type of dwelling,
Age,
Tenure,
Size of dwelling (number of rooms),
Whether in multiple occupation or not,
Possession of specific amenities,
Costs of installing absent amenities,
Costs of necessary repairs,
Whether the dwelling is unfit or not.

In addition the opportunity has been taken to obtain certain additional information about the privately rented dwelling sector at the request of the Rent Restriction Committee under the auspices of the Department of Housing, Local Government and Planning. The information to be collected in this inquiry covers the following matters in addition to those listed above:

Amount of rent,
Amount of rates,
Amount of rate rebate if any,
Execution of repairs over the last two years,
Satisfaction with house,
Preparedness to pay more for housing,
Preference for public rented or private rented housing,
Age of tenant.

The analysis, interpretation and possible publication of the results of this section of the survey are the responsibility of the Committee referred to above and not the Housing Executive.

Copies of the questionnaires and other documentation to be used in connection with the execution of these surveys together with the detailed instructions issued to the Surveyors (Inspectors) have been published by the Executive in [4]—see the list of *Additional References* below. It should be noted that in addition to the questions about amenities included on the questionnaire information is also to be collected on whether or not a mains electricity supply is available. In addition to the publication referred to above [4] a short *Explanatory Handbook* giving general information about the Survey has also been published by the Executive [3].

The Executive intend to publish the results of the main survey and a written report towards the end of 1974. Data will be provided at Local District Council level as well as for the whole Province. With regard to the availability of unpublished data the author is informed that unpublished tabulations would probably be made available to *bona fide* researchers. The raw data themselves are to be processed by computer and each record stored on magnetic tape; the actual survey forms are to be destroyed.

Tenure of the housing stock
Information about tenure will be obtained in the 1974 *House Condition Survey* referred to above.

Section 3.2   Changes to the Stock

Demolition, closure and repair
The second form of Return used for the collection of these statistics and reproduced in Appendix II was subsequently amended following the establishment of the Northern Ireland Housing Executive. The amendments made were small textual changes and not changes of substance. Currently the author is informed by the Department of Housing, Local Government and Planning that the return is now 'out of use' and that the whole field of 'redevelopment statistics' is being re-examined.

Section 3.3   Housing Needs

The House Condition Survey referred to above—Addenda Section 3.1—will provide some of the information essential for the assessment of housing needs.

Section 4.1   Financial Statistics—Public Authority Accounts, Rate Statistics

Rateable value of public sector houses
In April 1971 local authorities, the three Development Commissions and the Housing Trust authorities were required to submit returns to the Ministry of Development, in connection with a survey of rents, showing for pre-war and post-war houses separately the rateable values of its houses and the number of houses at each value. The information has not been published but may be made available by the Ministry on request. For further details of this survey see *Section 4.2* below.

Rates paid by tenants of privately rented dwellings
Information on this is to be obtained as part of the House Condition Survey to be carried out by the Northern Ireland Housing Executive in 1974. This particular information, however, is being obtained for the Rent Restriction Committee and publication will depend upon the decision of this Committee—see Addenda Section 3.1 above for further details.

Section 4.2   Rents

Public authority dwellings
Reference is made in the main text to two official surveys of rents charged for local authority houses in 1956 and 1966. Two further official surveys have now been made to obtain information about weekly rents one as at 1st April 1971 (Ministry of Development Circular HG 9/71 refers) and the other as at 3rd April 1972 (Circular HG 10/72 refers). In each survey, local authorities, the Development Commissions and the Housing Trust were asked to provide returns to the Ministry of Development distinguishing between pre-war and post-war houses, as in the earlier surveys but, unlike those, specifying individual rent levels and the number of houses with rents at these levels. The rents quoted were to exclude rates but to include any rent increases coming into effect on the survey dates. Overall averages (pre-war houses, post-war houses and total) from the 1971 survey were published in *Housing in Northern Ireland*, p. 258 [1]—see *Additional References* below. Apart from this none of the information has been published but it may be

made available by the Department of Housing, Local Government and Planning (formerly the Ministry of Development) on request.

Private dwellings
Information about the rents paid by private tenants will be obtained on behalf of the Rent Restriction Committee by the Northern Ireland Housing Executive in its House Condition Survey in 1974—see Addenda Section 3.1 above for further details. It is not yet known whether this particular information will be published or made available.

Additional References

[1] Centre for Environmental Studies, *Housing in Northern Ireland*, University Working Paper No. 12, by W. B. Birrell, P. A. R. Hillyard, A. Murie and D. J. D. Roche, The Centre, London, 1972.

[2] *Housing Executive, Annual Report*, first report for the period 13th May 1971 to 31st March 1972 published in 1973. The Executive, Belfast. Annual.

[3] *Housing Executive. Northern Ireland House Condition Survey, Explanatory Handbook*. The Executive, Belfast. (No date—1973 ?)

[4] *Housing Executive. Northern Ireland House Condition Survey, Surveyor's Instructions*. The Executive, Belfast. (No date—1973 ?).

List of Abbreviations

ABCS	Annual Bulletin of Construction Statistics
APTC	Administrative, Professional, Technical and Clerical
MBCS	Monthly Bulletin of Construction Statistics
NHBRC	National House Builders Registration Council
WP	Working Principals

I   Introduction

Most of the statistical information about housing in Northern Ireland is collected by Departments of the Northern Ireland Government, the most important Department concerned since the end of the Second World War being the Ministry of Health and Local Government until 1964 and then the Ministry of Development.* Other Departments with current responsibilities in this connection are the Ministry of Commerce, the Ministry of Health and Social Services and the Economic Section (currently part of the Ministry of Finance, formerly the Cabinet Offices). A curious and, in some ways, inconvenient feature of the publication of statistics, however, is that whilst some series are published by the Northern Ireland Government, others are to be found, in whole or in part, only in publications of the United Kingdom Government.

The end of the Second World War marks a clear division in the statistics available. Most of the information relates to the post-war period, but where appropriate, references have also been included here to information for pre-war years. In comparison with Great Britain the information available is sparse; improvements have been made in recent years, particularly since the mid 1960s, but despite these the statistics collected or published are still deficient in a number of respects.

The available statistics are considered by subject, rather than source, under five subject headings followed by a concluding summary section on desirable improvements, as follows:

Section 2 Output Statistics
       3 Statistics concerning the Housing Stock and Housing Needs
       4 Financial Statistics
       5 Building Costs, House Prices and Land
       6 House Building and the Building Industry
       7 Desirable Improvements—Summary

It should be noted that we use the term 'house' not in its strict sense, but, following common practice, to refer to all types of dwelling.

Quick Reference List of Current Sources (QRL). A summary guide to sources of the principal current statistics, prepared for quick reference purposes, is to be found immediately following the main text.

Publication References. All publications have been grouped into two lists—a Quick Reference List Key to Publications, which gives full details of the sources listed in the QRL, and a Bibliography of other references—both of which are placed at the end of this study. Each publication has been given a serial number, those from the first list being prefaced with the letters 'QRL' and those from the second list with the letter 'B', and references to them in the text are generally made by means of this serial number (shown in square brackets) only.

* The housing functions of the Ministry of Development were transferred to a newly-established Department of Housing, Local Government and Planning with effect from 1st January 1974.

2   Output Statistics

Two broad categories of data are available, one referring to the number of dwellings and the other to their value, providing information about dwellings completed in a period and also those at earlier stages of the construction and planning process. Information about the characteristics of new houses is very limited.

2.1   Data in Physical Units

Details of the statistical information available and its sources are most clearly and concisely presented in tabular form, and this is done in Table 2.1 below where the information is arranged according to type of statistic. There is no one source which may be regarded as primary in the sense of containing the full range of published information, and it has been necessary therefore to direct attention to several publications. It seems desirable to do this in any case since many Northern Irish publications are probably not readily available outside Northern Ireland. The table is meant to be self-explanatory and comment below is confined to more general matters.

2.1.1   *The number of dwellings*

The Period prior to 1st June, 1944
The only statistics available for the pre-war period were compiled through the administration of legislation providing for financial assistance towards the building of certain categories of house in both the public and private sectors of the economy. The statistics, therefore, are incomplete and, as we indicate in Table 2.1, only an estimate of the total number of houses built without financial assistance in the inter-war period as a whole is available.

The Period since the 1st June, 1944
The statistics available for this period were collected at first by the Ministry of Health and Local Government and then, from 1965, by the Ministry of Development as part of the process of administering regulations relating to housing subsidies and planning. All local authority★ housing schemes and contracts for them have been subject to the scrutiny and approval of the Ministry and, during the process of construction, sites have been subject to inspection by Housing Inspectors who are employed by the Ministry and are responsible for making statistical returns about progress. Thus a great deal of detailed information about various aspects of the nature of schemes and the rate of progress in construction becomes available to the Ministry. The information published, however, has been confined almost wholly to statistics about the latter. The contracts of the Northern Ireland Housing Trust† were not subject to the same detailed scrutiny, and it provided separate returns to the Ministry but site progress was subject to the same system of inspection and statistical reporting as for local authorities. Houses of the new Housing Executive will also be subject to inspection by the Ministry.

For houses in the private sector the collection procedure is substantially the same except that a distinction has to be made between subsidised and unsubsidised categories. For unsubsidised houses the statistics are collated by the Ministry from returns made by local authorities. These returns specify the persons authorised to build and house

★ The housing functions of local authorities (including development commissions) were transferred to a central housing authority—the Northern Ireland Housing Executive—during 1972/3.
† The Northern Ireland Housing Trust was dissolved on 4th October 1971, and its functions transferred to the Northern Ireland Housing Executive.

TABLE

NEW DWELLING

(A cross (×) indicates

Type of Statistic*	Period Covered and Frequency§	Public Total	Public Breakdown	Private Total	Private Partial	Private Full	By Agency & District‡
					Breakdowns		
(A) Statistics for the Period							
1(a) Completions	1919–23 (Total) } 1924–1944 (A) }	×		×			see Remarks
(B) Statistics for the Period							
1(b) Completions —cumulative	{ 1944–53 (A)		×			×	×
	{ 1944– (Q)		×			×	×
1(c) —time series	{ 1944– (A), 1948– (Q)		×		×		see
	{ 1949– (A), 1957– (Q)		×	×	×		Remarks (from 1965)
	{ 1945– (A), 1950– (M)	×		×			
	{ 1944–50 (Total), 1951–(A) } 1964–(Q), July 1967–(M) }	×		×			
2(a) Under construction at end of period	1944–53 (A)		×			×	×
	1954– (Q)		×			×	×
2(b) Under construction at end of period	{ 1949– (A), 1964– (Q)		×		×		
	{ 1950– (A), 1953– (Q)	×		×			
	{ 1965– (A), 1968– (Q)		×	×	×		
3 Starts	1944–50 (Total), 1951–(A) } 1964–(Q), July 1967–(M) }	×		×			
4 Approved, not started at end of period	1944–53(A),		×			×	×
	1954– (Q)		×			×	×
5 New contracts	1950–54(A), 1953–54 (Q)	×		×			
	1950–54 (A), 1953–54 (Q)	×		×			
	1965– (A), 1968– (Q)	× see Remarks					

2.1

CONSTRUCTION STATISTICS

the availability of data)

Publication	Remarks
Prior to 1st June 1944	
Ulster Yearbooks [B 20], 1947 p. 206 and 1950 p. 230.	Statistics are incomplete: the analyses relate only to housing built with financial assistance. An estimate for unassisted housing built in the inter-war period as a whole is to be found in the Yearbook [B 20] for 1947, p206. An analysis of the total number built in each urban area over the war and inter-war periods is to be found in [B 6] App. IX.
A. Abstract [QRL 1, B 27] see Remarks.	The early post-war editions of [QRL 1] included series for pre-war 'unassisted' housing.
Since 1st June 1944	
Ann. Rept [B 14] to 1953. *Hsg. Ret* [QRL 4] from 1954	The only sources of statistics for each local authority district. Fully detailed summaries for whole province also included (except for period 1966–68). Cumulative totals run from 1st June 1944 to the current period.
Digest [QRL 3] No. 1, Mar 1954 *et seq.* *Hsg. Ret* [QRL 4] Dec 1958 *et seq.*	Fully detailed time series were published up to 1964 in [B 20] and up to 1961 in [B 14].
M. Digest [QRL 7] May 1952 *et seq.*	⎫
Hsg. Stats [QRL 5] No. 7, 1967 *et seq.*	⎬ The only sources of monthly data. Annual series are reproduced in [QRL 1].
Ann. Rept [B 14] to 1953 *Hsg. Ret* [QRL 4] from 1954	⎫ Current period only. Fully detailed summaries for whole province omitted 1966–68. ⎬ See item 2(b) below for less detailed time series.
Digest [QRL 3] No. 26, Sept 1966 *et seq.* *M. Digest* [QRL 7] Sept 1954 *et seq.* *Hsg. Ret* [QRL 4] Mar 1969 *et seq.*	See also item 2(a) above for 'under construction' series.
Hsg. Stats [QRL 5] No. 7, 1967 *et seq.*	The only source of monthly data.
Ann. Rept [B 14] to 1953 *Hsg. Ret* [QRL 4] from 1954	Current period only. Fully detailed summaries for whole province omitted 1966–68. A less detailed time series (annual from 1965, quarterly from 1968) for the province was introduced in *Hsg. Ret* [QRL 4] from March 1969—as in item 2(b) above.
M. Digest [QRL 7] Sept 1954–Mar 1955	
M. Digest [QRL 7] Sept 1954–Mar 1955 *Hsg. Ret* [QRL 4] Mar 1969 *et seq.*	Analysed according to: (a) no. of persons each dwelling is designed to accommodate (separate category for old persons) (b) storey heights, (c) method of construction: traditional/industrialised (from 1966).

Footnotes for Table 2.1 are given on page 14.

locations. For subsidised housing approval statistics are based on approval certificates issued by local authorities, copies of which are sent to the Ministry. These certificates (and subsequent completion certificates) contain details of the size of house (superficial area and number of apartments) and type of construction but no analyses of this information are made. Statistics of other stages of work are based on the reports of the Ministry's housing inspectors referred to above. It may also be noted, incidentally, that these inspectors also carry out inspections for the local committee of the National House Builders Registration Council (NHBRC) which extended its operations to Northern Ireland in 1970.†

It will be seen from Table 2.1 that the most detailed sources are the Ministry's *Annual Report* [B 14] prior to 1953 and its *Housing Return* [QRL 4] subsequently; these contain the most detailed

† Separate statistics about houses that fall within the NHBRC scheme are not readily available; the author is informed by the Ministry that such houses amount to about ninety per cent of total private enterprise building. The local committee of the Council does not publish statistics but it keeps a record of the number of houses registered and their cost (the latter is provided by the builder on the registration form and may or may not be accurate).

breakdowns by subsidy category and are the only sources of information for each local authority area. As sources of time series data, however, they are deficient, for much of the information is provided in cumulative form only. Time series for the province as a whole are available in a more convenient and accessible form in other publications.

In contrast to Great Britain, subsidies for private as well as public sector housing have been available for the whole period from 1944. The distinction between private subsidised and unsubsidised housing is one of size of dwelling. Regulations governing the entitlement to subsidies ('grants' in the private sector) and their value in both sectors are to be found in *Statutory Rules and Orders* made by the Parliament of Northern Ireland.

Northern Ireland Housing Trust. Additional information about the activities of the Northern Ireland Housing Trust is to be found in its annual reports [QRL 10]. These include statistics of the number of dwellings completed, or at earlier stages of construction, for individual sites and details of the acreage of land on each site, as well as a complete and detailed time series for its activities as a whole (introduced in the fifteenth annual report [QRL 10], 1959–60). Separate analyses have also been included

---

* *Definitions* of the terms used are not published. The Ministry state that they are as follows:
Completion—when the dwelling conforms to standards and is ready for occupation.
Start—when the foundations have been concreted.
Approval—when in the public sector a tender has been approved by the Ministry, in the case of a local authority, or by the Housing Trust (in future by the Housing Executive), when in the private sector a local authority has issued a certificate of approval to an applicant entitling him to construct a house under the subsidy scheme or for unsubsidised houses a certificate of approval has been issued.

† *Agencies:*

	Public	Private	
		Partial	*Full*
		Breakdown	*Breakdown*
Local authorities		Without subsidy	Without subsidy
N. Ireland Housing		With subsidy	With subsidy
Trust		(total only)	Letting
Other			Owner-occupation
			Industrial workers
			Farmers and farm-
			workers

The fully detailed sources also provide separate statistics for "War damage 'Cost of Works'" houses (i.e. rebuilt war-destroyed houses), aluminium bungalows and 'Arcon' temporary houses provided in the early post-war years.

‡ *District:* Each local housing authority area—i.e. each county borough, borough, urban district, rural district and in recent years, development commission or county council.

§ *Frequency;* A—Annual Q—Quarterly M—Monthly.

since the fourteenth annual report [QRL 10], 1958–59, of its activities in the 'Belfast Area' (see also the twelfth annual report for comment).

Development Commissions.★ Additional information about the housing activities of the three development commissions established during the 1960s, including expenditure, is to be found in their annual reports [B 33, B 35, B 36].

2.1.2 *Characteristics of New Housing*

Information about the characteristics of new housing is very limited in scope and has been published only for the period since 1965 for dwellings in new contracts in the public sector only. Details are shown in Table 2.1. Little comment is required except with regard to the definition adopted for 'industrialised building'. This is drawn very widely to cover:

> '. . . all measures to enable the industry to work like a factory industry . . . this means not only new materials and construction techniques, the use of dry processes, increased mechanisation of site processes, and the manufacture of large components under factory conditions of production and quality control; but also improved management techniques, the correlation of design and production, improved control of the selection, and delivery of materials and better organisation of operation on site. For this purpose, industrialised buildings include schemes using fully rationalised traditional methods.'

It is not readily apparent how, at the approval stage, contracts can be classified according to some of the elements of the definition, for example, the use of 'improved management techniques'. The definition lacks precision and the data based upon it must be treated with reserve. The information would be more useful if it were to be broken down so that at least dwellings to be built using proprietary 'systems' of construction were identified. Statistics of industrialised housing built by the Northern Ireland Housing Trust using proprietary 'systems' in the period 1945–66, the year 1965–66 and under construction at 31st March, 1966, each according to type of system, are to be found in its

★ The housing functions of the Development Commissions were transferred to the Northern Ireland Housing Executive during 1972-3.

twenty-first annual report [QRL 10], 1965–66, p. 10.

With regard to the size of houses built in the public sector the only published information, apart from the time series introduced from 1965 (see Table 2.1), is an analysis of the area (sq. ft.) and the number of apartments provided in houses approved for local authorities in 1956 which was included in the Ministry's *Annual Report* for that year [B 14], Cmd.379, p. 65. No information about the size of contracts in the public sector is available except for an *ad hoc* analysis of official records made by the author for the period 1964–5 which was published in [B 32].

In the private sector virtually no information is available about the characteristics of new houses, although some inferences about size may be made on the basis of the distinction between subsidised and unsubsidised houses. Mention may be made of the statistical analyses made from time to time by the Nationwide Building Society (formerly the Co-operative Permanent Building Society) of the houses mortgaged by it in the United Kingdom, although regional analyses other than for house prices and purchasers have not been published; the only published data about the characteristics of houses in Northern Ireland related to the provision of central heating [QRL 11], No. 98, November 1970.

2.1.3 *Desirable improvements*

The information published is notable for its paucity. The greatest deficiencies are information about the characteristics of new housing in terms of their size and other standards of accommodation and equipment provided, and about contracts and contracting methods.

Information about standards is of obvious social and economic importance. Official approval of houses in the public sector is governed by regulations concerning standards, but these are minima only, and it is useful to know how far the minima are exceeded in practice. Information of the kind published in Great Britain, about the extent to

TABLE 2.2

STATISTICS OF THE VALUE OF HOUSING WORK

(a cross(x) indicates availability of data)

Statistic	Analyses				Time Series and Frequency	Source		Remarks
	New Work		Repairs & Maintenance			Government Department	Publication	
	Total	By Sector	Total	By Sector				
Gross Domestic Fixed Capital Formation	x	x	not applicable (see Remarks)		1950—(A) see Remarks	Economic Section Ministry of Finance	Digest [QRL 3], No. 11, March 1959 et seq. (A period of eight or nine years is covered each time)	Constant price series by sector from 1958 (annual) are available in the *Economic Rept.* [B 10] 1964 *et seq*; the same price indices are used for deflation purposes as in the statistics for the U.K. as a whole. Current-price analyses by sector (public/private) have been published only from 1961 and were introduced in [QRL 3] No. 32 Sept. 1969. Separate accounts are included for capital formation by local authorities on a financial year basis in [QRL 3].
Output—Work Done by: Contractors Direct Labour	x	x	not published		1966—(Q) not published	Ministry of Commerce	Digest [QRL 3] No. 30, Sept. 1968 et seq. For secondary sources see Remarks	Contractors employing 7 or more operatives only. See text for discussion of register on which the surveys are based. Conversions, extensions and alteration work are not counted as new work. Secondary sources: *Ec. Rept.* [B 10], 1966 *et seq*., *MBCS** [QRL 6] Sept. 1968 *et seq.* Annual series in *ABCS†* [QRL 2] No. 10, 1968 *et seq.*

		Date	Source	Reference				Remarks
7*	New Contracts and Orders received by Contractors	1966—(Q)	Ministry of Commerce	As for 'Output' above	×	× (see Remarks)		Contractors employing 7 or more operatives only. The 'housing' classification excludes orders of less than £2,500 in value and work to be carried out by the contractor on his own initiative. Statistics of the total value of work to be carried out by the contractor on his own initiative are published in [QRL 6] and [QRL 2] as above†; in the Northern Ireland *Digest* [QRL 3], the series is aggregated with that for orders of less than £2,500, and called 'work not covered by orders'.
	Output—Work Done by Contractors & Direct Labour	1951 & 1954	Ministry of Commerce	*Censuses of Production* 1951 & 1954 [B 17, B 18]	×	× (partial)	×	The censuses covered only establishments employing 11 or more persons in the construction industry defined according to the SIC 1948 [B 26]. Analyses by sector only for larger contractors. The 1951 report distinguished flats and tenements from other types of dwelling and 'prefabricated dwellings' from other types of construction—for further details see the reports themselves. It is not known how far the register of contractors used as the basis of the census was complete; in 1951 it must be assumed that it was, since licensing was still in operation at that time; by 1954 *ad hoc* methods would have had to have been used to maintain it.

* MBCS: Monthly Bulletin of Construction Statistics [QRL 6]
† ABCS: Annual Bulletin of Construction Statistics [QRL 2]
‡ The series is now also published in the later issues of [B 10].

which the houses being built measure up to certain desirable norms of design and equipment such as those recommended in the report of the Parker Morris Committee [B 22], is valuable.

With regard to contracts, information about their size is of value in assessing performance in the house-building field, since size of contract has been shown to be an important factor affecting efficiency. Information about types of contract (fixed price or not) and about the methods used for letting contracts (open or selective competition, negotiation) together with information about the use of 'serial' tendering and 'package deals' is also of value, since they too are important matters affecting house-building efficiency and costs.

Much of this information, it may be said, already becomes available to the Ministry by virtue of the exercise of its powers of approval over all local authority contracts. In the future the consolidation of all public house-building functions in a central Housing Executive will facilitate still more the preparation of detailed housing statistics and it is to be hoped that the opportunity is taken and the data published. In the private sector the administration of grants for private building provides a source of information which could be exploited.

2.2 Data in Monetary Units

Details of the information available are set out in Table 2.2. There are three statistical series as such, two relating to housing 'output' and the third to the value of new contracts and orders placed with contractors*. The latter and one of the output series are both obtained in the same return so that these data may be conveniently considered together. The other output series forms part of statistics on gross fixed capital formation. We discuss these data below but at this stage it may be worth emphasising that the two output series

*Additional statistics about housing work ought to be available as a consequence of the licensing of building operations which was required under Defence Regulation 56A until its repeal in November 1954; official searches, however, undertaken on behalf of the author have revealed none.

should be treated with a certain amount of caution since there are discrepancies between the two series which it is difficult to explain satisfactorily; we return to this question later. An additional source of information is the censuses of production which have distinguished housing as a separate category at times in the past.

2.2.1 *Gross domestic fixed capital formation— housing*

These statistics do not form part of the United Kingdom series but are prepared independently by the Economic Section of the Ministry of Finance. Unfortunately, no information is published about the sources and methods used in deriving the estimates nor about their reliability. In general the same principles are followed as in the national accounts for the United Kingdom (see [B 21]), thus in addition to containing an estimate of the value of new work, the value of grant-aided conversions and improvements is included, and the figures should also include the cost of architects' and surveyors' fees. Estimates of the value of new house-building as such are based on the number of dwellings completed multiplied by average prices. The reliability of the figures, therefore, depends largely on the reliability of the price information though it may be noted that houses completed in a year are not the same as housing 'output' in that year nor necessarily the base of new housing expenditure in the year because of stage payments. In the public sector price information is available to the Government department concerned and thus the estimated values for this sector should be reasonably reliable. In the private sector the estimates are built up currently (at least) by taking separate figures for letting and owner-occupation (subsidised houses), Housing Associations, non-subsidy houses and new farmhouses. The only direct price estimates relate to the last category (separate Housing on Farms grants scheme) and owner-occupation, for which the Nationwide Building Society prices are used (see section 5.2). For non-subsidy houses a notional price is used and for the other categories local authority house prices are taken as being equivalent. It is almost certainly true to say that the reliability of the estimates has improved over time for certain price information was not available when the series was commenced; it is difficult to date any improvements precisely but there are grounds for thinking that the series from around the early 1960s may be more reliable than that preceding.

2.2.2   *Output and Contractors' New Orders Series— Housing*

From the beginning of 1966 quarterly returns have been obtained from contractors and the building and civil engineering departments of public authorities showing the value of work done, the number of operatives employed* and, in the case of contractors, the value of contracts and orders obtained for new work (i.e. excluding repairs and maintenance). The returns from contractors are obtained under the terms of the Statistics of Trade Act (Northern Ireland) 1949, which, amongst other things, renders the provision of the return compulsory. The enquiry is conducted by the Ministry of Commerce on behalf of the Economic Section, but the questionnaires are modelled on those which are used by the Department of the Environment (formerly Ministry of Public Building and Works) in Great Britain. The questionnaires themselves are reproduced in Appendix I, in order to indicate the range of information collected, together with the instructions given with regard to their completion. Details of the information published are to be found in Table 2.2; it will be seen that important parts of the information collected are not published.

In this section consideration is given to certain general matters which are pertinent to the interpretation of these statistics. A matter of crucial importance is the extent to which comprehensive coverage of house-building activities (including in this term work of repairs and maintenance on housing) is obtained. The statistics are collected not

about construction activities as such but from establishments classified to the construction industry, in accordance with the *Standard Industrial Classification* [B 26]. Thus construction work undertaken by organizations and individuals that do not fall within the definition of the industry is not covered. The main importance of this with regard to housing is that the substantial amount of work, especially repair, maintenance and alteration work to housing, which is undertaken directly by owners and occupiers using their own labour and by individuals employed in a private capacity escapes coverage.*

Even within the industry as defined it is not easy to ensure comprehensive coverage, for the number of enterprises is very large, most of them are very small and highly dispersed geographically, and the population of firms is continually changing because of the ease with which it is possible to enter (and leave) the industry. Many builders do not operate from a recognisable business address, and the fact that the work itself is undertaken at particular sites and not at a fixed location, as in a factory or workshop means that there is not necessarily any identifiable 'establishment' from which to collect information. There is no system of compulsory registration of building enterprises and in the absence of such a system these facts pose severe difficulties in the way of maintaining a comprehensive register of enterprises upon which to base the statistical surveys.† It would seem virtually inevitable, therefore, that the register on which the surveys are based is rarely, if ever, complete.‡

The main deficiency in the register is likely to be of small firms (including one-man enterprises) whose activities are particularly important in the housing field for both new work and repairs, main-

---

* Information about the average expenditure of households on repairs, maintenance and decorations, however, is available from *Family Expenditure Surveys* [QRL 9]. It may be noted too that information for local authorities is available from their Housing Repair Accounts in [B 8].

† Compulsory registration under national war-time Defence Regulations ended in November 1953.

‡ Some evidence of this was obtained, incidentally, in a study by the author ([B32] see section 6.1 below).

---

* These statistics are considered in section 6 below.

tenance and alteration work, especially the latter. In recent years this problem has been aggravated considerably by the growing practice of 'labour only' sub-contracting in which a gang of men undertakes part of the work on a contract, often merely by verbal agreement with the main contractor or another sub-contractor, by supplying their labour and perhaps some tools and equipment but not materials. Since the members of such groups often retain the status of 'self-employed' workers and their association is often both informal and transient, the difficulties of data collection are increased.

Finally, it is important to note, although attention is not directed to the fact in the currently published statistics, that only contractors employing more than seven operatives are covered*.

Output

The major matter of importance with regard to output in particular is the question of the measurement of work and its valuation since most construction jobs take a considerable period of time to complete. The value is meant to be an estimate of the work actually done in the preceding quarter, not merely the value of contracts completed nor the value of payments received for work done, including the value of work done on site preparation and demolition. The value of work done on the contractors' own initiative on houses destined for eventual sale or lease is also included, but it will be appreciated that in these cases the valuation inserted by the contractor is to be treated with more discretion since there is no predetermined contract sum to act as the basis of valuation, and the sale price may not have been determined. In the case of the direct labour of public authorities, the valuation of work is somewhat different inasmuch as it does not include a profit element. The costs of land, legal charges and professional fees are excluded.

---

* This statement is based on information supplied to the author by the Economic Section in June 1971. The only published references to this fact are in the *Economic Reports* [B 10] for 1967 and 1968.

Contractors are instructed not to include the value of work done by sub-contractors nor payments made to 'labour only' sub-contractors since these should be covered on separate returns, but, for the reasons discussed earlier, it is virtually inevitable that some of these sub-contractors, especially those operating on a 'labour only' basis should escape the net. Since 1969 contractors have been required to state the value of wage payments made to operatives employed on a 'labour only' basis separately, but the information is not published.

New orders

Statistics of new orders and contracts placed are collected only from contractors. It is to be expected that such statistics should be more reliable than statistics of output for they can be precisely defined at a point of time whilst the latter, carried out over a period of time, will normally need to be based, at least partly, on estimates. In addition, since information about new orders is collected for the order as a whole, and not separately for such parts of it as are let under sub-contract, the problem of ensuring full coverage by collecting information from 'labour only' and other small sub-contractors is of much smaller significance. The value of a new order will normally be explicit being the price accepted by the client, but there are certain instances where this is not the case or where the value has to be estimated (see the instructions for completing the return in Appendix I).

We direct attention to the deficiencies in coverage of this series in the remarks to Table 2.2. A major deficiency in the publication of results is the failure to distinguish the housing element of the work to be undertaken by the contractor on his own initiative ('work not covered by orders'). Such work is likely to be largely house-building, though not wholly for it may include other buildings such as offices or storage premises, built speculatively for sale or letting or for the builders' own use. Practice in this respect is contrary to that adopted with regard to the comparable series for Great Britain where such work is not only published as a separate series but is also allocated according to type of work. 'Own-initiative' work is also in a slightly different category inasmuch as the value the builder is instructed to include is the value of buildings upon which foundation work was actually started in the period covered by the return, so that these figures, therefore, represent 'starts' rather than work planned.

Another factor to note with regard to coverage is that the limit of £2,500 for small contracts has remained unchanged since the introduction of the series so that the real volume of work coming above the limit will have been increasing over time because of rising prices.

From the point of view of forecasting future output it should be appreciated that the new orders series may be affected by alterations in the work to be done, postponements, and possibly also cancellations, although once a job has progressed as far as the letting of a contract it would normally be expected to continue. In addition, of course, the value of work done on a particular contract may not be the same as that recorded as a new order, for although an accepted contract price will form part of a contract, such contracts often include clauses to allow changes in the costs of material and or labour which may take place during the construction period to be recouped. In addition, the two values may differ as a result of variations in the work itself, arranged after the award of the contract. No information is published about time lags from the start, or the award of a contract, to completion.

2.2.3 *Comparison of the housing output series*

The two series of statistics on the value of new housing—that of gross domestic fixed capital formation and that of work done by contractors—provide estimates which are in marked disagreement. The former is generally half as big again as the latter, a large part of the difference occurring in respect of dwellings in the private sector. Further, the two series do not always agree in the relative magnitude of the change which they show from one period to the next. Great caution is required, therefore, in using the two series and some attempt at explanation is called for.

There is no official explanation, and what follows is the explanation offered by the author. Part of the reason is that the series of work done by contractors and the direct labour of public authorities suffers from the deficiencies of coverage and incomplete publication which have been discussed above, whilst the capital formation series is meant to be comprehensive. The greater magnitude of the deficiency in respect of output in the private sector is undoubtedly due in large part to the lack of coverage of the small contractors who are important in the private house-building market because of the small size of jobs. Another difference between the two series, though it goes little way towards explaining the discrepancy between them is one of timing, in that the capital formation estimates are built up on the basis of houses completed, whilst the work-done series represent estimates (as made by the contractor) of the value of work done during a period regardless of whether construction was complete or not. The capital formation series would be expected to be larger, however, inasmuch as they include architects' and surveyors' fees and the transfer costs of land and buildings. Further, the capital formation series includes the value of grant-aided conversions and improvements whereas such work is not counted as new work in the value of work-done series.

More reliance must be placed on the capital formation series as an indicator of the value of housing output than on that of work done because it aims to be comprehensive and is based to some extent on physical data about the construction of dwellings which are themselves regarded as reliable. The degree of reliability that may be attached to it, however, is not clear since no official assessment is provided about the likely margins of error and the general lack of information (other than that provided in this study) about sources and methods of estimation precludes the user from forming his own judgement.

2.2.4 *Desirable improvements*

The most desirable improvement that could be suggested in connection with the gross domestic fixed capital formation series is that full information should be provided about the sources and methods used in its calculation and the likely margins of error of the estimates.

With regard to the work-done and new-orders series perhaps the most desirable improvement would be the publication of more of the information that is already collected. At present, as we have indicated, the housing series published in respect of both output and new orders are incomplete and indeed, not fully comparable. The new housing output series, as published, covers only the work carried out by contractors whilst the contractors' new-orders series fails to distinguish housing work carried out on their own initiative, a part highly important in the private sector of the market, as well as small housing contracts in both the public and private sectors. Thus both series provide only a partial picture and despite the fact that both relate solely to contractors, cannot be correlated except for work undertaken for public clients. Despite the great importance of the repair and maintenance of the housing stock, no information at all is published about the value of this work, and it is also desirable that this deficiency should be remedied. Information could also be provided about the number and size of contracts on the basis of the returns already obtained (see Appendix 1).

It is unfortunate that it should be necessary to entertain doubts about the adequacy of the register of contractors used as the basis for the enquiries. The difficulties that must be contended with are acknowledged and it may not be possible to resolve them satisfactorily without a system of compulsory registration of builders, but it would be useful to know what methods are used to maintain the register and how large and frequent the revisions are. Large and infrequent revisions, of course, are likely to lead to discontinuities in the statistical series, and it is desirable to know whether these are significant. It would also be useful to know what is done about the problem of non-response. The problem of the register is probably of greater importance than the exclusion of the smaller contractors, though their inclusion would be desirable and could usefully be reconsidered on the basis of a complete register.

3 Statistics Concerning the Housing Stock and Housing Needs

This section is concerned with statistics relating to not only the size and characteristics of the housing stock but also to activities such as demolition or improvement which affect both of them.

3.1 Size and Characteristics of the Housing Stock

Size and Composition of the Stock
The principal information about the number of houses in existence is that obtained as part of the periodic censuses of population. Like the corresponding statistics for Great Britain, these also provide information about the characteristics of dwellings in terms of the number of rooms and, more recently, the extent to which certain basic amenities are provided and the basis of tenure of the dwellings. This information is considered, along with the corresponding British data, in the companion study of *Housing in Great Britain*, App. I.

With regard to the number of houses, information additional to that collected in the censuses of population has also been obtained in four *ad hoc* surveys as follows:

Some interesting information about the characteristics of housing and its occupants in six areas of Belfast designated for redevelopment in 1965 based on sample surveys is to be found in [B 37]. Information is included about dwelling type and tenure, amenities available, number of bedrooms, number of persons per household, incomes and rents.

Age and Condition of the Stock
Age. Little information is available about the ages of houses. Estimates were published in 1962 in [B 25], Appendix XIII, of the percentages of the stock built before 1919 and before 1880 and in [B 23], p. 175, of the percentage over 80 years old in 1965. No information is available about the bases of the estimates and their reliability.

Condition. There are three sources of information about housing conditions each of which has been referred to above in connection with statistics about the size of the housing stock. The first is the periodic census of population which, as we indicated above, provides information about the provision of certain basic amenities; this information

TABLE 3

	Date	Ministry	Coverage	Analyses	Source
1.	1943	Home Affairs	All houses	Each local authority except rural districts (by county only)	[B 6]
2.	1956–8	Health and Local Government*	All houses	Each local authority	[B 11]
3.	1956	Health and Local Government*	Local authority houses	Not published. Surveys made in connection with analyses of rents (see section 4.2)	
4.	1966	Development*			

* Returns submitted by local authorities

is considered in the study *Housing in Great Britain* (Book 5 in this series). The other two are the surveys carried out in 1943 [B 6] and in the period 1956–1958 [B 11], the latter being referred to as the '1958 survey'.

(i) *The 1943 Survey*, This survey was the first comprehensive review of housing conditions in Northern Ireland and was undertaken by the Ministry of Home Affairs. The subjects dealt with included overcrowding, structural condition, light and ventilation, sanitation, water supply, heating and lighting. Analyses of the results and details of the standards used in the survey were published in [B 6]; a description of the basis of the survey and the methods employed in carrying it out was published separately [B 15]. Sampling methods were employed but no information is provided about the sampling frame or sampling errors.

(ii) *The '1958 Survey'*. Each local authority was required under the terms of the Housing (Miscellaneous Provisions) and Rent Restriction Law (Amendment) Act (Northern Ireland), 1956, to submit to the Minister of Health and Local Government, within a period of two years from the passing of the Act (November 1956), proposals for dealing with unfit houses in its area. It was necessary, therefore, for each local authority to ascertain the number of unfit houses by means of a general survey. The results of this survey were published in [B 11] which provides statistics for each local authority of:

> total number of houses in each area,
> number of unfit houses: repairable/non-repairable,
> estimated time to deal with all unfit houses,
> number of new houses required,
> number of houses to be demolished } by the
>   or closed } end of
> number of new houses required } 1961

The results of this survey must be treated with a certain amount of caution. The standard of 'fitness for human habitation' applied in the survey, an amended standard laid down in the 1956 Act (s. 33)

referred to above, is adumbrated in very broad terms and it is not clear how it was applied in practice in the survey nor how far the results for different authorities may be held to be comparable. Unfortunately no commentary is provided about these matters nor about the criteria adopted as the basis for classifying a house as 'repairable' or 'non-repairable'.

Tenure

Statistics about tenure are available from the *Censuses of Population* (discussed in the study of British housing statistics, *supra*). Some information is also available from *Family Expenditure Surveys* [QRL 9] in which it is used as a characteristic for the analysis of household income and expenditure.

3.2   Changes to the Stock

Demolition, closure and repair
Time series (as such) of houses demolished or closed were first published in the *Housing Return* [QRL 4] for March 1969 (annual series from 1965, quarterly from 1968 together with aggregates for 1964–68, 1959–63 and 1958). A distinction is drawn between fit and unfit houses demolished and gross and net* statistics are provided of houses closed in this and subsequent *Returns* [QRL 4]. It should be noted that the statistics would not include houses demolished by private persons unconnected with statutory action; it is felt, however, that few dwellings would fall within this category.

Statistics on these matters were published prior to 1969, but not as time series and they are subject to important qualifications. These statistics were presented in cumulative form and for part of the period (March 1965 to March 1967) were presented as houses demolished or closed 'since 1.1.58'; in fact, the statistics included such houses *as were known* to have been demolished prior to 1958—this

---

* Net statistics allow for houses subsequently demolished or made fit.

is made clear in the *Housing Return* [QRL 4] for March 1969 which publishes the relevant figure for the first time. Another deficiency in the early published statistics was an element of duplication in the combined figures of houses demolished and closed since the latter were not adjusted in respect of houses subsequently demolished or made fit. Such adjustments were introduced in the *Return* [QRL 4] for March 1966, but it would appear from an examination of their size in this and the following issues of the *Return* that the first few figures must be treated with care.

The Returns used for the collection of these statistics are reproduced in Appendix II together with the covering Ministry circulars. It will be seen that the information for 1958 was collected retrospectively since the first return was issued in January 1959, requesting information for the year 1958 and subsequent quarters on a continuing basis. A revised form of return was introduced in April 1962 which it was hoped would be used from the beginning of the year. As late as 1967 it appears that there was some doubt as to whether houses entered in the Return under item (3) should also be included under item (1) and authorities were asked to re-examine their returns back to 1st January 1962*. The possibility that all errors were not eliminated as a result of this request should be borne in mind. Initially, statistics were classified according to houses demolished under Demolition Orders or under Clearance Orders, etc., but this presentation was abandoned in the revised format adopted in 1969. Statistics under the individual categories of items (1) to (3) and items (1) to (4) of the first and second, revised, Returns (Appendix II) respectively, however, were published in the Ministry's *Annual Reports* [B 14] for a number of years after 1958.

War-time destruction. Statistics of the number of houses destroyed or damaged during the war are to be found in [B 1] p. 238.

Comprehensive redevelopment. Particulars of individual redevelopment schemes approved since

* Ministry of Development Circular HG 12/1967 dated 22nd November 1967.

1956 have been published, irregularly, in the Ministry's *Annual Reports* [B 14].

Conversions, improvements, reconditioning and the provision of standard amenities

A distinction has to be drawn between grant-aided and non-grant-aided work. A scheme for the provision of financial assistance to owners of property for the conversion of houses and other buildings into flats and houses and for the improvement of existing houses was introduced with effect from 15th April 1957, under the terms of the Housing (Miscellaneous Provisions) and Rent Restriction Law (Amendment) Act (Northern Ireland), 1956. Prior to this date financial assistance was available only for the reconditioning of farm dwellings under the Housing on Farms Act (Northern Ireland) 1948. Statistical time series were introduced for the period from 1958 together with aggregate data for the preceding post-war period showing for both periods the number of conversions, improvements and farm dwellings reconditioned covering both grant-aided and non-grant-aided work, no distinction being drawn between the two. How comprehensive the statistics for non-grant-aided work were is not clear. Statistics for these, however, have not been kept since 31st March 1969 and from that time the series published have related to grant-aided schemes only. Additional financial assistance towards the provision of certain basic amenities was introduced in 1963 in the Housing Act (Northern Ireland) 1963 and separate statistics are published relating to action under this legislation.

Information on these matters is collected by the Ministry of Development (formerly the Ministry of Health and Local Goverment) on the basis of its own approval machinery in public sector cases and returns from local authorities in private sector cases. Details of the statistical information published are set out below in Table 3.1 except for financial statistics which are considered in Section 4. Attention is drawn in particular to a pitfall in the use of the statistics about conversions inasmuch as most of the data relates to the number of conversions and

TABLE 3.1

CONVERSIONS, IMPROVEMENTS, RECONDITIONING AND PROVISION OF
STANDARD AMENITIES—STATISTICS OF WORK COMPLETED*

Item	Period Covered	Analyses	Time Series and Frequency	Publication
1. Conversions† Improvements Farm dwellings reconditioned	From 1944	By: sector (local authority/private) See additional notes below regarding conversions	From 1958: Annually & Quarterly (from 4th qtr)	[QRL 4] 31st Dec. 1958 issue *et seq.*
2. Provision of Standard Amenities‡	From 1964	By: (a) sector—as above (b) number of dwellings concerned (c) amenity	From 1964: Quarterly	[QRL 4] 31st March 1965 issue *et seq.*

* Statistics were also published for item 1 in the table relating to earlier stages of work: 'in progress' and 'approved not started' quarterly from December 1958 to December 1964 in [QRL 4] and 'started' and 'approved' in [B 14] from 1958 to 1964.

† *Conversions* Statistics of the net number of new dwellings produced by conversion (total only) were regularly published in a footnote to the table until 1969.

Statistics (cumulative from 1944) of the number of conversions according to each local authority district are also published in [QRL 4].

‡ *Standard Amenities:* bath, wash-hand basin, hot water supply, W.C., food store, new bathroom, septic tank, cold water supply and sink. The last three amenities were not grant-aided until 1967 for pre-war houses and 1968 for post-war houses.

not to the net number of dwellings provided by conversion (see the footnotes to Table 3.1). No information is provided on whether it is dwellings or other buildings which are the subject of conversion.

3.3 Housing Needs

Statistics about housing needs are in a completely different category from most of the other statistics considered in this paper for they cannot stand in their own right as the outcome of a discrete collection process. They represent less statements of fact than statements of opinion for they must be based partly upon assumptions of one kind or another about desirable standards of accommodation and possibly about future developments. The subject is of such importance, however, as to

justify its inclusion, more especially since a great deal of the statistical information considered here is required precisely for this purpose. Judgement of the validity of such statistics must depend upon individual assessment of the nature and reliability of the underlying statistical information, the assumptions made and the methods of estimation used.

In fact there is very little information to which to refer. Indeed no real appraisal of housing needs has been published since that in the report of the Planning Advisory Board [B 6] in 1944, work which is now largely of historical interest. This provided estimates of immediate need, based upon considerations of overcrowding and the number of houses needing replacement which, in turn, were based upon the results of the house condition survey carried out in 1943 and reported in [B 6] and [B 15]—see section 3.1 above for details. A survey of housing conditions was carried out in 1958 and reported in [B 11]—see section 3.1 above for details—but it was not followed by a published assessment of housing needs. Attention may also be drawn perhaps to figures published in 1962 in [B 25], Appendix XIII, but these were concerned less with assessing needs than with comparing the likely sizes of the housing stock and population in 1981 on the basis of certain broad assumptions.

An estimate of housing need in the Belfast Urban Area for the period up to 1986 was published in [B 34]. But beyond providing a breakdown showing how the total estimate was arrived at, no analysis of the figures is provided such as would enable an independent appraisal of the estimate to be made.

3.4 Desirable Improvements

Undoubtedly the most desirable improvement relates to statistics about the housing stock. Up-to-date information about its physical condition, composition and occupancy is an essential prerequisite for a reliable assessment of the scale and nature of current housing problems and the formulation of sound housing programmes and policies. By comparison other desirable improvements are insignificant.

Statistics of conversions could be improved by the re-introduction of series showing the net number of new dwellings provided and revising the series for individual local authorities accordingly. Statistics about improvements would seem to be of little value without knowing something of the nature of the improvement and perhaps the cost of the work carried out.

4 Financial Statistics

This section covers all statistics dealing with the financial aspects of housing and housebuilding including subsidies and rents, but excluding building costs and house prices which are considered separately in section 5 below.

4.1 Public Authority Accounts

Useful consolidations of the financial accounts of the central and local government sectors based on national income accounting principles are published in [QRL 3]. It is stated that as far as possible the same principles are applied as in the accounts for the United Kingdom as a whole which are described in [B 21]. Unfortunately little or no information is provided about the differences between the two sets of accounts in sources and methods though this would be valuable.

Currently the accounts are presented in two ways. First, separate capital and revenue (or current) accounts are included for the central government and the local government sector in which items are shown for housing in respect of subsidy payments, rental income, capital grants and direct capital expenditure. This series is available annually from 1953/54 and was first published in [QRL 3], No. 11, March 1959. Secondly, a separate 'functional and economic analysis of public expenditure' (both central and local) has been included for financial years from 1968/69. This series was first published, with housing shown as a separate category, in [QRL 3], No. 34, September 1970 (prior to this, housing was incorporated with environmental services). The primary sources of information for each sector are considered below.

Central government

The statistics of expenditure by the government on housing are to be found in its annual financial accounts. The most important item is subsidies for new housing paid to local authorities, both in respect of their own building and as contribution towards the grants for private building which are paid by the local authorities, and as subsidies paid to the Northern Ireland Housing Trust and Housing Associations. An important matter with regard to the interpretation of the subsidy statistics, however, is that the housing authorities in Northern Ireland, unlike those in the rest of the United Kingdom, have been able since 1947 to commute their entitlement to sixty annual contributions from the central government and take an equivalent lump sum*. Insofar as use is made of this facility, expenditure by way of annual contributions is thereby reduced so that the two types of expenditure, details of which are published separately, need to be taken in conjunction; in fact, considerable use has been made of the facility. Statistics of annual contributions are published in [B 4]. With regard to commutation, a special fund, the Housing Commutation Fund, was established in 1947; details of payments from it, however, have been published only from 1952–3 in [B 3]. Prior to 1952–3 it is understood that payments were not met exclusively from the fund, and information is available only from the Ministry of Finance.

Statistics about expenditure in connection with the schemes for house conversions, improvement, the reconditioning of farm dwellings and the provision of standard amenities (referred to above in section 3.2) are most conveniently presented in the Ministry's *Annual Reports* [B 14] where they are published alongside information about the number of dwellings concerned.

* The commuted subsidies are not paid to the local authority (or the Housing Trust) but are used to offset loan charges.

Local government
Housing accounts. Details of the financial transactions of each local authority on revenue and capital accounts including the Housing Revenue and Housing Repair Accounts are published in [B 8] for the period from 1953–4; earlier statistics were published in [B 19].

Rate statistics. Annual estimates of payments and receipts on which each local authority strikes its rates are published in [B 9]; this provides details for housing along with other services but excludes certain government receipts. No analyses are provided about the rateable valuation of houses.

Development Commissions
The accounts of the three development commissions are published annually in [B 33, B 35, B 36].

Northern Ireland Housing Trust
The accounts of the Housing Trust have been published annually in [B 7]; from 1958–9 they are also to be found in the Trust's *Annual Report* [QRL 10].

4.2   Rents
Statistical information about rents is very limited and it all suffers from a failure to take account of the widely varying characteristics of housing in terms of size, physical condition, amenities, etc. The only information which covers housing in the private as well as the public sector is that obtained in surveys of family expenditure; these are of value in providing information about the whole range of family expenditure against which housing expenditure can be compared. Separate official surveys for Northern Ireland were not undertaken until 1967 [QRL 9] but some information may be extracted from earlier surveys for the years 1953–4 [B 24] and 1937–38 [B 28] which covered the United Kingdom as a whole; some information from the 1937–38 survey (unpublished) is to be found in [B 2], p. 168. The only other published information about rents in the private sector would appear to be data collected in sample social surveys

carried out in six designated redevelopment areas in Belfast around 1966–67 [B 37].

In the public sector two official surveys have been made, one in 1956 and the other in 1966. In each survey local authorities were requested to submit returns to the Ministry showing as at 31st March in each year: the number of houses owned, the total annual rent from those houses taking rent levels as at 31st March and the total rateable value ('Poor Law Valuation') in respect of pre-war and post-war houses separately. This information was used to calculate average rents. The results of the 1966 survey have not been published; those for 1956 were published in the Ministry's *Annual Report* for 1956 [B 14], Cmd. 379, p. 65; the only distinctions drawn are between pre-war and post-war houses in rural and non-rural areas respectively. Information about the expenditure (including rent) of tenants of the Northern Ireland Housing Trust, now of historical interest, was obtained in a survey of estates in the Belfast area in 1954 [B 28]. In addition the Housing Trust occasionally included details of the rents it was charging for new houses in its *Annual Reports* [QRL 10].

Rent income. Information about the rent income of the Housing Trust, local authorities and development commissions is contained in their annual financial accounts discussed above (section 4.1).

Rent restriction. No statistics about the operation of rent restriction legislation are published and very little information is available: the Ministry may be able to give the number of notices served but only for limited areas.

4.3   House Purchase
Details of average expenditure by householders on mortgage and 'other payments for purchase or alteration of dwellings' are obtained in *Family Expenditure Surveys* [QRL 9], [B 24].

Annual series from 1966 of the average amounts advanced on mortgage for the purchase of 'new dwellings' and 'other dwellings', based on a regular sample survey of building society mortgages, is available from the Department of the Environment (U.K.) together with a complementary analysis of the average prices of the houses. Apart from statistics for the year 1966, which appeared in [QRL 5], No. 5, April 1967, Table VII, the data have not been published. The information collected in the surveys covers a number of matters relating to the dwelling, the mortgage and the applicant: the details may be seen from the questionnaire which is reproduced in the companion study to this, *Housing in Great Britain* (Appendix II). It should be noted that the part of the sample relating to Northern Ireland is very small and thus the figures have large standard errors; it is for this reason that an annual series only is made available although the survey itself is carried out monthly.

Information which is similar in kind to that obtained in the official survey of building society mortgages is also produced in surveys by the Nationwide Building Society (formerly the Co-operative Permanent Building Society) from time to time, although these relate only to houses on which it has advanced loans itself. Financial statistics analysed on a regional basis have covered such matters as the amount of loan advanced, the size of deposit, the income distribution of purchasers and monthly outgoings [QRL 11], No. 100, December 1970.

Statistics of the total amounts advanced by Building Societies on mortgage are published in the reports of the Northern Ireland Registrar of Friendly Societies [B 13]. For the period from 1961 (quarterly) more useful information, distinguishing new houses and other houses, has been published in [QRL 3], No. 18 *et seq.* Statistics of advances for house purchase made under the Small Dwellings Acquisitions Acts are to be found in the Annual Reports of the government department concerned [B 16, B 14] and also, for each local authority, in [B 8].

5 Building Costs, House Prices and Land

5.1 Labour and Material Costs

There are no statistics about the costs of labour and materials which relate to housing specifically. The usual statistics about wage rates and earnings for the building industry as a whole are available. Information about the prices of selected building materials in Belfast has been published in the *Ulster Builder* [B 38] since 1953; price indices based on this source were published by the author in [B 31], Appendix A.

5.2 House Prices and Land

In this section the terms 'costs' and 'prices' are used synonymously to refer to the amount paid by the buyer.

Public sector

In the public sector information about the prices submitted in tenders to local authorities is obtained by the Ministry of Development (currently) in the exercise of its powers of approval. Analyses of this information are made as the basis for adjusting the level of subsidies but none of them are regularly published. Indeed there are only three official pieces of information to which attention may be directed and these solely of historical interest. The first and most important is an analysis for the year 1956, included in the Ministry's *Annual Report* for that year [B 14], Cmd. 379, p. 65, which provides statistics of the average tender prices and average floor areas (sq. ft.) of houses in tenders approved for local authorities in urban and rural areas respectively. The second is a series of annual estimates of the cost of building an 800 sq. ft. house over the period 1954–61 published in [B 25], Appendix XIII. How far this series is based on actual tender prices is not clear, but a certain reservation must be expressed in view of the fact that the cost is shown as an un-

changed round figure in each year from 1956 to 1960 (despite a consistent upward trend in building wage rates, earnings and materials prices over this period). The third is a very limited comparison of some house tender prices in Britain and Northern Ireland in 1946 published in [B 5]. Some additional information about public sector house prices is also to be found in a study by the author relating to the period 1964–5 [B 30] although this was concerned with assessing the effect of the scale of operations on prices and does not contain overall averages.

Post-war prefabricated house costs. An analysis of the costs (components, transport and erection) of prefabricated dwellings erected at the end of the second world war is to be found in [B 12], p. 20.

Private sector

House prices. In the private sector information about average purchase prices, distinguishing between new and other dwellings, has been obtained monthly by the Department of the Environment (U.K.) as part of a sample survey of building society mortgages in the U.K. since 1966 (the questionnaire used is reproduced in Appendix II of the companion study of *Housing in Great Britain*). Apart from the analyses for that year, which appeared in [QRL 5], No. 5, April 1967, Table VII, the information is not published but it is available from the Department on request on an annual basis. These statistics complement analyses of average mortgage amounts referred to above— section 4.3. Again it should be noted that since the part of the sample relating to Northern Ireland is very small the figures are subject to large standard errors and for this reason are analysed on an annual rather than monthly basis. We discuss this series further below after considering a similar series published by the Nationwide Building Society.

The Nationwide Building Society publishes analyses in [QRL 11] of the prices of houses on which it has itself provided mortgages. These have their limitations inasmuch as they cover a range of different types of house, as does the official series described above, and furthermore it is not clear how far the houses mortgaged by this one Society are representative of all transactions in the market. Nonetheless it provides a valuable source of information which has been maintained over a long period of time—details are set out below (Table 5.1).

In addition to the regular surveys made by the Society, special surveys are made from time to time providing, among other things, more detailed regional analyses of prices according to type of house [QRL 11], Nos. 76 December 1966 and 100, December 1970.

Information about costs, it may be noted incidentally, is also provided by registered builders to the local Northern Ireland branch of the National House Builders Registration Council but its accuracy is open to doubt and it is not published (see Section 2.1.1).

Land. Estimates of site values have been published by the Nationwide Building Society since 1968 in [QRL 11]—the only source of such information which appears to be available.

The interpretation of the average house price series prepared by the Department of the Environment and the Nationwide Building Society needs to take into account two major factors. First is the fact that the composition of dwelling types upon which the averages are based may vary over time and differ between regions and thus bias comparisons. The value of the analyses would be enhanced if information were to be provided for different house types. Information about the degree of price variation would also be useful. The second major factor—important in regional comparisons—is differences in the extent to which purchase prices include or exclude freehold title to the land on which the house stands as well as the house: insofar as land is excluded prices will, of course, be lower and insofar as there are regional differences in the incidence of this factor, regional comparisons will be distorted accordingly. This is particularly important in Northern Ireland where it is often the case that house prices do not include freehold title to the land. The Nationwide Building Society endeavour to place the prices of freehold and leasehold properties on a comparable base by adjusting the price of the latter by a figure representing fifteen years' ground rent. For example, a leasehold property selling at £4,500 with an annual ground rent of £22 would be regarded as equivalent to a freehold property valued at £4,830 (£4,500 + 15 × £22) and the notional price of

TABLE 5.1

REGULAR ANALYSES OF HOUSE PRICES AND LAND PRICES MADE BY THE NATIONWIDE BUILDING SOCIETY

Data	Type of House	Time Series and Frequency
House Prices:		
Index Nos.	Second-hand—3 classes	1939*, 1951–62 (quarterly to 1956, then 2nd & 4th qtrs. only)
Averages	New / Second-hand—2 standards (from 1965)	From 1963 } 2nd & 4th qtrs. each year
*Site Values**	New	From 1968 }

* Surveyors' estimates

6 House Building and the Building Industry

The sector of the building industry which undertakes housing work is not well documented statistically since most of the information available relates to the industry as a whole. More information is available about labour employed on housing work than about other inputs or about the structure of this part of the industry.

6.1 Labour and Other Inputs

Labour
Information about the labour employed on housing work is collected by the Ministry of Commerce and by the Ministry of Health and Social Services as follows (Table 6.1):

The statistics collected by the Ministry of Commerce are obtained as part of the quarterly enquiry into the value of output and new orders. As we indicate, only limited information is published and, curiously, appears only in British publications. We have discussed this particular enquiry at some length elsewhere in this study (section 2.2.2) and need not repeat that discussion here, but we would emphasise that the statistics suffer from certain basic deficiencies of coverage as well as from incomplete presentation. Interpretation of the labour statistics in particular must also take into account the following additional points. First, since self-employed workers who do manual work, 'Working Principals', are not counted as operatives, the expansion of labour-only sub-contracting in recent

TABLE 6.1

STATISTICS COLLECTED ABOUT LABOUR EMPLOYED ON HOUSING

(a cross (×) indicates availability of data)

Collecting Agency	Type of Work			Labour Analyses				Time Series & Frequency
	New Work		Repairs & Maintenance	By Occupational Group*			By Occupation	
	Total	By Sector		Operatives	A.P.T.C.	W.P.		
A. Ministry of Commerce	×	×	×	×				From 1966. Quarterly
B. Ministry of Health and Social Services	×		×	×	×	×	×	From 1965. Annually

* A.P.T.C.: Administrative, Professional, Technical and Clerical. W.P.: Working Principals

Publication of Results:
A. *Ministry of Commerce.* Only the series for operatives employed by contractors (i.e. excluding direct labour) on new housing by sector is published.
  Sources: quarterly series: [QRL 6], annual series: [QRL 2].
B. *Ministry of Health and Social Services.* Only percentage analyses of employment by occupational group on new house construction are published: [QRL 8].

years is likely to have depressed the statistics of operative employment since, quite apart from the problem of covering them in the enquiry, it is likely that most of this labour will be recorded not as operatives but as working principals (see the questionnaire in Appendix I). Secondly, when comparing the employment series with the value of work done, a difference in timing needs to be noticed: employment refers to one week in each quarter whilst work done refers to the whole quarter.

The surveys carried out by the Ministry of Health and Social Services are undertaken on behalf of the Construction Industry Training Board (Northern Ireland) under the terms of the Industrial Training Act (Northern Ireland) 1964. In these enquiries, the industry has been defined in accordance with the *Standard Industrial Classification* [B 26] except that no direct labour departments of public authorities and of private firms in other industries are covered except those of local authorities. The Ministry has to face the same problem with regard to compiling a register of firms (as referred to earlier), and it is likely that it suffers from deficiencies. Some indication of this was obtained incidentally in a study made by the author [B 32], Table I, based partly on the register for 1964, which showed that information was not available for a quarter of contractors winning public sector housing contracts in the period 1964–5 either because returns had not been submitted or because the firms were not on the register. Admittedly this was the first register the Ministry had attempted to compile and may have been improved subsequently, but since it was based partly on that maintained by the Ministry of Commerce it provides evidence of deficiency in the latter.

It will be noted that more information is collected than is published, in particular information about occupation as distinct from occupational

£4,830 would be used in the calculation of average prices*. Unfortunately, no information is provided about the number of houses for which a notional

* Information kindly supplied by the Society's Planning Department.

price is calculated nor about the levels of ground rents. The average house price series prepared by the Department of the Environment incorporates both types of property, but no adjustments are made to bring their prices on to a comparable base.

6 House Building and the Building Industry

The sector of the building industry which undertakes housing work is not well documented statistically since most of the information available relates to the industry as a whole. More information is available about labour employed on housing work than about other inputs or about the structure of this part of the industry.

6.1 Labour and Other Inputs

Labour
Information about the labour employed on housing work is collected by the Ministry of Commerce and by the Ministry of Health and Social Services as follows (Table 6.1):

The statistics collected by the Ministry of Commerce are obtained as part of the quarterly enquiry into the value of output and new orders. As we indicate, only limited information is published and, curiously, appears only in British publications. We have discussed this particular enquiry at some length elsewhere in this study (section 2.2.2) and need not repeat that discussion here, but we would emphasise that the statistics suffer from certain basic deficiencies of coverage as well as from incomplete presentation. Interpretation of the labour statistics in particular must also take into account the following additional points. First, since self-employed workers who do manual work, 'Working Principals', are not counted as operatives, the expansion of labour-only sub-contracting in recent

TABLE 6.1

STATISTICS COLLECTED ABOUT LABOUR EMPLOYED ON HOUSING

(a cross (×) indicates availability of data)

| Collecting Agency | Type of Work | | | Labour Analyses | | | | Time Series & Frequency |
| | New Work | | Repairs & Maintenance | By Occupational Group* | | | By Occupation | |
	Total	By Sector		Operatives	A.P.T.C.	W.P.		
A. Ministry of Commerce	×	×	×	×				From 1966. Quarterly
B. Ministry of Health and Social Services	×		×	×	×	×	×	From 1965. Annually

* A.P.T.C.: Administrative, Professional, Technical and Clerical. W.P.: Working Principals

Publication of Results:
   A. *Ministry of Commerce.* Only the series for operatives employed by contractors (i.e. excluding direct labour) on new housing by sector is published.
      Sources: quarterly series: [QRL 6], annual series: [QRL 2].
   B. *Ministry of Health and Social Services.* Only percentage analyses of employment by occupational group on new house construction are published: [QRL 8].

7 Desirable Improvements—Summary

A comparison of the scope of the statistical information available about housing and house-building activity in Northern Ireland with that available for Great Britain would reveal many deficiencies. But whether this would be a useful way of defining desirable improvements is questionable, and it is not followed here. For one thing it would provide no indication of the relative importance to be attached to particular improvements and, moreover, it would rest on the questionable assumption that the existing scope of British statistics represented a desirable norm. Instead attention is concentrated on those areas where it appeared to the author that deficiencies were most marked. Various gaps in the information available have been identified, and improvements suggested at several places in the text and three specific sub-sections on the subject have been included—sub-sections 2.1.3, 2.2.4, and 3.4. The purpose of this section is to draw this material together and direct attention to what are considered to be the most important areas for improvement.

Housing statistics may be divided into two broad categories: statistics about the housing stock and statistics about changes to the stock including a wide spread of information about the economic activities involved in these changes. Of these two the first undoubtedly suffers from the greatest deficiencies. Very little information indeed is available about the characteristics of the stock and its occupancy, information which, as we stress in sub-section 3.4 above, is essential for the appraisal of the housing situation and the development of housing policies with regard to the needs for new building, replacement, repair and improvement.

Statistics about changes to the stock may themselves be conveniently considered in two parts, first additions and removals, from it and second changes to existing constituents of it. With regard to the first, statistics of the numbers built or at various stages of construction is adequate but information about their characteristics is lacking in a number of respects as we have indicated in sub-section 2.1.3. It is an essential complement to information about size and composition of the existing stock. In the public sector the information has been readily accessible in the past as part of the centralised system of approval, but not exploited; in the future the centralisation of housing functions should facilitate data collection and analysis still further. In the private sector the operation of the subsidy system for most houses provides a ready-made channel which could well be exploited for obtaining information. Statistics about demolitions resulting from statutory action are now probably accurate but coverage of other demolitions may remain incomplete and it would be useful if this could be clarified. It would also be useful if the statistics were to specify the number of dwellings involved rather than 'houses' since the latter may have provided accommodation for several families.

The second part of changes to the stock consists of changes to existing dwellings. Statistics here serve the purposes of keeping information about the stock up-to-date and judging rates of maintenance and improvement in relation to needs. Both of these, however, require data about the stock itself which, as we have emphasised, is largely lacking. At present statistics of conversions and improvements are confined to grant-aided work and provide no indication of the nature of the work or, often, of the net number of dwellings provided by conversion or indeed of the gross number of dwellings, as distinct from other buildings, converted. Refinements here, if possible, would be useful.

years is likely to have depressed the statistics of operative employment since, quite apart from the problem of covering them in the enquiry, it is likely that most of this labour will be recorded not as operatives but as working principals (see the questionnaire in Appendix I). Secondly, when comparing the employment series with the value of work done, a difference in timing needs to be noticed: employment refers to one week in each quarter whilst work done refers to the whole quarter.

The surveys carried out by the Ministry of Health and Social Services are undertaken on behalf of the Construction Industry Training Board (Northern Ireland) under the terms of the Industrial Training Act (Northern Ireland) 1964. In these enquiries, the industry has been defined in accordance with the *Standard Industrial Classification* [B 26] except that no direct labour departments of public authorities and of private firms in other industries are covered except those of local authorities. The Ministry has to face the same problem with regard to compiling a register of firms (as referred to earlier), and it is likely that it suffers from deficiencies. Some indication of this was obtained incidentally in a study made by the author [B 32], Table I, based partly on the register for 1964, which showed that information was not available for a quarter of contractors winning public sector housing contracts in the period 1964–5 either because returns had not been submitted or because the firms were not on the register. Admittedly this was the first register the Ministry had attempted to compile and may have been improved subsequently, but since it was based partly on that maintained by the Ministry of Commerce it provides evidence of deficiency in the latter.

It will be noted that more information is collected than is published, in particular information about occupation as distinct from occupational category; this information might be made available on request. An interesting feature of this collection is the classification of non-operative labour by type of work; this must be regarded with a certain reserve because of the difficulties that many contractors must face in allocating such labour in this way, given that it will often be employed on a range of activities not related solely to one type of work.

Labour productivity
The only information available about productivity on house building was obtained in a study by the author in 1967 [B 32] into the levels of productivity achieved and some of the factors affecting it.

Other inputs
No information is available about other housing inputs.

6.2   Structure of the House Building Industry
Information about the structure of the building industry as a whole is to be found in the *Reports of the Census of Production of Northern Ireland* and some analyses are prepared by the Ministry of Health and Social Services on the basis of the enquiry referred to in section 6.1 [QRL 8]. The only information about the house-building sector of the industry is an analysis made by the author of the size of contractors winning all public sector housing contracts, let in the period January 1964 to June 1965, analysed according to the size of contract obtained [B 32], Table 1.

Both the surveys for the Construction Industry Training Board and the quarterly enquiries into output, labour and new orders (section 2.2.2.) provide potential bases for detailed analyses of the house-building sector but ones which have remained apparently unexploited.

Statistics already collected about the value of re-pair and maintenance work could well be published although they would be more valuable if deficiencies in their coverage could be remedied.

With regard to statistics of the value of new house-building work it is important that the differences between the two available series—gross domestic fixed capital formation and value of work done—should be reconciled. Such an attempt must involve an appraisal of the estimation procedures and the quality of the information used for the first series and should lead to an expression of likely margins of error. As regards the second series attention must be paid to the likely deficiencies of coverage arising from deficiencies in the register of contractors from whom information is sought. A particular limitation in the scope of the survey needs to be publicised (see Table 2.2) and in general much more information needs to be supplied both about statistics collected but not published (Table 2.2) and the nature of the statistics themselves. The publication of statistics about the value of new contracts and orders obtained by contractors could also be improved since at present full details about housing orders are published only in two British departmental publications with a limited circulation (see Table 2.2).

Another major deficiency in available information is the lack of any published series about the costs of house-building in the public sector. More information is available about the private sector though here too improvements would be desirable to allow for differences with regard to land and house types (see sub-section 5.2).

Information about the resources absorbed in house-building, information of importance in assessing the economic implications of house-building programmes, is confined to labour. This is in need of the same improvement and clarification with regard to the coverage of contractors as we have indicated already in relation to the work-done and new-orders series. In addition improvements are desirable with regard to publication itself. Quite apart from the fact that more information is collected than is published, the major series that is published (operatives employed) suffers from the curious anomaly of appearing in no Northern Ireland publication despite the fact that it is collected as an integral part of the enquiries into work done and new orders—statistics which are not subject to the same restriction in publication (see Tables 6.1 and 2.2).

Finally it would be of great benefit to the users of those statistics which are available if much fuller information were to be provided about the definitions of all terms employed, terms such as 'approved', 'started', 'unfit', 'work done' etc., and about all other matters, such as methods of collection and collation, which would facilitate interpretation.

Quick Reference List—Table of Contents

QUICK REFERENCE LIST

Descriptive Title	Breakdown	Frequency	Publication (see QRL Key)	Text Reference and Remarks
Output				
In physical units				
Completions; under construction at end of period; starts	Sector and agency	Quarterly	[QRL 3], [QRL 4]	Table 2.1 and Section 2.1 [QRL 4] gives additional local authority breakdown by agency (subsidy category, etc.) for 'completions' (in cumulative form from 1.6.44 to current quarter) and for 'under construction' (current quarter only)
	Sector	Monthly/Quarterly	[QRL 5], [QRL 7]	Monthly series in [QRL 7] are for completions only. Secondary source (annual completions only): [QRL 1]
Approved, not started at end of period	By sector and agency	Quarterly	[QRL 4]	More detailed breakdown by agency, subsidy category, etc. and for each local authority are also included but for the current quarter only
New contracts	Public sector only.	"	"	Statistics refer to number of dwellings, not contracts
	House size; storey height; method of construction			
In monetary units				
Gross domestic fixed capital formation	Public/private sectors	Annual	[QRL 3]	Valued at current prices. See Table 2.2 for details of constant price series and a separate series for local authorities
Value of work done by contractors	"	Quarterly	[QRL 6]	See remarks to Table 2.2 regarding coverage. Northern Ireland Ministry of Commerce is source of data collection
Value of new contracts and orders received by contractors	"	"	"	Annual series (last 5 years) are reproduced in [QRL 2]
The Housing Stock				
Size, characteristics & tenure				Section 3. See the companion review on *The Housing in Great Britain.* (Note on housing statistics from the Census of Population in Northern Ireland)
Demolition and closure	Fit and unfit; gross and net	Quarterly	[QRL 4]	Section 3.2 The statistics refer to houses, not dwellings as such, and to houses demolished, closed or made fit generally as a result of statutory action only

Improvements, conversions and provision of standard amenities	By sector and amenity	"	"	Section 3.2 and Table 3.1 Grant-aided schemes only. Conversions are gross, not net

Financial Statistics

Housing subsidies				See also **House Prices, Mortgages and Land** below
Household expenditure: Rent, rates, etc.	By income and tenure	Annual	[QRL 9]	Section 4.1
Repairs, maintenance and decorations	"	"		Sections 4.2 and 4.3
Mortgage and other payments for purchase	By income	"		

House Prices, Mortgages & Land

Average purchase price and average mortgage amount	Private: new and other houses	Annual	Not published	Available on request from the Department of the Environment. (U.K.) Based on sample surveys of Building Society mortgages
Average purchase price and average site value	" "	2nd and 4th Quarters	[QRL 11]	Based on mortgages provided by the Society. Site values relate to new houses only and are based on surveyors' estimates

Building

Labour employed	By sector—new work	Quarterly	[QRL 6]	Section 6 Section 6.1 Operatives employed by contractors only. Annual figures (last 5 years) reproduced in [QRL 2]. N.I. Ministry of Commerce is source of data collection
	By occupational group—new work	Annual	[QRL 8]	Table 6.1 Percentage analyses only by three occupational categories. N.I. Ministry of Health and Social Services is source of data collection.

QUICK REFERENCE LIST KEY TO PUBLICATIONS

Reference number	Organization responsible	Title	Publisher	Frequency or date of publication	Price and remarks*
[QRL 1]	Central Statistical Office	*Annual Abstract of Statistics*	HMSO, London	Annual since 1948	For earlier numbers in the series see [B 27]. £2.20 (£2.44) (1971).
[QRL 2]†	Department of the Environment	*Annual Bulletin of Construction Statistics*	DOE, London		Free. Ceased publication. after issue for 1970.
[QRL 3]	Northern Ireland, Ministry of Finance	*Digest of Statistics*	HMSO, Belfast	Biannual since March 1954	75p (83½p) (1972)
[QRL 4]	Ministry of Development	*Housing Return for Northern Ireland*	HMSO, Belfast	Quarterly from 1953	18½p Series back to 1944
[QRL 5]†	Department of the Environment	*Housing Statistics*	HMSO, London	Quarterly from March 1966 to Feb 1972	95p. Ceased publication in Feb 1972.
[QRL 6]†	Department of the Environment	*Monthly Bulletin of Construction Statistics*	DOE, London		Free. Ceased publication after issue for June 1972.
[QRL 7]	Central Statistical Office	*Monthly Digest of Statistics*	HMSO, London	Monthly from January 1946	60p (67½p) (1971)
[QRL 8]	Northern Ireland Construction Industry Training Board	*Report and Statement of Accounts*	Ministry of Health and Social Services/ HMSO, Belfast	Annual from 1967	First report published by Ministry, later ones as H. C. Papers. 16p. 1968 & 1969 in one volume.
[QRL 9]	Ministry of Finance, Economic Section	*Northern Ireland Family Expenditure Survey Report*	HMSO, Belfast	Annual from 1967	74p (81½p) (1972)
[QRL 10]	Northern Ireland Housing Trust	*Annual Report of the Northern Ireland Housing Trust*	HMSO, Belfast, 1946–1948, The Trust, Belfast, 1949–1971	Annua	5p (1971)
[QRL 11]	Nationwide Building Society	*Occasional Bulletins*	The Nationwide Building Soc., Research Section, New Oxford House, London WC1V 6PW	Quarterly	Free

★ In the case of an annual publication appearing over a number of years, the price given is for the latest year of publication (given in parenthesis).

† Most of the series formerly published in [QRL 2, 5, and 6] are now published in *Housing and Construction Statistics*, Department of the Environment, Scottish Development Department, Welsh Office, quarterly from No. 1, 1st quarter 1972, published in 1972 (HMSO, London, 75p). A separate *Notes and Definitions Supplement* is published annually; first published in 1972 (HMSO, London, 25p).

Bibliography*

I. PUBLICATIONS OF THE NORTHERN IRELAND GOVERNMENT

[B 1] Blake, John W. *Northern Ireland in the Second World War*. H.M.S.O., Belfast, 1956.

[B 2] Isles, K. S. and Cuthbert, N. *Economic Survey of Northern Ireland*. H.M.S.O., Belfast, 1957.

[B 3] House of Commons Papers. *Accounts of Capital Receipts and Payments*. H.M.S.O., Belfast. Annual.

[B 4] House of Commons Papers. *Appropriation Accounts*. H.M.S.O., Belfast. Annual.

[B 5] Command Paper. *Housing Costs Inquiry*. Cmd. 240. H.M.S.O., Belfast, 1946.

[B 6] Command Paper. *Housing in Northern Ireland, Interim Report of the Planning Advisory Board*. Cmd. 224. H.M.S.O., Belfast, 1944.

[B 7] House of Commons Papers. *Housing Trust Accounts*. H.M.S.O., Belfast. Annual from 1945–6.

[B 8] Command Papers. *Local Authority Financial Returns*. H.M.S.O., Belfast. Annual from 1953–4 (for earlier publications in the series see item [B 19]).

[B 9] Ministry of Health and Local Government to 1964–5, then Ministry of Development. *Local Authority Rate Statistics*. H.M.S.O., Belfast. Annual from 1954–55.

[B 10] Economic Section—Cabinet Offices, later Ministry of Finance. *Northern Ireland Economic Report*. H.M.S.O., Belfast. Annual from 1964.

[B 11] Command Paper. *Proposals for Dealing with Unfit Houses*. Cmd. 398. H.M.S.O., Belfast, 1959.

[B 12] House of Commons Paper. *Report from the Select Committee on Public Accounts 1946–7*. H. C. Paper 817. H.M.S.O., Belfast.

[B 13] Command Papers (1947–62)/Departmental Reports (1963–66)/House of Commons Papers (since 1967). *Report of the Registrar of Friendly Societies (for Northern Ireland)*. H.M.S.O., Belfast.

[B 14] Command Papers. *Report on Health and Local Government Administration* (1948–66). *Report of Ministry of Development* (since 1967). H.M.S.O., Belfast. Annual from Report for 1938–46 (1948) For earlier reports see item [B 16].

[B 15] Command Paper. *Report on Health and Local Government Administration during the period 1st April 1938–31st December 1946*. Cmd. 258. Appendix LXXVIII, pp. 265–6 (1948). H.M.S.O., Belfast.

[B 16] Command Papers. *Report on the Administration of Local Government Services*. For subsequent reports see item [B 14]. Annual from Report for 1921–3 to Report for 1937–8. H.M.S.O., Belfast.

[B 17] Ministry of Commerce. *Report on the Census of Production of Northern Ireland, 1951*. H.M.S.O., Belfast, 1954.

[B 18] Ministry of Commerce. *Report on the Census of Production of Northern Ireland, 1954*. H.M.S.O., Belfast, 1956.

[B 19] House of Commons Paper (1921–22)/Command Papers. *Returns of Local Taxation in Northern Ireland*, continued as *Local Taxation Returns*. H.M.S.O., Belfast. Annual.

[B 20] *Ulster Yearbook*. H.M.S.O., Belfast. Triennial for 1926–38 and 1947–68, annual from 1969.

II PUBLICATIONS OF THE UNITED KINGDOM GOVERNMENT

[B 21] Maurice, R. (ed.). *National Accounts Statistics—Sources and Methods*. Central Statistical Office. H.M.S.O., London, 1968.

[B 22] Ministry of Housing and Local Government. *Homes for Today and Tomorrow*. H.M.S.O., London, 1961.

[B 23] Command Paper. *The National Plan*. Cmnd. 2764. H.M.S.O., London, 1965.

[B 24] Ministry of Labour and National Service. *Report of an Enquiry into Household Expenditure in 1953–4*. H.M.S.O., London, 1957

[B 25] Command Paper. *Report of the Joint Working Party on the Economy of Northern Ireland*. Cmnd. 1835. H.M.S.O., London, 1962.

[B 26] Central Statistical Office. *Standard Industrial Classification*. H.M.S.O., London, 1948, 1958, and 1968.

[B 27] Command Papers. *Statistical Abstract for the United Kingdom*. H.M.S.O., London. Annual up to No. 83, published 1940. For later numbers in the series see item [QRL1].

[B 28] Ministry of Labour and National Service. *Weekly Expenditure of Working-Class Households in the U.K. in 1937–38*. Unpublished Report. July 1949.

* See also Addenda—Additional References

III OTHER PUBLICATIONS

[B 29] Field, Dorita and Neill, D. G. *A Survey of New Housing Estates in Belfast.* Queen's University, Belfast, 1957.

[B 30] Fleming, M. C. 'Conventional housebuilding and the scale of operations: a study of prices.' *Bulletin of the Oxford University Institute of Economics and Statistics,* **29**, 2, 1967, pp. 109–37

[B 31] Fleming, M. C. 'Costs and prices in the Northern Ireland Construction Industry 1954–64.' *Journal of Industrial Economics,* **14**, 1, 1965, pp. 42–54.

[B 32] Fleming, M. C. 'Housebuilding productivity in Northern Ireland'. *Urban Studies,* **4**, 2, 1967, pp. 122–36.

[B 33] *Antrim and Ballymena Development Commission Annual Report.* Annual from 1968. The Commission, Ballymena.

[B 34] Building Design Partnership. *Belfast Urban Area Plan.* 2 vols. The Partnership, Belfast. 1969.

[B 35] *Craigavon Development Commission Annual Report.* The Commission, Portadown. Annual from 1966.

[B 36] *Londonderry Development Commission Annual Report.* The Commission, Londonderry. Annual from 1969.

[B 37] Building Design Partnership. *People and their Houses, City of Belfast.* The Partnership, Belfast, 1967.

[B 38] *Ulster Builder,* Belfast. Monthly.

Appendix I

Questionnaires used in Quarterly Enquiries into Construction Work

Two enquiries are undertaken, one with respect to the work carried out by contractors and one for that carried out by labour directly employed by public authorities. A separate questionnaire is used for each enquiry and specimen copies of each of these are reproduced below. Both enquiries were instituted in 1966. The questionnaires themselves were modelled on those used in similar enquiries undertaken in Great Britain by the Ministry of Public Building and Works and subsequently the Department of the Environment and, apart from an addition noted below, have remained substantially unchanged since then. The information obtained in these enquiries is considered above in sub-sections 2.2.2., 2.2.3., 2.2.4., 6.1 and 6.2. We summarise below relevant details about the completion of the returns and their subsequent processing and availability.

(1) *Contractors. Form Stats/CR/2*

QUARTERLY ENQUIRY INTO LABOUR, OUTPUT AND CONTRACTS

(a) Issuing Authority: Ministry of Commerce.

(b) Circulation: Contractors classified to the Construction industry on the register maintained by the Ministry of Commerce (see sub-section 2.2.2. regarding coverage).

(c) Person Making the Return: the Proprietor, Director, Manager, Partner or Secretary of the enterprise.

(d) Frequency of Return: quarterly.

(e) Processing of Returns: Ministry of Commerce.

(f) Availability of Data from Individual Returns: individual returns are treated as strictly confidential and no information from them is made available.

46

Stats/CR/2/

BUILDING, CIVIL ENGINEERING AND ALLIED INDUSTRIES

TO :

These numbers should
be quoted in
correspondence

From : MINISTRY OF COMMERCE
64 Chichester Street
Belfast
BT1 4JX

Dear Sirs,

DATE AS POSTMARK

QUARTERLY ENQUIRY INTO LABOUR, OUTPUT AND CONTRACTS

QUARTER ENDED..............................

(1) Under Section 4 of the Statistics of Trade Act (Northern Ireland) 1949 you are required to complete and forward this return in the enclosed envelope WITHIN TWO WEEKS OF THE END OF THE QUARTER. If exact figures are not available by that time do not hold up the return but make the best estimate you can.

(2) Subject to the provisions of the Act all the information you give will be treated as strictly confidential and will be used solely for the compilation of general statistics.

(3) Where the construction activities are only part of an undertaking the return should give information about that part only.

(4) All sections of the return should be completed, if in any section there is nothing to record a "nil" entry should be made.

(5) A separate return should be used for business carried out or proposed in Great Britain or the Republic of Ireland. Extra forms can be obtained from the Ministry of Commerce, 64 Chichester Street, Belfast BT1 4JX. Telephone 34488, ext. 338.

Yours faithfully,

(Miss) M. P. LECKY

for the Secretary

TO BE COMPLETED AND SIGNED BY THE PERSON MAKING THE RETURN ON BEHALF OF THE UNDERTAKING

Trading Name of Undertaking..

Full Postal Address (including ....

Town and County) to which ....

correspondence should be sent..

Is this the address of your Registered Office?...

If your name and
address is correctly
printed above
you need only
state "as above."

Are you a "labour only" subcontractor? Yes/No   (Delete whichever does not apply)

Telephone Exchange and Number...

I certify that to the best of my belief the particulars in this return are correct.

Signed ....Date..................................

(Please state whether Proprietor, Director, Manager, Partner, Secretary)

PART I
RETURN OF WORK DONE AND LABOUR EMPLOYED DURING THE QUARTER

A WORKING PRINCIPALS

State here the number of WORKING PRINCIPALS (i.e., Self-Employed Owners, Managers, Partners, etc., who do manual work). DO NOT enter them again in column 2 below.

B VALUE OF WORK DONE AND OPERATIVES EMPLOYED (all work, including repair and maintenance).
PLEASE READ PART I OF ENCLOSED NOTES

COLUMN 1 Value of work done last quarter	TYPE OF WORK	COLUMN 2 Operatives employed
£	**Work on Houses and Flats**	Number
(1)	1 New HOUSING construction for Government Departments, Local Authorities (e.g., Council houses) Housing Trust, Housing Associations and New Town Corporations (include site preparation and demolition).	(1)
(2)	2 New HOUSING construction for private owners and private developers (include site preparation and demolition).	(2)
(3)	3 Repair and maintenance of dwellings (include house/flat conversions, extensions, alterations and redecorations in this section).	(3)
(4)	**Non-Housing** 4 New* INDUSTRIAL construction; factories (including Government factories) warehouses, and other industrial plant.	(4)
(5)	5 New* schools, technical colleges and universities.	(5)
(6)	6 Other PRIVATE new* construction; offices, shops, hotels and public houses, places of worship, clubs, places of entertainment, road goods transport depots, etc.	(6)
(7)	7 Other PUBLIC new* construction; excluding roads (see 9 below) but including other building and civil engineering work for U.K. and Northern Ireland Government Departments, Local Authorities (other than housing), Hospital Boards, Public Corporations (E.B.N.I., Harbour Commissioners, etc.)	(7)
(8)	8 Repair and maintenance not included in Item 3, (including repair and maintenance of builder's plant).	(8)
(9)	9 Roads : New* construction and repair and maintenance of all public roads, highways, bridges and footpaths.	(9)
	10 Enter in column 2 the number of operatives who cannot be classified to the types of work listed in 1 - 9 above, e.g. transport workers, stores and warehouse staff, operatives employed in the manufacture of goods for sale.	(10)
TOTAL		TOTAL

*In the non-housing section the term "new construction" includes extensions; major alterations (i.e. improvements); site preparation; demolition; work done on building and civil engineering projects e.g. roads, harbours, sewage works, etc.

C VALUE OF WAGE PAYMENTS MADE TO AND NUMBER OF SELF-EMPLOYED OPERATIVES ENGAGED ON A "LABOUR ONLY" BASIS (See Notes, Part 1 (2))

Value of wage payments	Number of operatives

PART II

RETURN OF CONTRACTS AND ORDERS FOR NEW CONSTRUCTION OBTAINED DURING THE QUARTER

Report only contracts awarded to you direct by clients and not by another contractor.

Include the whole value of the building and civil engineering work but not the site value.

Exclude contracts, etc., for repair and maintenance work.

If you have nothing to report please write nil in all 3 sections of this part of the return.

PLEASE READ PART II OF ENCLOSED NOTES

Column 1	Brief description of the job			Column 5
Full site address. If not known, place name and county where the job is to be done.	**Column 2 — Type of work** (a) For jobs £¼ million or over give a brief description in your own words. (b) For jobs under £¼ million give a brief description or one of the suggested descriptions at note 2.	Column 3 'Private' or 'Public' (see note 3)	Column 4 Expected Completion date (month and year)	Total contract value (see note 4)

1 List of contracts and orders of £2,500 and over obtained during the quarter for new construction

2 List below new construction projects of £2,500 and over undertaken on your own initiative on which you started work on the foundations during the quarter (see note 1e)

3 Enter below the total value of all contracts and orders for new construction under £2,500 each obtained during the quarter. Include also those projects under £2,500 undertaken on your own initiative on which you started work on the foundations during the quarter. Contracts, etc., for repair and maintenance work and sub-contracts should not be included.

NUMBER OF JOBS (UNDER £2,500) [   ]   TOTAL VALUE OF JOBS (UNDER £2,500) £ [   ]

PLEASE READ THE NOTES BEFORE COMPLETING THE RETURN

NOTES TO PART I

1. Estimates entered in column 1 should include the following:
   - (i) the amounts chargeable to your customers for building, civil engineering and associated work done by you during the quarter;
   - (ii) the value of work done by you on the construction and maintenance of your own premises;
   - (iii) the value of work done by you on your own initiative.

   The estimates should refer to the value of work actually done rather than to jobs completed or payments made. The value of goods made by you for use in the work should also be included but not the value of goods made for sale.

2. Main contractors should NOT include the value of any work done for them by sub-contractors of any type but should include the value of materials supplied (but not sold) to "labour only" sub-contractors. Value of wage payments made to, and the number of self-employed operatives engaged on a "labour only" basis should be entered separately in Section C of Part I.

3. Labour only sub-contractors should enter all payments received from main contractors.

4. Electrical contractors, plumbers, heating engineers, etc. should show the value of installation work (including materials where supplied by them) associated with buildings and structures.

5. Painters and decorators should show the value of work on new structures as "new construction" and all other painting and decorating, etc. as repair and maintenance.

6. Enter in column 2 the number of operatives on your payroll on the ..... day in the week ending.............................. Include all persons age 15 years and over whose National Insurance cards you held on that date and who were employed on manual work whether full or part-time. Do not enter the same person on more than one line. Do not include administrative, technical or clerical workers. Main contractors should not include workers employed by any of their sub-contractors (but see note 2 above).

7. Labour only sub-contractors should enter in column 2 only the number of operatives employed. The number of working partners in the undertaking should be shown in Part C above.

NOTES TO PART II

1. New construction includes extensions, major alterations (i.e. improvements), site preparation and demolition except for housing where conversions, extensions and alterations should be excluded.

Include (a) All new contracts and orders for new construction obtained by you in the period shown;

   (b) extensions to existing contracts or orders;

   (c) the total value of serial or "run on" contracts. If the estimated total value is not known, enter in column 5 the value of work done in the period and enter "X" after the figures;

   (d) the estimated value of the building, civil engineering and associated works in "package deals";

   (e) (At section 2) new construction to be undertaken on your own initiative, i.e., work for which you have not been awarded a contract or order by any other party on a site already owned or leased by you or your subsidiary or associated companies (see Note 4).
   (EXAMPLES: a house or houses, for eventual sale or lease to other persons or companies, or for occupation by yourself, OR buildings such as offices, for occupation by yourselves or your subsidiary or associated companies, or for eventual sale or lease.)

Exclude (a) Contracts, etc., for repair and maintenance work;

   (b) sub-contracts obtained by you from other contractors;

   (c) the cost of architects', quantity surveyors', consultants' services, etc;

   (d) the site value.

2. Suggested descriptions   Examples of the kind of work covered:

   AGRICULTURE   barns, animal houses and fencing, and buildings for market gardening and horticulture. Houses on farms should be described as "DWELLINGS."

   AIRFIELDS   include hangars and buildings on airfields.

   CHURCHES   all places of worship and buildings connected therewith.

D060228 5m 11/73 WSM Gp139 A5883/1061

50

2. **DWELLINGS** houses, flats, maisonettes, cottages, etc., including the provision of roads and services within the site for gas, water, electricity, sewage and drainage.

ELECTRICITY power stations, dams, sub-stations and the laying of cables and erection of overhead lines.

ENTERTAINMENT theatres, cinemas, clubs, hotels, public houses, restaurants, holiday camps, work for radio and television and for sport and other recreations.

GARAGES include repair garages, petrol filling stations, transport workshops, bus depots, road goods transport depots and car parks.

GAS gas works, gas mains and gas storage.

HARBOURS and WATERWAYS harbours, wharves, docks and piers, jetties, canals and waterways, dredging, sea walls, embankment and defences.

HEALTH hospitals, medical schools, clinics, nursing homes, nurseries, ambulance stations, etc. Laboratories for industrial undertakings should be described as "Industrial".

HIGHWAYS public roads, bridges, footpaths, lighting, tunnels, etc.

INDUSTRIAL factories, warehouses, etc.

LAND DRAINAGE include surface drains, etc.

OFFICES include mixed development where offices form the major part of the job.

OIL oil refineries and distribution pipelines.

RAILWAYS permanent way, tunnels, bridges, stations etc.,

ROADS see HIGHWAYS

SCHOOLS include technical colleges.

SEWERS include sewage disposal works.

SHOPS include department stores, showrooms, etc.

UNIVERSITIES include halls of residence.

WATER reservoirs, dams, aqueducts, wells, conduits, waterworks, trunk distributing and service mains and hydraulic works.

Jobs forming part of a larger or existing project should be included in the main description, e.g., a private road or an office block to be constructed as part of a factory development should be described as "INDUSTRIAL" work; shops with dwellings above should be described as "SHOPS" if the shops are the major part of the job.

PRIVATE OR PUBLIC

3. (a) Private If the work is for a private owner or organisation or private developer "private" in column 3.

   (b) Public Enter "public" in column 3 if the work is for any public authority such as:

   Government Departments (including Water Supply Undertakings and New Town Corporations)
   District Councils
   Harbour Boards
   N.I. Electricity Service
   Health and Social Services Boards
   Northern Ireland Railways Company Ltd.
   Ulsterbus and Northern Ireland Carriers
   N.I. Housing Executive
   B.B.C. but not U.T.V.
   Universities
   Atomic Energy Authority
   etc.

4. Total contract value: Enter in column 5 the total value of the contract, order or project less any architects' or consultants' fee and site value. Include the value of any work you propose to sub-let to other contractors. For projects started on your own initiative you should enter the estimated total value of only those buildings on which you actually started foundation work in the period covered by the return.

(2) *Public authorities. Form Stats/CR/3*

QUARTERLY RETURN OF LABOUR AND OUTPUT

(a) Issuing Authority: Ministry of Commerce.

(b) Circulation: Public Authorities which employ labour directly on building and civil engineering work. (See the Notes to Part II, item 3 of the questionnaire to Contractors—form Stats/CR/2 below for a list of public authorities). With regard to housing work the main public authorities concerned are the local authorities.

(c) Person Making the Return: the Town Clerk or Surveyor, etc.

(d) Frequency of Return: ⎫

(e) Processing of Returns: ⎬ as for Contractors above.

(f) Availability of Data from Individual Returns: ⎭

D060225.1m.11/73.D.gp.181

Stats./CR/3/

These numbers should be
quoted in correspondence

MINISTRY OF COMMERCE

Telephone No. Belfast 34488
Extension 335

64 Chichester Street
Belfast
BT1 4JX
DATE AS POSTMARK

Confidential

PUBLIC AUTHORITIES

Building and Civil Engineering

QUARTERLY RETURN OF LABOUR AND OUTPUT

QUARTER ENDED....................

Dear Sirs,

A wide range of statistical information is needed to help in framing economic policy and up-to-date information about construction is particularly important because of the large part which the industry must play in developing the Northern Ireland economy. For this purpose public authorities are being asked to make a quarterly return of the labour employed and value of work carried out on building and civil engineering work. The statistics obtained will give the Government earlier and better information about the load of work, enable it to plan its programmes more precisely and take account of local as well as country-wide problems.

Information is required about those employees of the authority who are employed wholly or mainly on building and civil engineering work i.e., work which would otherwise be undertaken by building and civil engineering firms. This return is similar in scope to that issued by the Ministry of Public Building and Works to public authorities in Great Britain.

The earlier that the statistics based on the return are available the more valuable they are and your co-operation in carefully and promptly completing this form will therefore be of real assistance to the Government. As the late return of even a few forms must lead to delay in the publication of results, please do not hold up this return until audited figures are available but give the closest possible estimate. The completed form should be returned to above address WITHIN TWO WEEKS OF THE END OF THE QUARTER.

All the information you give will be treated as strictly confidential and will be used solely for the compilation of general statistics.

Yours faithfully,

(Miss) M. P. LECKY

for the Secretary

INFORMATION

1. All information given by you will be treated as strictly confidential and will be used solely in the compilation of general statistics. The results will be prepared and published in a way which will not reveal the particulars relating to any individual authority unless previous consent is given by the authority.

2. If you wish to keep for reference, a record of the information supplied on this form, further copies of the form will be sent on application to this office.

3. In all correspondence with this office, the reference number given in the address panel at the head of page 1 should be quoted.

NOTES FOR GUIDANCE IN COMPLETING THIS RETURN

GENERAL

1. THIS RETURN RELATES ONLY TO THOSE EMPLOYEES DIRECTLY EMPLOYED BY THE AUTHORITY WHO NORMALLY ARE WHOLLY OR MAINLY ENGAGED ON BUILDING AND CIVIL ENGINEERING WORK, i.e. WORK WHICH OTHERWISE, WOULD BE UNDERTAKEN BY BUILDING AND CIVIL ENGINEERING FIRMS.

EMPLOYEES

2. INCLUDE employees (male and female) aged 15 years and over who were employed (i.e. whose National Insurance Cards were held) by the Public Authority on building and civil engineering work.

3. INCLUDE employees (craftsmen and manual workers together with foremen and charge hands) engaged on the construction or repair and maintenance of:
    (a) houses and flats,
    (b) highways (roads, bridges, footpaths, installation of street lighting, surface drains, etc.),
    (c) harbours, wharves, docks, piers, canals, waterways, sea walls and embankments,
    (d) waterworks (including reservoirs, aqueducts, wells, mains, hydraulic works and pumping stations) sewers and sewage disposal works.
    NOTE : Exclude employees engaged on plant maintenance other than building and civil engineering plant,
    (e) tramways, trackless trolley omnibus and motor-coach services (permanent way, bridges, overhead wires, depots, workshops and other buildings concerned with the services),
    (f) railway services (permanent way, roads, bridges, signals, tunnels, stations and other buildings concerned with the services),
    (g) other buildings owned by the Public Authority,

4. EXCLUDE (a) administrative, technical and clerical workers,
    (b) all contractors' and sub-contractors' labour,
    (c) labour employed on scavenging and street cleaning, the disposal of house refuse, the maintenance of street lighting, snow clearance, and the cleaning of public conveniences,
    (d) "odd job" workers engaged on the day to day maintenance of the authority's offices, etc.

VALUE OF WORK DONE

5. THE VALUE OF BUILDING AND CIVIL ENGINEERING WORK DONE is an estimate of the value of the output of the employees described in notes 2 and 3 above, i.e. a sum calculated to cover the cost of materials, wages and the establishment charges attributable to the work carried out.

6. EXCLUDE the value of work done for the authority by contractors and sub-contractors.

7. EXCLUDE the cost of land, legal costs and architects' fees, etc.

Confidential

PUBLIC AUTHORITIES

BUILDING AND CIVIL ENGINEERING

QUARTERLY RETURN OF LABOUR AND OUTPUT

> THIS RETURN RELATES ONLY TO THOSE EMPLOYEES DIRECTLY EMPLOYED BY THE AUTHORITY WHO NORMALLY ARE ENGAGED MAINLY OR WHOLLY ON BUILDING AND CIVIL ENGINEERING WORK

The Notes on page 2 should be read before completing the return below

Employees engaged on building and civil engineering work and value of building and civil engineering work done.

	A Type of Building and Civil Engineering Work	B Operatives employed on the pay day in the week ending .... (see notes 1–4) Number	C Estimated value of work done in the quarter (see notes 5–7) £ (omit shillings & pence)
(I) HOUSES AND FLATS	(a) New Dwellings, including site preparation and demolition. (1)		
	(b) Repair and Maintenance, including extensions and alterations. (2)		
(II) WORK OTHER THAN HOUSING	(a) New Non-Housing Work (including new roads): site preparation (including demolition), construction, extensions and major alterations. (3)		
	(b) Repair and Maintenance, other than houses and flats, including road maintenance and minor improvements and repair and maintenance of building and civil engineering plants. (4)		
	Totals of Cols. B and C (5)		

To be completed and signed by the person making the return on behalf of the Authority.

Name of Public Authority ....

Full Postal Address ....
(including Town and County)

....

Telephone Exchange and Number ....

I certify that to the best of my belief the particulars above are correct.

Signed ....Date ....
        (State whether Town Clerk, Surveyor, etc.)

Appendix II

Statistical Returns of Houses Demolished, Closed and Repaired

Returns on the above matters were introduced in 1959 and the form of return revised in 1962. Specimen copies of both are reproduced below together with copies of the covering Ministry circulars issued when the returns were introduced as follows:

  (i) Ministry of Health & Local Government Circular No. H.G. 2/1959,
  (ii) Ministry of Health & Local Government Circular No. H.G. 8/1962.

Since 1962 the form of return has remained substantially the same. It will be seen that the first return introduced in 1959 required information retrospectively back to the beginning of 1958 and thereafter on a regular quarterly basis, the initiative for making the return resting with the local housing authority. It should be noted that in the future it is hoped that all statistics relating to these matters will be supplied direct to the Ministry by the Northern Ireland Housing Executive once the organisation of that body is complete and all public authority housing functions have been transferred to it.

  The information published on the basis of these returns is considered in sub-section 3.2 above. We summarise below certain details about the completion of the returns and their subsequent processing and availability.

  (a) Issuing Authority: Ministry of Health & Local Government and subsequently the Ministry of Development.
  (b) Circulation: each public housing authority in Northern Ireland.
  (c) Person Making the Return: Town Clerk, Clerk of the Council, etc.
  (d) Frequency of Return: quarterly.
  (e) Processing of Returns: the Ministry as under (a) above.
  (f) Availability of Data from Individual Returns: the Ministry may provide information on request.

Ministry of Health and Local Government,
Stormont,
Belfast.

Circular No. H.G. 2/1959   13th January, 1959.

Statistical Return of Houses Demolished, Closed and Repaired

Sir,

   I am directed by the Minister of Health and Local Government
to say that he is anxious that complete statistical information
should be available to show the progress which is being made by
local authorities under Parts I and II of the Housing Act of 1956.
Authorities will be aware that a Housing Return is published by the
Ministry at quarterly intervals, giving information as to the
numbers of new houses which have been built or are under construction in the area of each local authority.   In view of the increase
in slum clearance and in the number of improvement and conversion
schemes being undertaken the Ministry considers it would be
desirable to include in the Return particulars of improvement and
conversion schemes and action taken in regard to unfit houses.
The Ministry is itself in a position to compile particulars of
improvement and conversion schemes but the co-operation of your
Council in furnishing details relating to the action taken on unfit
houses will be greatly appreciated.

   The form in which this information should be supplied is given
in the Appendix to this Circular and I am to request that you will
be good enough to furnish –

   (1)   a Return, not later than 30th January, showing as far as
         possible the total number of houses in each category for
         the year ended 31st December, 1958;   and

   (2)   a Return for each quarter year in future, beginning with
         the quarter ending on 31st March, 1959, – to be sent to
         the Ministry within eight days of the close of the
         quarter.

                          I am, Sir,
                          Your obedient Servant,

To each Housing Authority in
Northern Ireland.

Appendix to Circular H.G.2/1959

County Borough)
Borough)
.... Urban District) Council
Rural District)

Houses Demolished, Closed and Repaired

Quarter ended..................

(1) Number of Unfit Houses demolished:-

    (a) following making of Demolition Orders   ....

    (b) following confirmation of Clearance Orders   ....

    (c) by Local Authority other than by action

        following (a) or (b)   ....

    (d) by other agencies or persons   ....

                    Total number demolished

(2) Number of Unfit Houses closed for human habitation:-

    (a) in pursuance of Closing Orders made by

        Local Authority   ....

    (b) in pursuance of undertakings to close   ....

                    Total number closed

(3) Houses Repaired:-

    Number of repairable houses

    (a) made fit following notices under Section 30 of the

        Planning and Housing Act (Northern Ireland), 1931   ....

    (b) repaired under Section 110 of the Public Health

        (Ireland) Act, 1878   ....

    (c) reused for human habitation following

        cancellation of undertakings   ....

(4) Fit Houses demolished:

    By local authority   ....

    By other agencies   ....

SPECIMEN

Ministry of Health and Local
Government,
Stormont,
BELFAST, 4.

Circular No. H.G. 8/1962
830/59

2nd April, 1962.

Sir,

Statistical Return of Houses Demolished, Closed and Repaired

1. I am directed by the Minister of Health and Local Government to refer to the Ministry's Circulars Nos. 2/1959 and 4/1959 requesting Returns of houses demolished, closed and repaired. Following a review of the statistical information supplied by local authorities in the past three years the Ministry now considers that some slight changes in the form of Return are required.

2. Progress in re-development schemes has made necessary the provision of information in relation to houses demolished in pursuance of such schemes whether carried out directly by local authorities or by arrangement with the Housing Trust. Information as to the numbers of houses already demolished in pursuance of re-development schemes may already have been included in earlier returns but to complete the Ministry's records any such figures should be repeated in the return for the current quarter with a note appended indicating that they have been included previously.

3. It is also considered that the section of the Return dealing with the repair of houses should be completed in future in a slightly different form. The Ministry is primarily concerned to ascertain the number of unfit houses which are made completely fit by local authority repair action. The Ministry appreciates that, in some cases, such repairs are carried out by informal agreement with the owner of the property and without recourse to formal statutory action under Section 30 of the Planning and Housing Act of 1931. Houses made fit by informal action should be included at 4(a) in the Return and those which have been the subject of formal statutory proceedings at 4(b).

4. In order to assess the activity of local authorities in preventing unfit houses falling into a worse state of disrepair the Ministry would also wish to to kept informed of repair action taken under Section 110 of the Public Health Act. In these cases (4(c) and 4(d) on the Return) the repairs carried out will not necessarily have made the houses fit. This information should as far as possible be recorded by reference to the number of houses repaired as well as the number of repair actions undertaken or notices served.

   The Ministry hopes that it will be possible for local authorities to give the additional information now required as from 1st January, 1962, and in all future quarterly returns. Copies of the revised form of Return are enclosed.

I am, Sir,
Your obedient Servant,

To each Housing Authority in Northern Ireland.
Copies to Health Committees for information.

NI H8/6/1,500/4/62R.

(1) Number of Unfit Houses demolished during period:-

    (a) following making of Demolition Orders

    (b) following undertakings to demolish

    (c) following confirmation of Clearance Orders

    (d) in pursuance of Re-development Schemes -

        (i) by the Local Authority
        (ii) by the Northern Ireland Housing Trust

    (e) by Local Authority action other than (a) to (d) above

    (f) by other agencies or persons

Total number demolished in period

(2) Number of Unfit Houses closed for human habitation during period:-

    (a) in pursuance of Closing Orders

    (b) in pursuance of undertakings to close

Total number closed in period

(3) Number of Houses demolished in period which were previously returned as having been closed in pursuance of Closing Orders or undertakings to close

(4) Unfit Houses Repaired during period

    (a) Number of unfit houses made fit as a result of informal action by the Local Authority

    (b) Number of unfit houses made fit following action under Section 30 of the Planning and Housing Act (Northern Ireland) 1931 (including houses re-used following cancellation of undertakings under Section 30 or Section 29)

    (c) Number of notices served under Section 110 of the Public Health (Ireland) Act, 1878.

    (d) Number of houses repaired under Section 110 of the Act of 1878

(5) Number of houses included at 4(a) or 4(b) above which were previously returned as having been closed.

(6) Fit Houses demolished during period:-

    (a) in pursuance of Re-development Schemes -

        (i) by the Local Authority
        (ii) by the Northern Ireland Housing Trust

    (b) by other Local Authority action

    (c) by other agencies or persons

(7) Number of Council houses (provided before 1940) included at (1) and (6) above.

Town Clerk/Clerk

Date _____

NI H8/6/1,500/3/62R.

Subject Index